The A-Z of facilities and property management

David Martin

Thorogood Publishing Ltd
10-12 Rivington Street
London EC2A 3DU
Telephone: 020 7749 4748
Fax: 020 7729 6110
Email: info@thorogoodpublishing.co.uk
Web: www.thorogoodpublishing.co.uk

© David Martin 2006

A CIP catalogue record for this book is available from the British Library.

PB: ISBN 1 85418 313 3
978-185418313-2

RB: ISBN 1 85418 318 4
978-185418318-7

Cover and book designed and typeset by Driftdesign

Printed in India by Replika Press

The author

David M Martin FCIS FCIPD FIoD

The author David M Martin has been Assistant Secretary of two public companies, Scaffolding Great Britain and Gaskell & Chambers, where he was directly involved in property and contractual matters as well as personnel and corporate administration. He was subsequently appointed Secretary and then Director and Secretary of one of the top 250 listed PLCs where he remained for nearly ten years.

David was responsible for a range of disciplines – including property and insurance as well as statutory and legal requirements and corporate/internal communications. The property portfolio comprised over 400 units including retail, manufacturing, warehousing and domestic premises.

Following a takeover, he founded his own business consultancy – Buddenbrook – in 1985. Buddenbrook carries out various projects for a range of clients, large and small, including conducting property negotiations, acquisitions and disposals, rent reviews and renewals etc.

David is also an employer's representative for the panel of members for the Employment Tribunals and a member of one of the Registrar of Companies committees. He speaks at around 90 seminars each year and is author of around 40 business books. A fifth edition of his title *The Company Director's Desktop Guide* and a second edition of his *The A-Z of Employment Practice* are now available from Thorogood.

Foreword

It's for you!

"I'm not into property – I just want to make widgets." This is entirely understandable, but whether your organization is making widgets, selling insurance or leasing aircraft – or, indeed making and/or selling anything else, then, like it or not, you **are** in property. Property is often the most valuable of an organization's fixed assets; for example, trading in UK property portfolios reached a record £9 billion in 2005. Here, however, we are concerned not so much with property as an investment (other than as a one-off) but with its use and administration for the purpose of an organization's own business.

Some entities employ managers to specialize in property administration; in most, however, either the duties relating to such assets are allocated to a manager already fully committed to his or her 'real job' – or they are not properly administered at all. Such a 'property admin. vacuum' is not restricted to smaller organizations. In an investigation of a hundred of the largest 1000 UK companies, property surveyors DTZ Debenham Thorpe discovered that:

- only 20% of those surveyed had a comprehensive database concerning the properties they occupied, and

- 10% had such incomplete databases that not even addresses and details of tenure were recorded centrally!

The survey also disclosed that 66% of organizations were investigating how to minimize their occupation costs – though how this could be achieved without an accurate database is difficult to reconcile!

A property strategy

It may help planning and administration in this area if occupiers develop and adopt a property strategy. For example:

Whilst it is accepted that the [organization] needs to occupy property(ies) primarily to facilitate its aims, it is recognized that property occupation/ownership

a) *generates opportunities to trade in such assets and such opportunities will be explored and exploited*

b) *imposes responsibilities, obligations and liabilities, the full extent and effect of which will be established and considered as part of the regular planning process of the business*

c) *requires regular investment not only to comply with legal obligations, but also to maximize its value and protect the investment.*

Some organizations may wish to adopt a strategy which commits them to trade actively in the property(ies) they use as well as in their core business, although the dilution of management attention as well as the potential dislocation caused by repeated moves must be carefully considered.

'Occupational value' myopia

The DTZ report also stated that '…proactive management of occupational real estate will make a significant contribution to a company's performance'. Surely at a time when all organizations are looking at improving performance by realizing assets and cutting costs this strategy should include 'occupying (their) buildings more efficiently'. This point was emphasized by the Royal Institution of Chartered Surveyors (RICS) which stated that British industry is '…throwing away £18 billion every year' through inefficient control and use of its property assets. The RICS calculated that proper budgetary and cost control, space planning, disposing of surplus space, etc., could 'boost profits by 13%'.

Far too often organizations enter into the long-term commitment of property occupation without fully appreciating the obligations they have taken on, whilst the routine administration of the facility may be handled by a variety of different people perhaps leaving gaps and paying insufficient attention to gaining 'best value for money'. The DTZ survey suggested that only around 50% – 70% of occupiers monitor their property costs, whilst only 25% – 40% review existing and potential property values. Property can be improved, altered, have its use changed, be used as loan security and sold – all strategies which can work to the financial and efficient benefit of the business.

Duties

The obligations of those responsible by appointment (or default) for the administration of their organization's property assets are three fold:

1) Facilities administration, which the British Institute of Facilities Management defines as:

    - the integration of multi-disciplinary activities within the built environment and the management of their impact on people and the workplace

    - (combining) resources and activities (which) are vital to the success of any organization, by contributing to the delivery of strategic and operational objectives

    - providing a safe and efficient working environment which is essential to business performance whatever its size and scope

    - the provision, maintenance and development of myriad facility services which range from developing a strategy, managing space and putting in a communications infrastructure to building maintenance, administration and contract management.

2) Budgetary and expenditure control. In many organizations there is an apparent 'cost blindness' to property expenditure, so much so that facility costs are regarded as fixed and immutable as taxation. Indeed in some instances costs are passed for payment with hardly any examination as to correct calculation and/or appropriateness. This is doubly curious since presumably costs related to other purchases are surely not passed for payment without investigation. Of course property costs could be among the most expensive in the budget.

3) Property administration, which could include:

    - long-term planning of requirements

    - compiling and administration of records

    - interfacing with regulatory bodies involved in building, fitting out and occupying properties, and those having access to them

    - interfacing with landlords and/or agents

    - administration of cleaning, security, reception, housekeeping and safety, waste disposal, gardening etc services

    - ensuring compliance with covenants under leases

    - interfacing with, providing information to, and making claims on insurers

- interfacing with utility and other bought in service providers
- preparing and updating contingency and/or disaster recovery plans
- interfacing with neighbours and trespassers
- assisting with planning and implementation of relocation
- overseeing the renegotiation of leases, agreeing rent reviews and renewals

and so on – and on – and on!

With this range of obligations it is obvious that in any organization with more than a few properties (particularly if leased) this should not be a job to be added to the duties to be undertaken by someone who already has enough to do. It poses specific problems and challenges which, if not dealt with properly, could involve (and often does) considerable cost, waste and inconvenience.

The challenges of the 21st century

Both the working environment and the location of such work are subject to considerable change and, assuming these changes continue in their current direction, present new problems for the property administrator. For example, around 3 million people in the UK work at home and this number has been projected to grow to around 9 million by 2010. If correct, this would mean roughly a third of the UK workforce could be working at home within the next decade, which, apart from the beneficial effect it would have on public transport and road congestion, could mean a substantial reduction in demand for commercial property. After all, if an organization can operate effectively with only two-thirds of its workforce commuting to, and working in, its traditional workplace, at the very least the size of those workplaces should be re-assessed. Organizations should ensure NOW that they do not commit on a long-term basis to space which could become a costly surplus in the future.

Our aim

Having been involved with the negotiations to acquire, dispose of and administer facilities within a number of portfolios over 30 years, I have tried in this book to address aspects of property and facilities strategy, and administration and control with practical suggestions drawn from a distillation of experiences (good and bad!) during that period. In some instances, expert input should be sought but at least the content should allow the reader to know the right questions to ask and be able to brief the experts accordingly.

David M Martin
Buddenbrook
Summer 2006

Using this book

1. This book is presented in the expanded index format which enables attention to be concentrated on one particular subject at a time, rather than the item being buried along with other items in a long chapter.

2. Using the expanded index leads to some duplication of content but this is deliberate in the interests of a comprehensive treatment of each subject.

3. Short case studies have been incorporated to demonstrate aspects of this fascinating area of administration.

4. Leasehold occupation is governed by Landlord and Tenant Act legislation. A lease is a contract between a lessor (the landlord) and a lessee (the tenant). The description 'lessee' has been used here partly to underline the need to have regard to the obligations in the lease.

5. Examples of forms, checklists and registers are incorporated for the personal use of the reader. In addition, a 'Useful contacts' section provides brief details for some additional reading, sources of advice and guidance etc.

6. Other than where it is inappropriate, the masculine includes the feminine.

Contents

Access   3

Accommodation planning   9

Acquisition   13

Archiving   23

Budgetary control   31

Building works   35

Condition survey   45

Contaminated land   47

Contingency planning   51

Cost checklist   57

Covenants   65

Dilapidations   75

Disability discrimination   79

Electronic security   85

Energy   89

Environmental obligations   93

Fire precautions   101

First aid   111

Freehold ownership   117

Guarantees   123

Health and safety   127

Homeworking   133

Insurance and incident reporting 143

Internal rents 153

Janitorial duties 157

Keeping property records 165

Landlord's rights and duties 177

Leasehold commitment 181

Lessee's Works 187

Licence 193

Maintenance 199

Marriages of interests 207

Neighbours 213

Notice Boards 219

Notice serving 223

Option to break 229

Outsourcing 233

Planning 239

Privity of contract 243

Quiz 249

Rating 255

Reinstatement 261

Relocation 263

Rent review 271

Repairs and redecoration 285

Risk management 287

Safety communication 299

Security 307

Service charge 319

Tenancy agreements   325
Termination   329
Terrorist precautions   333
Trespassers   339

Underletting   345
Upwards only rent review (UORR)   347
Use and user clause   349

Valuation   355
Variation of orders/lease   357
VAT on rent   361

Waste   365
Work/leisure occupation   373

Xmas precautions   377

Yearly projections   383

Zoning   391

Useful contacts   397

Cases   401

A

Access   3

Accommodation planning   9

Acquisition   13

Archiving   23

Access

Introduction

Every property occupier needs to allow access to those working at the facility – and needs to control or prevent access to others. In addition, access rights (increasingly on a forcible basis) are possessed by many regulatory bodies. Control thus needs to be exercised over all access in the interests of security, safety and confidentiality.

Types of access

Those gaining access can be divided into five categories:

1. Those who are employed at and/or are required to visit the premises in the ordinary course of their or the occupant's business e.g. employees, suppliers, visitors. If members of the public need access (e.g. to a theatre, sports stadium, doctor's surgery etc) this adds an additional sub-category.

2. Those who own the business (for example shareholders) who have a number of rights of access – mainly to inspect statutory records.

3. Members of the public and creditors of limited companies who have rights of inspection of statutory records.

4. Official/regulatory bodies whose representatives are entitled to gain access under authority vested by statute, contract etc.

5. Trespassers.

1. Employees and visitors

The most numerous of those requiring access are employees, and visitors related to the organization and/or with the goods or services being produced. Whilst few organizations would wish to unduly restrict such access, there may be occasions when general and/or particular restrictions to 'sensitive' areas of the premises may be essential. Procedures (see JANITORIAL DUTIES) should be developed and promulgated so that employees are aware of such restrictions. This is particularly relevant to computer suites (see ELECTRONIC SECURITY) and to those organizations vulnerable and attractive to TERRORISTS, or to industrial espionage. Electronic access equipment may not only solve some of the security problems but may also provide employees' attendance records and input to payroll.

2. Owners

Shareholders in limited companies have a number of rights of access allowing them to inspect the following statutory registers:

- Members or shareholders **
- Overseas branches **
- Directors and secretary **
- Directors' share interests **
- Significant shareholdings **
- Disclosure of holders under section 212 **
- Charges **
- Debenture holders
- Transactions not disclosed in the accounts under Companies Act 1985 section 330

as well as:

- minutes of general meetings, and
- directors' service contracts.

These documents and registers must be made available for a minimum of two hours each working day. A procedure similar to that devised for employees' access might be advisable.

* *

Procedure example: Shareholder access

1. Those wishing to inspect company records may do so only between [time e.g. 9.00am and 11.00am].
2. They must register in the same way as other visitors but in addition will be asked for evidence of their shareholding.
3. On receipt of such evidence (ideally a share certificate) the Company Secretary (or a person in his/her department) will meet the visitor.

4. Having checked with the Register of Members that the visitor does have shareholder rights, the shareholder will be escorted to [location].

5. The shareholder will be asked which document and/or registers they wish to inspect and (assuming these are subject to inspection results) these will be presented for inspection. On no account will the person dealing with them leave the item with the shareholder.

6. If the shareholder wants a copy of the item, the standard charge allowed by law will be levied.

7. Once the inspection/copying has been completed the shareholder will be escorted back to Reception.

This procedure envisages that the records are kept in hard copy. They may, however, be computerized and indeed, since most of these records are available virtually instantly in electronic form via the duplicate records kept at Companies House, such physical inspections are likely to be very rare.

3. Public and creditors

In the above list those registers followed by a double asterisk must also be made available to the public.

Again it may be helpful to draw up a procedure to ensure such requests (likely to be even more rare than those made by shareholders) are dealt with efficiently.

4. Official visitors

Many regulatory organizations have rights of access to the premises for the purpose of inspecting records and checking legal compliance. Other organizations may have similar rights derived from contractual relationships (e.g. because the premises occupied are leased, and/or because of membership of a trade or similar organization and so on). The principal bodies having such rights are set out below. Receptionists should be briefed on the manner of dealing with such persons.

i. Government and statutory regulatory agencies

Department of Trade and Industry (DTI), Financial Services Authority (FSA which took over the role of the Self-Regulatory Organizations SRO), Serious Fraud Office (SFO), European Union competition law inspectors (EU).

- **DTI** has power to investigate company affairs, ownership, dealings in shares, including insider dealing. Exact nature of investigation should be ascertained.

- **FSA** has powers under the Financial Services Act to investigate the affairs of organizations required to register under the Act.

- **SFO** has powers, wider in many cases than those available to the police or SROs, to investigate matters of fraud likely to total in excess of £2 million and to be of public concern.

- **EU** – inspectors have rights (without notice) to enter the premises of organizations of member states under EU law, although it has been stated that, in doing so they should try to act in accordance with the laws of the member state (and in concert with the domestic regulatory agency) concerned.

- **Competition Commissioner** – The Office of Fair Trading has an obligation to investigate whether supplies of goods or services breach the principles of the Fair Trading Act 1973 i.e. whether control of a market is monopolistic. Under the Competition Act as enhanced by the Enterprise Act, the CC/OFT also have rights of access and enquiry regarding suspected price fixing, operating a cartel etc.

ii) Statutory reporting agencies

HM Revenue and Customs (covering the previous and separate responsibilities of the Inland Revenue, the Contributions Agency and Customs and Excise) (HMRC), Wages Councils (WC), Rating Authorities (RA), Pensions Regulator (PR).

- **HMRC** powers of access tend to be exercised by the Audit Department of the Inland Revenue Compliance unit, which has the duty of checking the validity of the way an employer has paid and deducted tax from employees. However, the new body also has wide powers of access in respect of VAT and duty collection and it is anticipated that in future a single inspection will cover all areas under the aegis of this 'super-regulatory' body.

- **WC** officials have a right of access to check the display of the current Wages Council edict and to ensure payments etc., are being made in accordance with it.

- **RA** have access rights to check the valuation for the purposes of the Uniform Business Rate (or any appeal in respect thereof).

- **PR** has a right of access to check compliance with requirements – proper deduction and paying over of pension contributions, obligation regarding the provision of access to stakeholder pension scheme etc.

iii) Emergency and utility services

Fire, Police, Health and Safety, Environment, and Factory Inspectorates, Gas, Water and Electricity utilities:

- **Fire** – right of access to premises mainly for the purposes of checking occupier's compliance with the requirements of the Regulatory Reform (Fire Safety) Order 2005 and any requirements regarding fire safety made by an enforcement officer.

- **Police** – unless in the belief that a crime is about to, or is being committed, or in pursuit of a suspected person, (or with a search warrant) the police have no immediate right of access to premises other than with the permission of the owner.

- **Health and Safety Executive, Environmental Health Officers, Factory Inspectors** have a range of powers depending on individual industries. In addition, operators of large (and potentially hazardous) facilities are obliged (under the Control of Industrial Major Accident Regulations 1988) to file and keep up-to-date details of plans and emergency evacuations etc which will require an interface with the appropriate department which may well wish to check the site.

- **Utilities** – have rights of access to read meters and, if leaks/breaks are suspected, to rectify on an emergency basis, which could even entail forced entry.

iv) Others

- **Dept of Transport** – to inspect any transport operators licence and administration.

- **Local authorities have an increasing range of obligations** – particularly under the Food Safety and Environment Protection Acts.

- **Trading Standards Officers** – to ensure compliance with the relevant trading law.

- **Landlord and agents** – to inspect condition and use of premises, assess value for insurance, prepare dilapidations reports, etc., under the provisions of lease and/or licence.

5. Trespassers

Whilst trespassers are not present by invitation of the occupier and/or owner, the latter have obligations under the various Occupiers Liability Acts to them, particularly for the safety of children who trespass.

Case study

In *Margereson & Hancock v J W Roberts Ltd,* the company was held liable to the widow of a man who had contracted a disease as a result of him playing, as a child, in the asbestos-ridden dust of a loading bay – where he had no right to be. Occupiers must be proactive to ensure trespassers safety is maximized and their own liability is minimized.

Accommodation planning

Introduction

Commercial property is usually required for occupation – the main subject here – but sometimes it is treated as a commodity and used for speculation. When used for occupation the organization should assess its requirements and seek a facility to suit (see RELOCATION) or should mould premises to suit those requirements.

Basics

Property occupation can be expensive and an occupier's aim should be to minimize costs whilst maximizing the use of the space, purchased or rented, not only for the present but also for the projected term of occupation. An audit of present and future requirements (a 'space audit') should be completed identifying:

- projected growth (or otherwise). 'Space and people' forecasts should be projected as far into the future as possible,

- type of work, type of employees engaged upon that work and any special needs,

- history of space occupation. What has been utilized previously can be a guide (but only that) to what is required in the future,

- workflow, employee and departmental relationships. For instance, does the organization want open plan or individual offices (which may be a philosophical decision as much as anything else),

- technological requirements. In an increasing number of organizations employees need access to computer linkage, telecommunications etc,

- comfort of working environment. If an employer wishes to obtain and retain the 'best employees', providing well-designed and suitably comfortable premises may be essential,

- costs – see BUDGETARY CONTROL and YEARLY PROJECTIONS.

Layout

For offices, the choice is between individual offices (which would normally be accompanied by at least some open plan areas) and 'open plan' (with a minimum of, or even a complete absence of, individual offices). However, with an increasing number of people not being based permanently in the traditional workplace – either being in the field or HOMEWORKING etc – both 'hot desking' (where there is no specific workstation allocated to an employee – they simply use whichever is free at the time of need) and 'hostelling' or 'hoteling' (where those not permanently located in the premises, book a workstation each time they wish to work at the location) are increasingly being utilized and thus these options may also need to be catered for:

- **Open plan: advantages**
  - higher occupancy per any given area
  - better interfacing, team building etc
  - better energy consumption
  - fewer items of equipment, since there should be increased shared use
  - potential reduction of demarcation disputes and departmental barriers
  - better communication

- **Open plan: disadvantages**
  - reduced privacy, although this can be overcome to some extent by the use of private areas for common use
  - distraction from other employees' work, movement, phones ringing etc. It may be possible to reduce this by using noise absorbent ceiling tiles, carpets and free standing partitions
  - loss of status by managers. This may be more perceived than real – not least since effective leaders should not need such status supports
  - managers, since there is no physical barrier between them and their teams, may find themselves involved in dealing with routine matters

- **Private offices: advantages**
  - privacy and security increased
  - recognition of career progression and/or status
  - ease of control by virtue of perceived status of room allocation

- **Private offices: disadvantages**
  - increased space requirement
  - can create more distance between manager (leader) and team and thus reduce rapport (although an 'open-door' policy may offset this)

- **Hot desking: advantages**
  - minimizes the space required
  - permits greater investment (and thus should generate better quality) in each 'workstation'

- **Hot desking: disadvantages**
  - not having an 'allegiance' to a particular location may reduce the user's rapport with the organization (perhaps generating a feeling of being an outsider)

- **Hostelling: advantages**
  - minimizes the space required
  - allows greater investment in each 'workstation'
  - being allowed to 'book' a dedicated workstation may overcome the disadvantage of the lack of 'allegiance' common with 'hot desking'

- **Hostelling: disadvantages**
  - such external users may also experience a feeling of not being part of the organization

Physical factors

That employees work best when they are comfortable and well-motivated should be self-evident. The workplace provider thus needs to address:

- *Heating and ventilation.* The provision of an appropriate working temperature is essential but sadly it must be said that it seems rare to find systems that can provide what is required. Often a so-called 'air-conditioning' installation seems to pump cooling air **into** the area (creating unwanted draughts) rather than extracting heated air **from** the premises (this improving the quality of the air generally).

- *Lighting.* Care must be given not only to the provision of an appropriate level of lighting but also to ensuring it does not create unwanted reflections (for example, on VDU screens). To avoid the waste of electricity because lights are left on unnecessarily, convenient (or 'time-delay') switches should be provided.

- *Noise*. Performance can be impaired by excessive noise and thus noise absorbing ceilings, panels, flooring etc may be needed to reduce noise to an acceptable level.

- *Colour*. Research indicates that output can be impaired by strident or 'clashing' colours. Neutral colours may be preferable.

- *Furniture*. Whilst expensive furniture may be unnecessary (unless a prestige environment is sought) a reasonable level of attractive, well-designed and ergonomically appropriate desks, chairs, filing and other cupboards and equipment should be utilized. Whilst many may be able to work well even in poor surroundings and with poor equipment and support, most will work more effectively and willingly with good surroundings and decent equipment.

- *Toilets and cloakroom areas*. To minimize unproductive time as well as for employees' convenience, such facilities (including facilities for the disabled) should be adjacent to each work area.

- *Refreshment areas*. To minimize unproductive time, (good quality) vending machines (or alternative facilities) should be located adjacent to each work area.

- *Access*. Increasingly employers are required to 'make reasonable adjustments' to allow the disabled to work productively, and thus consideration should be given to means of access – width of doorways, avoiding or circumventing stairs, lifts, hearing loops, notices in Braille, etc.

Acquisition

Introduction

Rights to property occupation, other than under licence, often entail a long-term commitment. Failing to appreciate the implications of such a commitment can come as an expensive surprise. The aspects and implications of the various types of occupation, covered in FREEHOLD, LEASEHOLD and LICENCE sections – should be referred to. Whilst the choice between the accommodation types may be predominantly a financial one there are a number of other considerations which need to be borne in mind.

Types of occupation

a) Freehold

The acquisition of freehold property entails a capital outlay which must be sourced and financed. However, investing in a freehold property may strengthen the organization's balance sheet since, in the long-term, property values tend to rise at around the level of inflation. Thus suppliers or creditors inspecting the balance sheet may derive some comfort from seeing such assets which, unlike most others, should appreciate. A freehold acquisition retains flexibility since:

- the business could raise capital on the property by means of a 'sale and lease-back' arrangement whereby, owning the freehold, the business sells that interest to a third party subject to the simultaneous grant of a lease to them of the premises (so that they retain occupation rights),

- subject to PLANNING restrictions and any restrictive covenants in the conveyance the owner can do with the property what it wishes.

- businesses operating an occupational pension scheme can reduce their levy to the Pension Protection Fund if they pledge property/ies to that scheme.

All aspects of the investment need to be identified and costed.

ACQUISITION JUSTIFICATION FORM – FREEHOLD

ORGANIZATION   FREEHOLD ACQUISITION ASSESSMENT

Property address _____

Purpose _____

A. RATIONALE

Is acquisition in plan? YES/NO* _____

If NO provide complete rationale and explain effect on plan _____

_____

_____

If YES – is timing in accordance with plan? YES/NO* If not provide explanation

_____

_____

B. COST

Purchase price   £

Purchase costs   £ (fees for agents, surveyors, solicitors; stamp duty)

Fitting out costs   £ (confirmed estimate)

                                                          _____

Total acquisition costs £

                                                          =======

Estimated annual charge £ per square metre/yard (so that an occupation cost per department can be calculated (see INTERNAL RENTS)

C. LOCATION

Explain rationale for selecting this site. _____

_____

What is the planning authority's designated use for the area? _____

_____

What are prospects for disposal in long-term? _____

_____

Any capital growth anticipated? YES/NO _____

_____

If YES explain type of growth/period etc. _____

_____

D. USAGE

Is whole property to be used YES/NO_____

If Yes – state annual income from purpose of occupation _____

If No – explain approach regarding surplus _____

Subletting – expected income (etc) _____

E. RUNNING COSTS

Annual operating costs_____

(Provide analysis for duration of plan span of [specify]) _____

(Note: This could include the 'annual charge' (see B above), internal rent, cost of money or depreciation, statutory imposition reserve, etc.)

F. ALTERNATIVE RATIONALE

(That is provide an explanation of how the situation will be addressed if this purchase does not happen.)

_____

_____

NOTES

i)   Unless the proposal has been previously addressed within the planning process the whole rationale needs to be examined.

ii) The means by which the operating department/unit etc is charged for the occupation needs to be determined either by means of a proportion of the original cost price, or by an internal rent or depreciation charge etc.

iii) The question of ultimate use or disposal should be addressed.

iv) The 'statutory imposition' reserve addresses the fact that increasingly commercial occupiers of property are required under legislation to carry out alterations etc., to their properties. For example:

- since October 2004, occupiers have been required to make reasonable adjustments to their premises to allow disabled access to members of the public;

- since November 2005, occupiers have been required to carry out an 'asbestos containing materials' survey of their premises and to protect any asbestos discovered from being disturbed;

- since April 2006 occupiers have been required to be pro-active regarding assessing FIRE risks in their premises.

All such requirements could, depending on the state of the building, be expensive.

b) Leasehold

A lease grants a right of occupation in return for which the occupier must pay rent and other outgoings for the premises and keep them in a state of good repair and decoration for the lease term. A lease is a binding contract with many clauses including a number of COVENANTS which can be onerous and restrictive. The implications of all covenants should be fully appreciated, particularly as failure to comply may mean that the lessee can be in breach of the lease which could lead to loss of occupation, and the payment of compensation in respect of the unexpired term. A lease usually also grants a right to the lessee to a new lease when the old expires unless:

- the landlord wishes to occupy the premises himself or to redevelop them, or

- the lessee has failed to comply with the covenants, or

- the lease is agreed (with Court approval) to be outside the Landlord and Tenant Act (the legislation which protects the interests of lessees).

Subject to some provisions a lease may be able to be sold (assigned).

ACQUISITION JUSTIFICATION FORM – LEASEHOLD

ORGANIZATION   LEASEHOLD ACQUISITION ASSESSMENT

Property address _____

Purpose_____

A. COMMITMENT RATIONALE

Is commitment in plan? YES/NO*_____

If NO provide complete rationale and explain effect on plan _____

_____

If YES is timing in accordance with plan? YES/NO* _____

If NO – provide an explanation _____

_____

B. TOTAL EXPENDITURE COMMITMENT

Expenditure: multiply commencing annual rent plus service charge (if any)
by term of lease or term to option date (if any) _____

_____

Projected additional rent and service charge from reviews _____

_____

Total commitment (i.e. figure to be justified)_____

What alternatives are there to the lease commitment? _____

_____

Can lease term be shortened and is this appropriate? _____

_____

If there is no option to break, can one be introduced?_____

_____

Possibilities of assignment (i.e. is lease marketable)? _____

_____

Any possibility of acquiring freehold? YES/NO

If YES, what price?

C. ANNUAL RUNNING COSTS

(Total annual expenditure inc. rent, rates, heating, lighting, statutory imposition reserve, maintenance, redecoration, dilapidation reserve.)

D. USAGE

Is whole property to be used? YES/NO _____

If NO, can surplus be sublet? YES/NO _____

If YES what is expected income to offset annual costs? _____

If NO – explain rationale re. surplus_____

NOTES

i) The requirement for prospective occupiers to state alternatives should approval for occupation not be granted is used widely in the USA. Such alternatives could, for example, include:

    a) a bought-in service

    b) short-term licensing

    c) outsourcing

    d) outworking, and so on.

ii) The requirement to consider the implications of commitment to a long-term lease is mainly to underline that very point i.e. it is a long term commitment and any method of achieving flexibility should be considered.

iii) See the notes to the Freehold acquisition form for other guidance to the questions asked above.

c) Licence

This is simply a 'right to occupy', usually only for a short period. Similar covenants to those in a lease may be contained but without any right to renewal of occupation at the end of the term. Occupying premises under licence provides little security, although usually it does have the advantage of low cost. It is very unlikely that the rights under a licence could be transferred.

Pre-commitment checklist

1. **Location**: Ideal locations are rare, but unless the required parameters are identified it will certainly be unlikely to find the ideal (see RELOCATION).

   There are a number of initiatives operated either by the State (DTI Enterprise initiative, Urban Regeneration), by local authorities (Enterprise Zones) and the European Union (Special Assistance Areas) giving financial assistance to businesses prepared to move to certain areas where employment is required. The Department of the Environment has issued over 20 guides giving information about development policies in various areas.

2. **Area**: Before making a decision, the long-term future of the area should be considered. Is it likely that, should the organization wish to dispose of the premises in the medium future, that there will be a market for such premises in such a location? If not, the possibility that disposal may be costly (or at a discount) needs to be borne in mind as part of the acquisition cost assessment. The position regarding Registration of Land on which the building stands should also be investigated. Although an increasing proportion of land in the UK is now registered (i.e. details of position, history, ownership, restrictive covenants etc., are on record with the Land Registry and allocated a Title Number) sizable areas (including much of London) are not yet registered which may make the investigation of title more difficult.

3. **Type of property**: Whilst using a property that fits the exact requirements of the organization is ideal, if such requirements are very unusual and the property is customized it may be difficult to dispose of it. Using a listed building may add to an organization's image, but there are severe restrictions regarding use and alteration of such a property – and its value on disposal may be reduced accordingly.

4. **Pre-acquisition survey**: Since failing to establish the true state of the property could prove costly, a full structural survey should be commissioned, despite the cost. This is especially the case with property subject to a full repairing lease. Under the terms of such a lease the landlord can force the lessee to rectify repairs etc, but if the clause states 'put and keep repaired', the lessee's obligation is extended, and requires the lessee to bring the property to a fair state of repair no matter how

dilapidated it may have been initially (and how blameless the current lessee is for its state). Establishing the state of the building enables the purchaser to take a commercial decision in recognition of such potential obligations. Indeed, the existence (and results!) of a professionally compiled and costed survey may be a valuable negotiating factor in arriving at the determination of price, rent and/or premium.

5. **Inherent defects**. Another advantage of the survey is that it may disclose any inherent defects in the building which, through negotiation, may be taken out of any commitment as far as rectification and/or repair.

6. **CONDITION SCHEDULE**: Such a schedule may also be negotiated to minimize onerous repairing/rectification obligations in a lease. An agreed schedule of the state of the property should minimize the lessee's obligations to repair to that state (and no better).

7. **COVENANTS**: The full effect of all the covenants required to be included in the lease should be explained to those who will actually operate in the building in case any (for example, unduly restrictive opening hours) would inhibit the required use of the building. Someone fully aware of the effect of covenants on the practical aspects of operating in the premises should review ALL covenants before commitment.

8. **PRIVITY OF CONTRACT**: If these requirements or their equivalent are included in the lease, permission for the lessee to sublet or underlet as an option to assignment should be insisted upon. In this way, should the premises become surplus to requirements, and an alternative occupier be found, the lessee can sublet or underlet (rather than assign), knowing that should the new occupier fail, they retain rights (usually lost in the event of assignment) to re-occupy and/or to re-let.

9. **PLANNING**: Any restrictions placed on occupation by planning consents and/or conditions, and/or covenants contained in the conveyance need to be fully appreciated (and costed).

10. **Acquisition costs**: As well as the actual purchase price, all solicitors' and agents' costs, stamp duty, land tax, insurance etc. should be built into the budget. For leasehold premises, some organizations require justification of the total rental exposure for the term of the lease (ignoring or including reviews) because this is the total commitment being entered into.

11. **Acquisition concerns**: When an organization acquires land or buildings, enquiry regarding pollution should be made. Land may previously have been used by organizations that contaminated the land and under the Environment Protection legislation if the polluter cannot be found then the occupier is responsible for an expensive

cleansing of the land. Since knowledge that the land is polluted may not be realized for some time it may be advisable to insure against this risk. Alternatively it may be possible to obtain an undertaking from the vendor to hold the purchaser harmless from such costs.

12. **Occupation costs**: The full costs of occupying and running the facility need to be assessed and justified. In a relocation, the current costs of heating and lighting may be extrapolated (to take account of buildings of different sizes and/or configurations). If an existing building is being acquired, enquiry of the previous occupier may also provide a guide to these costs. Obviously the effect of building costs as well as the investment, depreciation etc must also be taken into account. If the use of the building – or its configuration in terms of occupation – is to be changed, the question of the RATING valuation – and any appeal – should also be considered. It may also be necessary to check whether there is any breach of user or PLANNING requirements.

13. **Access**, car parking and relationships with NEIGHBOURS should be investigated: Where access could be denied e.g. because of (for example) fire of a neighbouring building, insurance against 'denial of access' (a particular consideration if a unit is for example in shared facilities such as a tower block, retail centre or park) should be considered and costed.

14. **Personnel**: Staffing costs and employees' travelling conditions may need consideration.

Commitment checklist

1. **Customizing**: Rarely will any building be ideal for immediate occupation and most will require some customizing. Such works need to be approved under building regulations and comply with the requirements issued in accordance with the latest fire precautions regulations. Where the occupation is leasehold the approval of the landlord must also be sought prior to any works being effected whilst the obligations under any REINSTATEMENT requirements should be assessed.

2. **Works approval**: Landlord's approval can be obtained either formally (under a LICENCE to carry out works or a Deed of VARIATION) or informally (by the landlord signing copies of the plans and specification setting out the work to be conducted). Usually the formal route is required which will not only require a deed to be drawn up, but will also set out

conditions regarding the works and an obligation on the lessee to REINSTATE the premises on lease termination. This requirement can have a triple cost: payment for the works, payment for them to be removed at lease termination and, since the premises must be left in a good state of repair, payment to make good.

3. **Funding the works**: Such costs can be met by either party. If the landlord pays, the costs could be recovered by the rent being increased. Although this makes the relationship somewhat 'tidier' since the lessee is simply occupying a facility, the entire cost of which has been met by the landlord, if the rent itself is increased it may have repercussions at times of RENT REVIEW when the occupier needs to relate its rent to rents commanded by similar properties in the immediate area. The 'rentalised' costs may be better dealt with as a charge entirely separate to the rent (even if collected at the same time). If the lessee funds the works, then not only should the triple cost effect referred to above be borne in mind but also the lease should stipulate that the effect of the works should be ignored when the rent is reviewed. If not, the lessee, having paid for works which have increased the value of the premises, be asked to pay rent enhanced by the value of the same works. If the landlord resists this 'ignore the effect of the works at rent review' argument and requires the full value to be reflected at review either the landlord should fund the works, or some dilution of other covenants (e.g. repairing and/or reinstatement obligations) should be negotiated.

4. **Accountability**: Ideally completion of the acquisition phase should take place in sufficient time for customizing and setting up work to be completed before occupation. Rarely does this occur and usually there needs to be some compromise – often with employees trying to commence working whilst builders are still finishing. Usually the terms of a building contract will require the builder to take responsibility for the property during the works (and to effect insurance related to this). If staff from the employing organization occupy the premises before the builder has 'handed over', responsibility, in the event of any loss or damage, may be blurred. In addition, the builder may be able to disclaim any attempt to enforce any penalties for late completion by virtue of his staff being 'hampered' by the occupation.

Archiving

Introduction

Control of property assets cannot be effected properly without information being available instantly to the property administrator. The sourcing and collation of such data (see KEEPING PROPERTY RECORDS) is essential. However, the source material for such information is often original documentation which may have a value in its own right (not least inconvenience should it be lost) and thus require adequate protection.

Freehold data

Transfer of freehold property is usually effected by means of a conveyance. Free-hold land in the UK has been required to be registered with the Land Registry (LR see USEFUL CONTACTS) since 1937. The LR keeps details of ownership of all registered land, but since registration is only required on sale or mort-gage, around a third of all UK properties (including most of the properties in London) remain unregistered. In terms of ownership, registration renders other title deeds somewhat superfluous, although they may contain details of PLAN-NING and building regulation consents as well as details of wayleaves etc. Most organizations are loath to dispose of old deeds even for registered land and on each successive transfer of ownership the bundle of documents evidencing title tends to grow. All such documents – easements, wayleaves, rights of access, consents, etc need protection, as should evidence of all alterations to the prop-erty – approvals, plans, specifications, etc. An index or schedule of the items should be prepared and copies kept both with the deeds and by the property administrator. Obviously the loss of a conveyance or other evidence of title of unregistered land can cause considerable inconvenience.

WARNING: Strict control over the protection of title needs to be effected since in any audit of the financial records in which reference is made to the value of its properties, auditors may wish to see evidence of ownership. Some form of control register such as is set out below may be advisable to record to whom deeds, etc were lent and when. In passing title deeds outside the immediate control of the Property Administrator, a receipt should be obtained and kept with the register. On return, the items should be checked against the schedule and a counter receipt issued.

Date	Property	Deeds schedule	Reason withdrawn	Sent to	Returned	Comments
1.10.06	St Albans	Conveyance etc		Sale to [name]	[Solicitors]	n/a
15.11.06	York	Lease etc	Termination/ new lease	[Agents]	1.1.07	

Note: Many historians and archivists are totally opposed to the destruction of 'title' deeds since they can provide such a valuable research source.

Leasehold data

A lease is not a document of title – it evidences a lessee's right of occupation of the property. Nevertheless leases should be preserved safely. Some leases have a financial value and the points referred to above in relation to the audit should not be overlooked. For similar reasons to those suggested for freehold data, all documentation relating to the occupation (plans, specifications, approvals etc) as well as any deeds of variation, rent review confirmations, etc should also be preserved. Where the landlord has granted approval to the lessee to carry out alterations by signing and returning plans (rather than insisting on a deed of VARIATION or licence evidencing the works) such plans must be preserved to evidence the variation. To ensure that all records (including those not related to property) are properly stored a policy/procedure should be adopted.

Document and records preservation policy [Organization]

1. Responsibility for preserving the various books, registers and records of the company, in order to comply with legislation and business practice is devolved to (Company Secretary/Property Administrator)

2. Such responsibility will include:
   - ensuring safe storage with reasonable accessibility whilst the items are current,
   - provision of adequate back-up systems capable of providing current record data, should originals be lost
   - archiving records in accordance with a procedure and timetable, and
   - ensuring preservation of records in those archives.

3. The various terms of retention as set out in [specify reference source – see suggestions in USEFUL CONTACTS]

   (subject to any extension, but not contraction, of the suggested time limits for reasons particular to the organization) are to be adhered.

4. Suitably secure premises/facilities will be utilized for this purpose. Such premises will provide protection from rodents, fire, flood, intruders etc.

5. If data is computerized, and software is changed, reformatting of the stored information should be undertaken.

6. The [Company Secretary or equivalent executive] will be required to report annually on compliance with the requirements of this procedure.

Item 5 seeks to protect against a situation where records have been compiled using a version of software or computerization which has been superseded. The old records should be reconstituted to avoid later finding that access is impossible due to the change and lack of retention of the software on which the records were compiled.

Case study

In 1086, William of Normandy (William I of England) decreed that a 'domestic day book' should be compiled recording everything going on in the country at that time. This 'domes day' (which quickly became known as the 'doomsday') book can, if a reader understands the Latin in which it was compiled, be read today. In 1986, to mark the 900th anniversary of the compilation of the Doomsday Book, the BBC commissioned a 20th century version using 12" video disks of pictures and text. Sadly the software and hardware has been replaced and now the 1986 version cannot be accessed although one can still read its 900 year old predecessor!. Technology is a wonderful invention – common sense sadly may be less common than its name implies.

Protection

All the deeds and documents referred to above require protection. In some cases they may be required to be deposited with (for example) the bankers of the organization as security for a loan. On making such a deposit those receiving the items should be asked to confirm that they will hold them securely, store them safely (in fireproof cabinets) and surrender them when the loan is repaid.

Other than when out on loan or held by third parties (e.g. solicitors) pending sale etc the items should be stored internally in fireproof cabinets or safes. Wherever possible, such cabinets should be stored on the ground floor or basement. If not, there is a danger in a fire that even though the cabinet can resist a fire, should it fall as a result of the collapse of floors, etc it could burst open (although burst proof cabinets can be sourced). In the aftermath of the terrorist campaign of the late 1980s and early 1990s, many organizations created bomb proof rooms within their facilities. Whilst there may be pressure on the space available, consideration should be given to storing property deeds and documents there.

Plans

Experience indicates that few purchasers (even of a freehold) stipulate that the vendor should provide plans and copies of the building specification – although having these could be invaluable. A similar request should be made regarding leasehold premises although such a request is even less likely to meet with success. Where alterations are required to leased premises it may be possible to gain the landlord's consent by simply supplying plans of the proposed alterations (in duplicate) asking for one copy to be signed as evidence of permission to carry out the works. If a signed copy is provided, this may also avoid the lessee being required to reinstate. All plans, regardless of origination, should be preserved safely (map chests can be used for flat storage).

Copies

It may be prudent to computer scan or microfilm original deeds, plans etc, both for instant access and also for recovery of data in the event of a loss of the originals. Reference should be made to British Standards guidance to ensure proper steps are taken when copying records. For microfilming, the standard is BS6498 whilst for information stored on electronic document management systems the reference is PD0008. Subject to proof of reliability, the Civil Evidence Act 1995 allows computer records (including records stored on compact disks) to be used as evidence.

Note: In TERRORIST PRECAUTIONS the concept of compiling contingency plans is addressed. Properly controlled archiving may be one of the ways in which it will be easier for an organization to recover following an emergency, particularly where alternative premises are to be used and access to the original premises is prohibited.

B

Budgetary control 31

Building works 35

Budgetary control

Introduction

Property must be carefully budgeted for and controlled. Whether it is appropriate for an organization to commit capital to a freehold purchase or to lease and incur an annual rental charge is an obvious question, nevertheless the costs associated with a leasehold acquisition should be quantified so that informed decisions can be made with the benefit of these facts or projections. Experience indicates this is not always the case.

Investigation

The forms set out in ACQUISITION can be used to identify costs likely to be incurred in connection with the ownership/occupation/use of the property. If total expense can then be related to the benefit likely to be derived from the investment, its viability can be assessed. These forms are suggested as examples and need to be customized to suit individual organizations. They assume that the organization prepares a long-term financial/sales plan, and commence with the requirement for individual parts of the organization to determine the space they need for at least the duration of such a plan. From that analysis the organization can devise a 'premises requirement' and work towards the provision of suitable areas accordingly. However, most organizations already utilize one or more properties and it is appropriate to consider and detail exactly what we have before we can decide 'where to take whatever it is we have'.

FORWARD PLANNING FORM

Organization	Planning period 20XX CURRENT SPACE USAGE	20XX ANNUAL CHARGES	Department CURRENT EARNING
Income generating			
Ancillary			
Storage			
Display/reception			
TOTAL			

Space req'd	20XX Annual projected			20XX Annual projected	
	Costs	Earnings		Costs	Earnings
Income generating					
Ancillary					
Storage					
Display/reception					
TOTAL					

Reasons for increase(s)

Space likely to be released from current allocation

	20XX Annual projected			20XX Annual projected	
	Costs	Income		Costs	Income
Income generating					
Ancillary					
Storage					
Display/reception					
TOTAL					

Reasons for increase(s)

Notes

i. The form should be geared to fit the span of time covered by the financial plan. Space could be indicated in square feet or square metres.

ii. Calculating the facility cost per department (no matter how crude – provided the same parameters are used for all) can aid the planning process itself. It might, for example, support an outsourcing proposal.

iii. The split of type of space has been provided as a guide – approaches will differ regarding the desirability (or even practicality) or otherwise of this.

iv. Annual charges could include an appropriate proportion of – rent (or INTERNAL RENT), rates, maintenance, decoration, heating, lighting, security and so on.

v. An assessment of 'income' or value of each part of the facility needs to be made. This may be the hardest part of the process – and the one open to most challenge by those using the space.

vi. Any requirement for additional space must be substantiated. Of course, such a development should have already been addressed during the main planning process.

vii. Space surplus to requirements can be identified in the same way as additional needs. Provided the space is freehold or leasehold where there is permission to sublet, the possibility of using this space to generate income needs to be examined

Cost control

By carrying out this kind of analysis, for every unit, opportunities may arise which can be exploited by the organization.

Case study

A multi-divisional organization requesting information in the above format discovered that four of its units, within a short distance of each other, were using up to 25% of their valuable in-town office space for storage of old records accessed infrequently. Over a three year period it arranged a 'bought in' archive operation at an annual cost of £5,000 to be shared by all units, consolidated the four units into three and reduced its total occupation costs by over £20,000 p.a.

Building works

Introduction

Official approval/clearance for building works and/or alterations to a building must be obtained not only from a landlord (if the property is leased) but also from local authorities under PLANNING and Building Regulations (BR) requirements. In addition to such permissions, full specifications and quotations for the costs must also be obtained.

Application

Other than relatively minor works and works subject to a number of exceptions in Schedule 2 of the Building Regulations 1991 (SI 1991 2768) amended by the Building (Amendment) Regulations 1994 (SI 1994 1850), work, whether erection of new, or alterations to existing buildings will usually require approval under BR. An application in respect of buildings being used for commercial purposes will also require clearance under the Fire Precautions legislation i.e. the 'Responsible Person' (see FIRE PRECAUTIONS) will need to have carried out full and appropriate risk assessments etc. The authority of the BR themselves, together with advice regarding their application which is listed in Approved Documents, emanates from the Building Act 1984. The BR (as amended from 2000) requires that where it is a 'new build' or making alterations to a building or materially altering its use, developers will need to:

- have means of early warning of fire to assist speedy escape
- use appropriate materials to reduce the spread of fire
- improve facilities to enable fire-fighters to save/protect life, and
- make suitable provision at the building for the easy access of fire appliances.

In addition, under the Construction (Design and Management) Regulations, for some works a safety supervisor must be appointed and a safety plan prepared and made available to all interested parties.

WARNING: Even the erection of a 'demountable' partition may, should it create 'an office within an office', infringe fire regulations. Thus advice regarding, and a full investigation of, the effect of even such minor works should be carried out.

Definitions

'Building works' for the purposes of BR are defined as:

- erection/extension or material alteration

- provision or material alteration of a controlled service (i.e. toilet, drainage, water, etc provisions)

- change of use and work in connection with a change of use

- underpinning and wall insulation work.

This is an outline only, the purpose of which is to demonstrate the widespread application of the regulations and the need to gain clearance of non-application or permission prior to any work taking place. Expert advice should be sought (see USEFUL CONTACTS) and reference should be made to the Regulations themselves.

Preparation

Obtaining approval under BR may be time-consuming particularly if the original suggestions are not agreed or it is indicated they will only be agreed subject to alterations. The compiling and submission of building plans for approval should be handled by an appropriately qualified person who, by virtue of experience and local contacts, may be able to save time (and cost) by ensuring that proposals which will not meet approval are not put forward. Informal contact with the appropriate officials, either by a qualified surveyor or the like, or even the property occupier, may save time.

Administration

BR requirements are administered by local authorities, and to obtain clearance those wishing to carry out building works must deposit full plans of the works contemplated. It is prudent to ensure the timetable allows for the time that will be taken by the local authority considering the proposals. Whilst it may be possible to start some works in advance of clearance, there is a risk that any work which does not comply with the regulations or requirements may have to be rectified – or even removed.

Appeal

Should a local authority reject their plans, applicants have a right of appeal to the Department of the Environment and, in some cases, of further appeal to the Office of the Deputy Prime Minister (ODPM). Whilst this may have some attraction, the delay before a decision is forthcoming should not be under-estimated.

Compliance

Should a person not submit plans required under BR, or should the regulations be contravened, fines of up to £5,000, plus a daily fine of £50 for the duration of the default can be imposed. The local authority can also require the person responsible to demolish any building erected without regulation approval and/or carry out alterations as required to make the building comply with the regulations. Should the owner not comply within 28 days the Authority has the right to enter the land, carry out the required works and recover its costs from the person responsible.

Documentation

No matter how small the works, a contract should be drawn up. Whilst for minor works this may seem unnecessary, the damage that could be done to a building (and the business being carried on from it) during building works can be immense. It is not unknown for millions of pounds of damage to be caused as a result of action (or inaction) during relatively minor building work (e.g. the fire at Windsor Castle). Agreeing a contract enables both parties to stipulate what is required as well as setting out the responsibilities of each during the works. This is particularly important when the works are to be carried out whilst the building is being used for its main purpose. Included in the contract should be:

- a detailed specification of the works (so that in the event of any dispute the parties can refer to it for determination)
- a detailed timetable and progress chart
- a time/cost analysis with details of any bonus payments for early completion (or penalties for late completion)
- the names and titles of those involved in the works with their authority levels (see below)
- details of the third party to be used in the event of any dispute between the parties.

Increasingly Alternative Dispute Resolution (ADR) is being used to determine disputes. Under this process both parties nominate a third party to determine their dispute agreeing to pay 50% of the costs involved – less expensive than using the legal profession.

Safety

Works

The safety both of those carrying out the works and of those working within the building during the works should be paramount. Under the Construction (Design and Management) Regulations 1994, for any building work which is to last longer than 30 days and involves more than four people, or is to boiler/ heating plant, or is to be carried on inside offices or shops without interrupting normal activities, a safety planning supervisor must be appointed and a suitable health and safety plan must be compiled.

The plan itself must address various phases in the process:

- the tender period (health and safety requirements must be given to those tendering for the work)

- the design period (the designer needs to consider health and safety requirements in planning the design and to advise the client of these and their implications)

- the construction phase (when health and safety becomes the responsibility of a planning supervisor who is required to coordinate and manage health and safety matters in liaison with the principal contractor).

The safety plan must be compiled, complied with at all times and made available to interested parties which can include members of the public.

WARNING: The foregoing is a brief outline only of the Construction (Design and Management) Regulations 1994. For greater coverage reference should be made to the Health and Safety Executive information sheets: Construction Sheets Nos. 38 – 44.

Premises

In many cases a contractor will be working on a client's premises whilst at least part of those premises are in ordinary use. It is important that the safety matters related to the works themselves are brought to the attention of the contractor, the occupier and their employees, subcontractors and their employees and all

others affected. A copy of the health and safety policy and any other requirements should form part of the contract documentation and a clause in the
contract should make it clear that the client expects adherence to the policy at
all times.

Other requirements:

- security rules to be observed

- disconnection of electricity (only to be made after at least a clear working
  day's notice to avoid losing computer data etc)

- builders refraining from commenting (in any way, but particularly
  verbally or by whistling) on any member of the client's staff – or on
  the public (if there are exterior works to the premises) – should also
  be made clear. Increasingly clients are also inserting a requirement that
  should they, for any reason, not wish a member of the contractor's staff,
  or any subcontractor or their employee(s) to work on the contract then
  that person or organization must be removed by the contractor.

Control

Normally a contractor will assume responsibility for the area covered by the
building works (i.e. the area delineated in the specification). Other than those
working on the project, official visitors and the contractor's staff, agents and
suppliers, no-one else should be admitted to the site without the contractor's
permission – and adherence to safety rules etc. This rule may need to be relaxed
where work is being carried on within a working environment conducting
normal business. Shared access/use can be a problem, since in the event of any
loss or accident it may be difficult to allocate responsibility. Since the contractor
will normally be required to effect insurance to cover the works and potential
liabilities, there is also a possibility of conflict between two or more insurers.
The problem may be alleviated by the client insisting that the contractor uses
their own buildings/contents insurer.

Variation

Few building contracts run to their completion without at least one variation
of the original specification. Whilst some of these may be the result of unforeseen snags and be requested by the builder, most tend to emanate from the
client. Accurate information – and contemporaneous confirmation to proceed
– of all VARIATIONS is essential.

WARNING: If the works covered by such a variation order are substantial it may be necessary to reconsider the safety plan prepared previously for any revisions.

Completion

The building profession is notorious for poor and/or late finishing. For this reason all building contracts should stipulate:

- practical completion and handover is not to be made until snagging is completed,
- a [six month] defects liability period, and
- [2.5 – 10%] retention.

Before the works are handed over to the client it is usual for the latter (or his agent, for example, an architect) to tour the works listing all items that need finishing or remedial attention. Only when such works are rectified should practical completion be certified and the works handed over.

Defects liability period

This period is usually six months during which time all problems, shortcomings etc should be noted by the client so that at the end of the period the contractor can be presented with a list of items which need rectification. A retention is merely a deduction (of 2.5%, 5% or 10%) from the total contract sum which is held by the client as a form of guarantee or incentive that the contractor will complete the full specification and, if necessary, will return to complete it satisfactorily. If there is difficulty getting the contractor to return to carry out the works, the retention sum can be forfeited and available to pay other contractors to finish the works. With a large contract, where payments are made in stages as the work progresses, the percentage retention is usually made from each stage payment. It may be helpful to link the release of the retention, subject to all works being completed, to the end of the defects liability period, although if the client is generally satisfied with the standard of the works, part of the retention may be released before that date.

Sub-contractor's retention

The contractor should be requested to deduct the contract rate of retention from payments made to any sub-contractor, so that there is an incentive to the sub-contractor to return and complete/rectify. Although the principle of the retention is sound and is likely to be effective where the rate is 10% or more, with rates of 5% or less, the sum involved may be so small that contractors can afford to ignore the 'incentive' offered to return and rectify, particularly if this means they have to pull employees off current jobs to do so. This negates the whole point of the retention and is a powerful argument against the lowering of the percentage from 10% to 5%.

WARNING: Where there are sub-contractors the client should check from time to time that they are being paid by the main contractor. It is not unknown for unscrupulous builders to retain the contract monies paid on account, withholding sums due in respect of work satisfactorily completed by the sub-contractors. Whilst the client has no liability to the sub-contractors they can still become involved in the ensuing argument – and it can delay completion.

Inspection

The contractor is normally required to rectify omissions and/or poor work at the end of the defects liability period. To help minimize the possibility of over-looking any item(s) on the day, before any joint inspection the client should carry out their own inspection (also referring to the specification and variations) preparing a ('snagging') list of items requiring attention.

C

Condition survey   45

Contaminated land   47

Contingency planning   51

Cost checklist   57

Covenants   65

Condition survey

Introduction

Property occupiers (whether freehold or leasehold) take on long-term responsibilities. Since a lease imposes enforceable repairing and redecorating covenants which could be invoked to require the lessee to put the premises into a good state of repair, a survey before lease commitment should be regarded as a necessity. Where a survey discloses that the premises are not in a good state of repair, consideration should be given to taking the matter one stage further by converting this assessment of the state of the premises into a schedule evidencing the standard, to which, but not beyond, which, the prospective lessee undertakes the premises must be repaired/redecorated.

Survey

A surveyor should inspect the property and prepare a report and schedule showing its state in general, and the areas where there needs to be work carried out in particular. In view of the potential liabilities and costs that could be incurred, any suggestion that the fee involved should be saved by waiving the need for a survey is likely to be a false economy. Generally landlords dislike schedules of condition since they not only negate the concept of the lessee bearing responsibility for repair and redecoration (thus restricting this valuable covenant) but also they have the effect of reducing the potential value of their investment. To a purchaser, a leasehold property with a schedule of condition is a less attractive proposition than a property where the lessee remains fully responsible for the state of the property. However it may be possible to obtain agreement to a schedule being written into the lease if, for example:

- the terms of trade are in favour of the purchaser (i.e. there is little demand for the property or its type), or

- the prospective lessee is attractive to the landlord (e.g. they are regarded as reliable tenants and/or have what is called a 'sound covenant – they are financially sound and always pay their rent on time) and the fact that they are in occupation may enhance the investment to an extent greater than the reduction occasioned by a schedule of condition.

Compiling the schedule

Although a surveyor's schedule may be sufficient to outline the condition of the premises, it may be preferable to record its state photographically or, preferably, by video. The advantage of using a video is that the film can encompass every aspect of the building which could probably otherwise only be covered by hundreds of photos. Cross-referencing the video image to the written schedule should provide a comprehensive and accurate guide to the state of the premises. A camera which inserts the date on the film should be used to evidence the date of the compiling of the record which itself should be at or around the commencement date of the lease and/or the commencement of the period during which the lessee accepts liability for the property. It is unlikely that the lessee will be able to prepare the schedule without some input from the landlord, and it may be the preparation of such a schedule will need to be done by, or at least under the control of the landlord or his agent. Regardless of who actions the schedule a written receipt should be obtained from the landlord. Obviously the schedule should be kept safely since it is a valuable part of the evidence of a limit on the repairing liability. A copy of the schedule could be written into the lease or in some way referred to within the lease so that its existence and scope cannot be ignored or challenged later (when one or even both parties to the lease may have changed).

Waiving – or buying out

Such a schedule is a protection for the lessee. However, it may be that the lessee would prefer the premises to be brought to a better condition. In this case there is no reason why such work should not be carried out – the schedule merely prevents the landlord from requiring 'betterment', that is work to be carried out which puts the premises into a better state of repair than that existing when the lessee took responsibility.

The landlord's preference, particularly should they wish to sell their interest, is for the lease to be free of such a schedule. It may be possible to negotiate value in return for the schedule being removed from the lease, for example, either a rent free period or even a cash sum.

Contaminated land

Introduction

With ever greater attention being given to environmental matters the question of the responsibility for and rectification of land contaminated as a result of commercial activities is assuming increasing importance. The thrust of legislation is increasingly to 'make the polluter pay' by either contributing to the cleansing of such land or by carrying out the cleansing.

Background

Under the Environment Protection Act 1990, local authorities were required to set up Registers of Contaminated Land. Land is determined to be 'contaminated' if it *appears to the local authority … to be in such a condition, by reason of substances in, or under the land, that (a) significant harm is being caused or there is a significant possibility of such harm being caused, or (b) pollution of controlled waters is being or is likely to be caused'*. 'Significant harm' includes harm to human beings and embryos, crops, livestock, buildings and ecological areas etc. Land so defined was required to be entered in the registers and, even if the land was subsequently 'cleansed', the land would remain listed (and as a result of such listing no doubt would command a lower value than land not so listed). In fact, these registers were not set up at the time due to the concern that in recording details of land when the property market was suffering from a slump in demand, it could lead to widespread property blight. However, under the Environment Act 1995, the concept of contaminated land was re-addressed in a diluted version of the original requirements:

- where there is contaminated land remedial action is required where there is 'significant harm' or 'pollution of controlled waters' and there are cost-effective methods of cleansing

- local authorities are required to identify land within their boundaries which is contaminated.

Under the Contaminated Land (England) Regulations 2000 (the '2000 regulations'), heavily contaminated land can be classified as a 'special site' requiring special provisions (for example, the land on which the Millennium Dome was built in Greenwich was so classified). In such instances the Environment Agency deals with the matter rather than a local authority.

Following a three month 'consultation period' the local authority can serve a remediation notice on the 'appropriate person'. If this notice is not complied with then the authority can enter the land and cleanse it – recovering the costs from the appropriate person. It can place a charge on the land if these costs are not reimbursed.

The 'appropriate person' is the person who caused the contamination. Obviously this may not be the current owner, although if the polluter cannot be found it may be the current owner who has to pay. However, a polluter who can be traced and who sells contaminated land at a reduced price has the possibility of a double cost: the fact that the price may have been reduced because of the contamination, and a later requirement to cleanse.

It may be some time before the requirements under this Act are fully brought into effect and the detailed codes of practice required under the Act need to be carefully studied. Those purchasing land which they believe may be contaminated, however, should consider inserting in the sale and purchase agreement, a guarantee whereby should they be required to cleanse the land, the vendor will reimburse them. Insurance can be effected covering the unexpected discovery of contamination of land included in a purchase.

Water

The 2000 regulations make detailed provisions to protect certain sites and enhance the requirements regarding polluted waters. Under the Water Resources Act 1991, any organization that discharges polluting material into controlled waters can be made subject to remediation notices and fines and the 2000 regulations enhance these requirements.

Case study

In September 2005, 'The Times' reported that the Environment Agency might have to prosecute its own contractors. The Agency had commissioned contractors to build a water monitoring station near South Molton in Devon. Cement waste entered the river – a tributary of the River Exe – which altered the alkalinity of the water and as a result killed hundreds of fish. Owners of fishing rights along the rivers claimed the cost of the damage could run to six figures and demanded compensation.

Waste

Commercial occupiers are increasingly required to minimize, and control the disposal of, the waste their activities create and to ensure it does not contaminate wherever it is disposed of (see WASTE).

Contingency planning

Introduction

Most businesses plan for the future assuming things will 'go right'. Unfortunately for a variety of reasons, some outside our control, things may 'go wrong'. We need to, at least, consider the answer to the question 'what happens if...' adding our worst nightmare to the end of the sentence and then (when there is no pressure for action) identify a number of alternative reactions.

Basics

The following areas should be addressed:

1. Communication. One problem often experienced when there is a major problem is alerting those that need to be involved. A priority should be to create a list of telephone contacts (including own staff and professional advisers) particularly when business continues outside normal office hours and/or remote from administration and/or responsible management.

2. Use, but extend, existing emergency procedures to address a 'recovery' mode as well as an 'immediate action' mode. For example:

SPECIMEN EMERGENCY PROCEDURE: FIRE

a) Sound alarm and evacuate

b) Check attendance register against evacuees

c) Advise firefighters of dangerous materials location

d) Shut off services

e) Information to neighbours, customers, media, etc

f) Postpone deliveries

g) Lay off staff (or find other work), retain key skills

h) Seek alternative premises (in accordance with requirements)

i) Cover dislocation to production, etc with identified temporary arrangements

j) Utilize back up services

k) Interface with media, industry body, trade unions, customers, suppliers, etc.

l) Liaise with landlords, planners, architects, builders, etc.

3. Administrative matters:

- Identify and train media spokesperson (not having someone available to interface is potentially dangerous)

- Set up a 24 hour a day telephone hotline

- Make available skilled personnel to counsel and console those suffering from any trauma, and to deal patiently with those making enquiries regarding information, details of relatives etc.

- Source lists of all services identified as being needed

- Record details of officials with whom the business may need to interface (e.g. investigation and government agencies)

- Source alternative sites for administration and/or production

- Keep up-to-date management succession plans showing who could take over in an emergency

- Devise recall procedures for faulty or contaminated product, and so on.

* *

Contingency planning example

The problem

You are the facility administrator of a widget producing company. They are a high value product which need careful handling and storage and have a relatively short shelf life. They are sold throughout the UK and exported to European countries (which are supplied direct). The company occupies three factories (two freehold and one leasehold; one large, two small) as well as a main warehouse (leasehold) plus a number of satellite warehouses supplying retail customers within 24 hours of order.

The production process is partly mechanized but requires some manual work. Since the manual operation requires dexterity, this part of the workforce is mainly female and essentially part-time. Flexibility of hours has been a recruiting guideline for some years. A severe downturn in demand has led to a lengthening list of debtors despite constant chasing by the credit control department. Meanwhile there has been a constant rise in raw material costs and difficulty in passing these on in the form of price increases to the market. Formerly a small amount of raw material was derived as a by-product of animal experimentation, but this has not been the case for several years.

Anonymous terrorist threats have been made against the company and a number of small incendiary devices have been received via the post at head office, factory and warehouse. The Board is concerned that its operations could become a target for some serious (i.e. large scale) terrorist activity and has asked you to prepare a report highlighting areas of weakness and vulnerability, suggesting initiatives that could be taken to defuse the situation and, should such activity occur, to recover the status quo.

Suggested areas of attention (note these are not exhaustive but provided purely as an example of areas to be considered):

1. Worst case scenario

Assess what is likely to be the worst disaster to hit the company and consider action, then next worst and so on. In this case it could be said that the worst case would occur should all productive units be wiped out simultaneously. This is probably so unlikely that it can be safely ignored, however, the next worst case could envisage the main factory being wiped out, followed possibly by the Head Office going and so on.

2. Research enemy

Trying to establish who is likely to be the enemy (whether animate in terms of this example, or inanimate in terms of a fire, etc) and what they need and what are their aims may help establish ways of dealing. For example, if the Animal Liberation Front were suspected in this example, it might be possible to contact them to explain the cessation of the work which seems to be the source of their complaints. Fire can be a serious hazard but needs three factors before it can cause damage: a source, raw material and time. Without any one of these, there can be little threat from such a source.

3. Consider advantages

The way this particular group is geographically spread provides an advantage. It has a number of sites and it is extremely unlikely that all could be hit simultaneously. Assuming multiple sites are required, the development of flexibility could be addressed, so that if one site is disabled, output could resume at another. Conversely, any inter-dependability of sites should be reduced.

4. Take advice

No-one can be expert in all areas. There are experts specializing in this field and their input could be sought. Even though the plan developed may never be used, the examination of procedures and practices could be valuable as a form of process re-engineering.

5. Examine vulnerability (examples only)

a) Post. Institute controls and examination. Arrange for delivery elsewhere than own premises – passing to premises only when opened safely.

b) Access. Examine security generally (entrances and exits, control, etc).

c) Deliveries. Issue letters of authority to ensure access provided only to genuine suppliers.

d) Publicity. Promulgate the organization's commitment to a 'clean hands' process. For example, a corporate social responsibility statement (as is required for listed PLCs) may assist.

e) Screen employees. Check references, institute right of search, control internal access to sensitive areas, maintain records of unsatisfactory employees.

f) Increase internal security precautions: fire, explosion, etc (creation of 'safe' areas).

g) Increase anonymity of units.

Case study

The Zodiac toy chain had around 80 shops throughout England and Wales. In one of the shopping centres where they were represented, they agreed to a neighbouring retailer's request to site Zodiac's delivery sign partly on the adjoining premises rear wall. Their neighbour – a jeweller – wanted anonymity of his premises rear access to aid his own security.

6. Consider means of recovery

   a) Relocation of workforce – difficult in view of nature of employment – consider 'bussing' workforce in.

   b) Possibility of production at warehouses (need to check authority in lease – if any – to do so).

   c) Need to check/circumvent lease restrictions.

   d) Keep watch on local property market for knowledge of what is available.

   e) Buy in product/assembly.

   f) Homeworking (check security and quality control).

   g) Media messages and spokesperson.

   h) Parallel working particularly of computer system (credit control is especially vulnerable)

   and so on.

Whilst businesses can recover from major dislocation, almost inevitably, should they have rehearsed the potential downside, they should be able to recover more quickly (see TERRORIST PRECAUTIONS).

Control of Major Accidents

The Control of Major Accident Hazards (COMAH) Regulations 1999 are designed to try to help prevent major accidents as well as limiting the consequences of those that occur to people and the environment. The schedule to the regulations lists various substances and two thresholds, requiring any establishment which keeps such substances in excess of these thresholds to comply with the regulations.

   A. If an establishment has substances in excess of the lower threshold the organization responsible must notify the appropriate 'competent authority' (in England the Health and Safety Executive and the Environment Agency) of:

   • their name and address

   • the location of the substances

   • the characteristics of the substances

   • details of the activities carried on in the establishment

   • details of the environment which could cause or aggravate an accident.

Operators must prepare a Major Accident Prevention Policy and must consult their employees or representatives about the preparation of on-site emergency plans.

B. If an establishment has substances in excess of the higher threshold, it must additionally:

- prepare safety reports and emergency plans which must show that all necessary measures have been taken to limit the consequences of an accident to people and the environment

- in conjunction with the local authority, prepare an off-site emergency plan.

Failure to notify the local authority and the other competent authorities, who can levy charges for their regulatory functions, is an offence.

Note: Consideration might be given to linking a home-based computer with daily updating of as much of the records as possible to the main computer so that should the main location be lost or damaged, or the operator be unable to access the premises, some continuation of the business could be carried on. (See Gee case study in TERRORIST PRECAUTIONS).

Cost checklist

Introduction

Every item of facilities expenditure should be checked before payment. Examples of facility costs, with guidance as to what should be checked to ensure the correct amounts are being charged, are set out below. Executive responsibility for property assets is often unclear and so it is not surprizing if some invoices and charges are passed virtually without challenge. Further, many feel that there is little that can be done about them – comments such as 'it must be right – it's for the property', or 'there's nothing we can do about it anyway' are common – but surely unacceptable.

1. Rent

Check amount demanded against the lease or précis (see KEEPING PROPERTY RECORDS). Although normally the amount to be paid will be a straight quarter of the annual rent, there may be a need to apportion the rent in respect of a split quarter, and the calculation basis may need clarifying. Rent claimed on the basis of a proportion of a quarter may give rise to a higher charge due than rent claimed on the basis of annual rent on a daily basis.

Example

The daily rent of a property with an annual rent of £10,000 is £27.40. If, instead of dividing by 365 as is normal, the rent is divided by four and then divided by the number of days in each quarter, different daily figures emerge since the days in each calendar quarter are not an exact quarter of the year.

Quarter   25th March to 23rd June: 91 days – daily rate £27.47

24th June to 28th Sept: 97 days – daily rate £25.77

29th Sept. to 24th Dec: 87 days – daily rate £28.73

25th Dec. to 24th March: 90 days – daily rate £27.77

Any attempt to use whichever method of calculation provides the higher daily rate should be resisted. The daily charge as a proportion of a year is fair to both parties and is also logical since most leases refer to the rent in 'annual' terms. If the lease refers to rent being paid as an amount 'per quarter' however, it may be difficult to resist the alternative method of calculation.

Case study

When a consultant was checking the occupation costs of a client he could not understand why for a lease at an annual rent of £10,000, the client's annual rental costs had been £10,486 for the past three years. It was eventually realized that the landlord had used the above method (i.e. calculating a daily rate for the shortest quarter and then multiplying that figure by the days in the other quarters).

Check:

- operative dates (the normal quarter days can be varied – see below):
- amounts and dates
- whether the lease allows for interest on late payment
- operative date if rent has been reviewed
- impact of any rent free periods etc.

2. Payment dates

Normally rent is payable on the quarter days of 25th March, 24th June, 29th September and 25th December. However, there can be variations on a regional or specific basis. Failing to realize that rent is due on dates other than the normal quarter days could mean late payment and the lessee incurring an interest charge. The dates stated in the lease should be checked and, although rent should not be paid late, there is no need for it to be paid early. Some older leases allow seven or 14 days grace following the quarter day and such days of grace should be used wherever possible, without endangering receipt of the payment before a date when interest would be payable.

Example

In a 25 year lease with a 14 days grace period in respect of each quarter, that concession equates to paying one quarter's rent 1400 days (or nearly four years) late. If the rent being paid is £100,000 p.a. and an interest rate of 10% is used – the interest saved by using the full days of grace in respect of each quarter's payment, is almost £10,000.

3. Payment methods

Rent is accepted by any reasonable means although payment by cheque is probably still the most common. Increasingly, however, lessees are pressurized (particularly by institutional landlords) to pay either by banker's order or by direct debit. Some lessees object to this manner of payment and it depends on the strength of each party during lease negotiations whether it can resisted. The practice of issuing post-dated cheques is best avoided. Banks are under no obligation to respect the post-dating of a cheque and thus if a cheque is presented 'early', the bank may honour it. This could have a number of repercussions including charges for operating an unauthorized overdraft – or even, if there are insufficient funds, and the bank will not allow it to overdraw the account, this could lead to the cheque being dishonoured which might be grounds for the lease being forfeited (issuing a cheque knowing there are insufficient funds to meet it is fraud).

4. Interest on late payment of rent

If interest is demanded on late payment, the lease should be checked to ensure this is permitted and that the rate charged is as stipulated – normally 4% or 5% above bank rate. The figure should be checked to ensure, if there are any 'days of grace', that due allowance has been made – and for any amounts paid on account. Most leases state 'rent is payable whether demanded or not'; thus non-receipt of demand is not a valid reason for non-payment. Late payment can attract an interest charge even though no demand is issued. Rent cheques should be ready for despatch in sufficient time to be received on the due date.

5. VAT on rent

At the option of landlords, VAT can be added to rent although landlords so electing (who must of course be VAT registered) are required to advise lessees before they take such action (see VAT).

6. Rent increase

On the first demand after a rent review, check the date from which the new rent is stated as being payable is as agreed and that the rate being charged is correct. If interest is payable on late settlement of a reviewed rent, check that the rate and amount charged are correct.

Case study

The £10,000 p.a. rent was due for review on 25th December but was not agreed (at £16,000 p.a.) until the following 29th September. Three quarters rent thus required to be adjusted and interest was payable on the difference between the old and new rents for the period of 'lateness'. The landlord's statement read:

Quarters rent at £10,000 due 29/9	2,500. 00
Four quarters rent at £16,000 less £10,000	6,000. 00
Interest on late agreement on £6.000	619. 80
Total now due	**£9,119. 80**

The interest charge was queried and it was discovered that (working on the basis that the demand covered four quarters i.e. a full year) the landlord's agents had simply charged a year's interest on the additional rent due i.e. £6,000. This was incorrect since:

a) the rent due on 29th September was being paid with the additional sum on time and no interest was due in respect of the additional sum for this quarter

b) the interest to be charged was nine months on £1,500 (December quarter increase), six months on £1,500 (March quarter increase) and three months on £1,500 (June quarter increase). Effectively this meant interest for 18 months on £1,500 or £232.43. The overcharge was £387.37.

Other 'mistakes' include:

- not giving credit for days grace allowed under the lease for payment of rent
- charging the varying quarters on a per day basis
- charging interest at a higher rate than that allowed by the lease, etc.

Rent increases should be evidenced by a Memorandum (see RENT REVIEW).

A review is not always backdated to the date of the review: the wording of the lease should be checked to determine the effective date. If the landlord was late starting the review process then some older leases may state that the new rent only becomes effective 'when agreed'. Further, it may be that interest on any 'late payment' can only be levied from that date. Any interest demanded should also be checked to ensure the calculation accords with the lease provisions.

7. Rent free period

If work is required to be carried out to the premises before occupation, the landlord may be prepared to allow the lessee a 'rent free' period whilst such work is completed (as their contribution towards these costs). Any such agreement should be evidenced in writing. Rent free periods can also be granted during the term of the lease (e.g. whilst works which impede the use of the subject premises, dislocate trade etc are being carried out). Not only should the period be confirmed in writing but the charge covering the period should be checked to ensure due allowance has been given. If a demand is not received, the rent should be paid with the estimated amount(s) in respect of the rent free period deducted. It would be advisable to include a statement showing how the deduction has been calculated.

8. Utility charges (shared supply)

The appropriateness of the apportionment should be checked and a copy of the original invoice should be requested. If metered, check the charge against the records. Meters should be read by an employee at the time of the supply inspection. Check against prior year usage.

9. Utility charges (individual supply)

Check against meter readings and review against prior year's usage.

10. Service charge

The services being charged for should only be those that are set out in the lease. The proportion being charged should be checked for accuracy and accord with the lease figure (or as otherwise agreed), and compared with the original estimate. If the lease states that any such statement is to be supported by an auditor's or other certificate, receipt and accuracy of such a certificate should be checked. Any suggestion that a lessee should bear a proportion of the amounts due in relation to other units (which may be empty), or regarding any under or non payment on behalf of any other lessee(s) (because of that non-payment), should be resisted.

11. Repairs and redecorations

The principle behind, as well as the responsibility for, such charge should be checked with the lease and to ensure that it is in accordance with a previously approved estimate. Usually the obligation is on the lessee to arrange for repairs etc and thus an approved estimate should already be available. The full contract sum should not be paid until the end of any defects liability period. A retention of between 5% and 10% of the contract sum should be deducted from each payment.

WARNING: The repairing clause wording should be carefully checked. If the lessee is required to 'keep' the premises repaired this would usually mean to the standard when the lease commenced (in which case photographic evidence or preparation of a CONDITION SCHEDULE is advisable). However, if the obligation is to 'put and keep' this could involve the lessee in upgrading the state of the premises to the level deemed by the landlord to be acceptable.

Check:

- competitive estimates obtained before work authorized

- scope of work is in accordance with lease obligations

- work is of acceptable standard

12. DILAPIDATIONS (or Wants of Repair)

Lessees are required to keep the premises in repair. At any time a landlord can require the lessee to repair the property by serving a schedule of items requiring attention. However, other than items which damage the value of the freehold interest, such works need not usually be carried out if there are more than three years before the lease terminates. Some leases are more onerous and can require lessees to 'put the property in good repair' which means that the current lessee will have an obligation to repair items which may have been in poor repair prior to them having any responsibility for the premises. Not only will any surveyor's costs for the preparation of a schedule have to be met by the lessee but so too will solicitor's costs serving the schedule.

Check:

- the lease gives a right to serve the notice

- who is responsible for cost of preparation of schedule

- items not properly included are deleted from the list

13. Rates

Ensure the demand is in accordance with any rating or re-rating proposal. Consider whether to appeal the assessment. Expert advice should be sought and if it is decided to appeal then the surveyor or other adviser dealing with the matter may be best paid on a '% of amount saved' or 'no win, no fee' basis.

14. Other occupational charges

Invoices re. regular maintenance contracts (e.g. roof and gutter clearing, window cleaning, gardening, janitorial and/or security services etc), may be provided centrally (e.g. in shared facilities) or commissioned by the occupier themselves. The range of charges will be set out in the lease.

Check:

- items being charged are properly chargeable
- service has been provided to acceptable level
- cost is reasonable

15. INSURANCE

Only if the lease retains the right to the landlord to insure should there be an external charge. Alternatively, the lease should be checked in case it requires the lessee to insure, in which case cover must be effected.

Check:

- covers stipulated
- premium is charged only for those covers
- the lessee's interest is noted on the policy

16. Service charge

In multi-occupational premises there may be areas and/or services used in common. Normally the costs of such works will be met by the landlord (or agents) and recharged.

Check:

- calculations (including apportioning with other lessees)
- coverage is only for items set out in lease
- benefit is being obtained regarding all items covered
- the proportion of costs in respect of empty properties is not charged against lessees in occupation.

Covenants

Introduction

Covenants are binding undertakings between the lease parties and comprise the greatest content of the average lease. Although many lessees tend to either ignore them or give them only cursory attention during lease negotiations – and even less attention during occupation, this is dangerous. Failure to comply with lease covenants can result in a breach of the lease, which, in turn, could lead to the loss of rights, for example, the right to exercise an OPTION to terminate.

Lessees covenants

A. Payment

i) **This prime covenant requires the lessee to pay rent on the due dates** – normally by the four quarter days (although there may be regional or specific variations). Some leases allow days of grace before payment (e.g. rent must be paid within 14 days of the due date) although this practice is dying out and increasingly not only is rent required to be paid on the due date but any late payment attracts interest – usually at penal rates. Rent is due whether demanded or not; non-receipt of a demand for rent is not a valid reason for late- or non-payment. Apportionment charges for odd days at the beginning or end of a lease should be clearly defined. Amounts can vary depending on whether the calculation is made on a per day basis (the rent divided by 365) or proportion of a quarter (the rent divided by four and then divided by the number of days in a quarter).

ii) **Rent can be made subject to VAT** – at the option of the landlord. If the lessee is VAT registered, apart from cash flow, this should have little effect, but it could have a severe effect on non-VAT registered lessees (e.g. charities) and thus may become a material factor in deciding whether to take the lease. It could also reduce the number of interested parties on disposal.

iii) **Other outgoings**. Normally the lessee will be responsible for heating and lighting costs as well as the business rates (applicable to their part of the premises) plus insurance and service charges recovered by the landlord. Most landlords prefer to insure the property in their own name and to pass the premium on to the lessee.

Case study

In *Havenbridge Ltd v Boston Dyers Ltd* the Court stated that there was no obligation on the landlord to 'shop around' to gain the cheapest premium. Despite this ruling it may still be prudent for a lessee, if a premium is thought to be excessive, to obtain an equivalent quote and approach the landlord and/or the insurers to try to gain a reduction.

iv) **SERVICE CHARGES**. In multi-occupation premises, each lessee will be responsible for a proportion of the costs of maintaining, heating, lighting and cleaning those parts of the premises in common use. In negotiation, any suggestion that should one (or more) lessee not pay the shortfall is recouped from other lessees, should be resisted.

v) **Landlord's costs**. Often leases specify that the lessee will pay the landlord's charges. If this arises as a result of a lessee's own action, for example, permission is required for alterations to the property, or where the lessee is in default (e.g. non-compliance with repairing covenants leading to the preparation of a DILAPIDATIONS SCHEDULE) it may be fair. However, it seems invidious for the lessee to pay for legal and other costs incurred by the landlord in effecting a rent review or lease renewal, and such suggestions should be resisted during negotiations. The Cost of Leases Act 1959 stipulates that each side should normally be responsible for its own legal costs.

If the lessee is responsible for insuring, the landlord will normally wish to see evidence of the setting up and renewal of the cover and to have their interest entered on the policy. If the landlord insures, then the lessee should ask for their interest to be endorsed. This is particularly important if the lease is 'full repairing' as, should the property suffer partial or complete damage, any shortfall in the landlord's insurance may otherwise be attempted to be recovered from the lessee.

Service charges should be checked to ensure only items stated in the lease as being the lessee's responsibility are charged for. Calculations should also be checked as should any proportion applied (if the charge covers other users).

vi) **Personal GUARANTEES**. Landlords dealing with newly formed or smaller organizations may require owners' or directors' personal guarantees. This means that should the business fail (or the rent and other outgoings required under the lease are not paid) then a guarantor becomes personally liable for these financial obligations. This suggestion should be resisted, but, if unavoidable, an option to break after, say, five years, should be sought.

B. Condition

i) **Redecoration and repair**. Most leases require the lessee to redecorate and repair the premises as well as to 'hand them back' in a reasonable state. If the repairing covenant includes the word 'put' as well as 'keep' in good repair, then, even if the premises were in a poor state when the lessee acquired the right of occupation, when the property is handed back it must be in a good state. Effectively this means the lessee could finish up paying for putting the property in a better condition than it was when they first became responsible.

Whilst repair is an ongoing obligation, redecoration tends to be linked to set periods, for example, 'redecorate externally every three years and internally every five years'. Few landlords seem to check that redecorating covenants (still less their timing) have been met. However, increasingly checks are made regarding compliance with repairing covenants. To ensure compliance, a landlord may prepare a schedule of works for the lessee to carry out to return the premises to a well-repaired/decorated state. This schedule of 'wants of repair' is usually termed a Schedule of Dilapidations. It may be possible to minimize the effect of 'repairing' covenants by agreeing a CONDITION schedule when agreeing the lease. This is a statement showing the state of the premises when the lease started or occupation commenced and demonstrates the level of redecoration/repair to which (but not beyond) the lessee must maintain the premises.

ii) **Wants of repair**. A lessee in receipt of a schedule of dilapidations in the early part of a lease could attempt to mitigate its effect (in full or in part) by arguing that, since the lease has a considerable time to run, the interests of the landlord are not being prejudiced by their failure to comply with the repairing covenants (although it should not be overlooked that a landlord might wish to sell the property and their interests could be prejudiced by the lessee's failure to comply with such covenants).

Case study

In *Jervis v Harris* it was held that despite there being a considerable time left before expiry (in this case around 900 years), the onus was still on the lessee to comply with the repairing covenants. Further, in the event of failure, the landlord had the right to enter the premises to carry out the works and to recover the costs from the lessee.

iii) **Keep in good condition**. Repairing and redecorating covenants should be clearly delineated. These can range from total responsibility for the whole building – internal and external – to internal responsibility for the area actually occupied, or even to nil responsibility. In multi-occupation buildings it is normal for each lessee to bear some responsibility for a proportion of the cost of repair of the roof (rather than this being the responsibility of the top floor lessee). This can be achieved either by a specific covenant or by requiring a contribution to a service charge.

iv) **Alteration**. Normally there will be a bar on the lessee carrying out any alterations or extensions (LESSEES WORKS) etc to the premises – or at least a bar subject to the landlord's permission required to be granted prior to the commencement of the work.

v) **REINSTATEMENT**. Should the lessee carry out such works then normally as a condition of the grant of the approval of the landlord to the works, the lessee will be required to put the property back to its state before the works.

vi) **Keep safe**. The lessee is using the landlord's property and there may be a covenant, that the premises will be kept safe and, when not in use, will be secured and protected.

C. Keep open and use

i) **Keep open**. Leases (particularly in retailing) usually include an obligation to keep the premises open for certain hours per day and to close them thereafter.

Case studies

1. In *Co-op v Argyll Stores*, the Court of Appeal held that Argyll (trading as Safeway) was obliged to keep its unit in the Hillsborough Shopping Centre at Sheffield open, even though the company, presumably since the unit was unprofitable, had closed it.

2. In *Retail Parks Investments Ltd v Royal Bank of Scotland plc*, the bank was held to be in breach of the covenant in closing a branch and merely leaving two automatic cash dispensing machines there. The Court of Session required the bank to keep its branch open.

3. In a dispute regarding a bridal gown and accessories hire and sale shop a draft lease of a new shop was given to the lessee's solicitor who recommended it for signing. Included in the covenants was an undertaking that the shop would be open from 8.00am until 5.30pm Monday to Saturday whereas the prospective lessee needed it to be open from 10.30am until 8.00pm (Monday to Saturday) and from 12 noon until 4.00pm on Sunday since those were the hours she felt would provide demand. Fortunately a colleague pointed this out along with a number of other restrictions before she committed herself to what was for her an unworkable lease.

ii) **Use for trade**. Many leases include an obligation to use the premises only for the purpose stated in the lease (i.e. in a USER CLAUSE). If lessees might want to change this use (or in an assignment of the lease a third party might want to use the premises for other purposes) then wording such as 'to use for [designated purpose] and such other use as may be permitted by the landlord, such permission not to be unreasonably withheld' should be included in the lease wording.

The question of whether to have a restricted or wide user clause can be double-edged. With a restricted clause it may be possible to argue that the rent on review should be restricted – because comparison should only be made with other similar users.

Conversely, if flexibility is retained with the 'such other use' wording, the rent review valuation can rely on other users which may inflate the figure.

With a designated use clause, applying for a change of use may provide an opportunity for the landlord to attempt to vary the rent – simply as part of the negotiations.

Case study

The landlords of some of the outlets approved to sell National Lottery tickets in late 1994 and in 1995 attempted to argue that this was an extension of the use of the premises and their permission was needed for this use. A few even succeeded in obtaining additional rent as a 'quid pro quo'.

iii) **Reasonable use**. Such clauses could include:

- dangerous material ban. A definition of 'dangerous' should be sought and compared with the requirements of the lessee's business. For example, such a ban might prevent a local shop selling fireworks

- prohibition of overload floor(s). Written clarification of the loading should be sought since lack of the provision of such a statistic (as in many cases it is unknown) may tend to negate its impact

- banning on the use of the premises for immoral purposes, to hold auctions and other (depending on circumstances) specific purposes

- bans on fixing advertisement hoardings to the exterior of the premises. This ban is often diluted so that the normal trade displays are allowed provided they are kept with certain dimensions etc.

D. Maintain occupation

i) **Not to leave vacant**. Vacant buildings tend to deteriorate and can be targets for vandalism. Lessees are usually required to occupy and keep the premises occupied other than for short periods. Landlord's permission is normally needed if the lessee needs to leave the property vacant for any appreciable length of time. If, without permission, the premises are left vacant at or just before the termination of the lease then the lessee may lose rights to a new lease.

Case study

In *Graysim Holdings v P&O Property Holdings Ltd* the House of Lords held that a landlord did not have to grant a new lease to a lessee who were no longer in occupation, having sublet the entire premises.

ii) **Bar on assignment**. A lease is a contract, and occupation under it is a right given specifically to the lessee. Such a right cannot be transferred (assigned) without the consent of the landlord. Some leases state that the leasehold interest cannot be transferred and although there is nothing to stop the lessee asking for such permission, the landlord may be able to resist assignment. If the lessee wishes to retain flexibility the wording of this covenant needs to be diluted so that the wording runs: 'not to assign or part with possession of part, or, without the permission of the landlord, such permission not to be unreasonably withheld, not to assign or part with possession of the whole'.

iii) **Bar on underletting**. Underletting may be a more attractive proposition to assignment since, should the underlessee default, at least the lessee still has control of the property and can either try to find another underlessee or re-occupy themselves. Whilst it may be possible to obtain a relaxation of a bar against subletting the whole, few landlords may allow subletting of part, basically since this tends to detract from the investment value of the property as well as leading to potential problems in its management. In the event that underletting is permitted, the underlease or sublease should repeat all the covenants in the lease – particularly those relating to rent review.

iv) **Peaceful occupation**. Most leases require lessees to occupy their premises peaceably. This is not only courteous to neighbours and in addition makes the management of the premises much easier.

v) **Surrender occupation on the due date** – that is on expiry of the lease.

E. Communicate

Post. Being in occupation, the lessee has control of receipt of post and other items delivered to the premises. Since some communications sent to the address will be for the owner rather than the occupier there is normally a requirement for the lessee to pass such items to the landlord within a reasonable time (or even 'immediately').

F. Indemnity

This entails the lessee confirming they will indemnify the landlord in respect of all occurrences arising out of their occupation of the premises.

Landlord's covenants

A. Maintain

Where a property is in multi-occupation the landlord will normally retain responsibility for maintenance of the common parts, the cost of which may or may not be passed on to the lessees.

Case study

In *British Telecom v Sun Life Assurance* it was held that a landlord had to comply with such a covenant 'at all times' and could not delay compliance for a 'reasonable time'.

B. Insure

Unless the lessee has negotiated permission to arrange their own insurance the landlord will normally have the right and responsibility for arranging insurance whilst re-charging the lessee.

Summary

The foregoing is an outline of the main covenants found in many leases but it is not exhaustive and individual leases may contain others. All covenants and their effect on the actual operation of the subject business (not just their legal effect) should be considered and understood. A brief summary of the most important covenants should be included in any lease précis (see KEEPING PROPERTY RECORDS) and known and understood by all involved in the occupation and administration of the premises.

D

Dilapidations 75

Disability discrimination 79

Dilapidations

Introduction

The right to occupy leased premises is not only subject to a payment of rent, but also to an obligation to keep the premises in a reasonable state of repair. If during the lease term (and possibly for some time after its expiry) a landlord feels the lessee has not maintained the property properly, he can serve a schedule of 'wants of repair' (or 'dilapidations') requiring the lessee to carry out the work on the schedule (or to make a payment to the landlord equivalent to the costs of the works).

Preparation

A landlord believing premises are not in a decent state of repair will usually instruct a surveyor to compile a list of all the items which they feel are not to the standard required. The lease may stipulate that costs of this inspection and schedule preparation should be met by the lessee. Whilst a schedule can be served at any time, under the Leasehold Property (Repairs) Act 1938, only if it is within three years of the expiry of the lease, can the landlord insist the work is done. However, if the poor state of repair is damaging the value of the freehold interest or affects the integrity of the building (e.g. the roof is not watertight), the landlord may be able to insist the work is done immediately.

Not everything listed, however, may legitimately be required to be rectified. Landlord's surveyors often include a great deal on a schedule including items which strictly should not be there. For example, if a property was supplied as a shell, with no fittings, a requirement to replace worn carpets or floor tiles, or light fittings should be deleted.

Case study

A loss-making shop had been occupied for some years by a company. As termination date approached the retailer served notice bringing the lease to an end (see below). The landlord accepted the notice but served a 20 page schedule of wants of repair. The total value was around £40,000 including the costs of the preparation of the schedule etc.

When the retailer examined the schedule they divided the contents into a number of categories:

A   genuine wants of repair, value about £11,000

B   items which if done would have improved the premises beyond a reasonable state of repair: £12,000

C   items which should not form part of any such schedule (replacing pictures, carpets and other floor and wall coverings, light fittings etc): £9,000

D   items which were not the responsibility of the retailer at all but of the landlord's tenant in the flat above the shop: £7000.

Their quotation for the items in A, for which they felt they were responsible was £4,500 and they commissioned the work immediately. Meanwhile they rejected all other items in the schedule. After several months of argument the whole matter was settled by the retailer's payment of a further £5,000.

They also assisted the tenant of the flat by providing evidence that when he took over the upper part there were no floorboards and various other unfinished items for the installation of which he had to be given credit.

Negotiations regarding what should be included and/or excluded from such a schedule can become acrimonious. The Royal Institution of Chartered Surveyors (RICS) has launched a service which can try and arbitrate or find an amicable solution to such disputes (see USEFUL CONTACTS).

Some landlords devise well-padded schedules sometimes as an attempt to pressurize lessees into agreeing to pay a sum to settle the liability. The landlord may spend a little of the sum (or even none of it) to improve the premises or simply attempt to lease them as they are – pocketing the cash thereby generated. Of course if the new lease stipulates 'put and keep in good repair' the full repairing obligation is immediately passed to the new lessee.

Expiry

As termination approaches, a lessee should ensure that the premises are repaired and redecorated to a reasonable level to try to minimize the extent of a schedule. Ideally a schedule should be generated in advance of termination so that the lessee has a chance to complete the work whilst still in occupation. However, a schedule can be served after expiry and if one has not been received by expiry it may be prudent for the lessee to take photographic evidence of the state of the building at expiry and to return the keys by recorded delivery. The lessee should not be held liable for any deterioration after expiry – and can use the photographic proof to evidence the state of the property at termination. Where the lease has already expired, it may be preferable to agree a sum of money to satisfy any breach of the covenants evidenced by the schedule or the landlord may be entitled to charge rent for the time taken by the works (post termination).

Disability discrimination

Introduction

Since October 2004, the Disability Discrimination Act has required all property occupiers who provide services or goods (churches, shops, food providers – restaurants, hotels, transport facilities etc) to the public to make 'reasonable adjustments' to help make their premises 'disabled friendly'. The definition of 'public' could include those attending commercial premises to (for example) apply for a job, and hence the requirement may apply to far more property occupiers than might at first appear. The new requirements are, however, conditional on the basis that alterations required are such that are 'reasonable in all circumstances of the case'.

Practical effect

It is common and almost inevitable when considering access for the disabled to think only of wheelchair users. However, there are many other disabilities and difficulties of access of those who are deaf, blind, have impaired speech and so on should be considered. The ability to 'make' the facility 'disabled-friendly' will depend very much on circumstances and it is for individual occupiers to examine their premises. However, a few examples may be helpful:

a) Where there is no level entrance or linkage between one part of the facility and another, ramps could be used to allow wheelchair access. Obviously this would only be possible where the 'gap' was relatively small – or the rake of the ramp is not too steep.

Case study

One of the first cases under this legislation is being brought against the UK department store, Debenhams. A wheelchair user has no way of gaining access to the men's clothing department in the company's Derby store. The only way he can inspect the clothes is for an assistant to bring them to him. He claims that this is a breach of the Act. It remains to be seen whether this will be successful but it may be unlikely bearing in mind the obligation is to 'make reasonable alterations' and if ramps are inappropriate, an elevator or 'chair-lift' may be the only alternative.

b) Where a ramp cannot be used, a notice could be displayed suggesting wheelchair users should ask for assistance, for example, by ringing a bell (located at wheelchair user height). This might only be possible, for example, in a small shop where more than one assistant is on duty.

c) For blind visitors handrails could be considered for uneven access and/or passage through the facility and any bar on animals could be relaxed to exclude guide dogs (although this might not be possible in a food and/or very small shop).

d) For deaf visitors a hearing loop could be installed.

e) Where there are people suffering from other disabilities, a bell to ask for assistance could be installed and/or writing materials made available.

f) Other items for consideration could include vision panels, notices in Braille, assessment of the height of call buttons and so on.

Case study

An employment agency (which is required to make 'reasonable adjustments since those entering its premises to seek employment are members of the public) has a notice on its door stating that since it is on the first floor, anyone with difficulty accessing their offices should telephone a contact number so that the agency can make alternative interviewing arrangements.

Guidance regarding assistance to the mentally ill can be sourced at **www.mindout.net**.

Somewhat unsurprizingly a number of advisory organizations now offer 'accessibility surveys' to assist those required to make reasonable adjustments under the Act. It must be said that in most cases all that is required is an objective viewpoint, an understanding of the difficulty a disabled person may have, common sense and a creative approach to try and help the disabled and to react positively should a disabled person ask for assistance.

E

Electronic security   85

Energy   89

Environmental obligations   93

Electronic security

Introduction

It has been estimated that 50% of UK organizations would go out of business within six weeks if they lost their electronic data processing systems for any appreciable length of time. Access to computers, computer suites and levels of information should be controlled and it be made known that there are severe sanctions against unauthorized access. Such sanctions, provided they are applied fairly, will normally be upheld in Employment Tribunals.

Criminal and civil offences

The Computer Misuse Act 1990 introduced offences of:

a)   unauthorized access to computer material – both hacking and access by unauthorized users,

b)   unauthorized modification of computer material – the insertion of time bombs such as the Friday 13th data destruction program,

c)   ulterior intent – unauthorized access for the purpose of committing a crime.

Giving publicity to the penalties for unauthorized access (i.e. up to five years imprisonment and/or an unlimited fine) may act as a deterrent. It should also be made clear that unauthorized access to such systems or levels within the system is also a disciplinary offence – that is gross misconduct.

Case study

In *Denco v Joinson*, the Employment Appeal Tribunal (EAT) held that an employee was fairly dismissed when he gained unauthorized access to his employer's computerized payroll files, even though no 'loss' (other than that of damage to the integrity of the system) occurred. The EAT advised employers to make it clear to their employees (e.g. via procedure handbooks, manuals etc) that they could be dismissed if they breached such rules.

Protection and prevention

The Home Office (contact 0207 273 4001) recently advised that thefts of most computer equipment result from specific 'orders' for such equipment, and that which is not 'stolen to order', appears for sale in adverts (a third of adverts for computers in Loot are placed by convicted dealers of stolen property). Computer users could take what may be regarded as fairly elementary steps in the protection of computer equipment and computer suites within the facility. Around a quarter of such thefts are repeat crimes. As the thieves know the computers will need to be replaced and will probably be located in the same position as those they have already stolen, they repeat the theft after a few weeks with the advantage on their second visit of knowing exactly where to look!

Computer facility/installation checklist

1. All computer systems should be protected by alpha-numeric passwords, the master list of which is held by [name]. Passwords will be changed on an irregular time basis with a minimum of notice to those affected.

2. [Name] will keep copies of the password master list personally with a spare set at the company's bankers.

3. Passwords will not be made available other than to those authorized who may not part with them or divulge them. The computer department will regularly publish a list of those permitted to have access to stated levels of computerized material.

4. Only those authorized may access the levels to which they are entitled. Attempted or actual access to an unauthorized level is gross misconduct.

5. No password will be written down, disclosed to an unauthorized third party, or, particularly, attached to the computer itself or stored in an adjacent desk.

6. All computers will be connected to the burglar alarm so that in the event of unauthorized tampering the alarm will be activated.

7. In the event of a computer theft, additional security measures will be installed immediately.

8. The retention of high visibility offices and public access (which may allow thieves to 'case' the premises whilst posing as members of the public etc) will be subject to periodic review.

9. Access to premises will be controlled by electronic access systems.

10. Serial numbers of all computers will be recorded.

11. Ownership marks will be added to items using ultra violet markers.

12. Each day's work will be backed up as advised by the computer department.

13. Any employee found to have purposely interfered with the organization's computer system so that loss is caused will be regarded as having committed an act of gross misconduct and will also be in breach of the Computer Misuse Act 1990 which entails criminal penalties.

Policy and procedure

1. The computers and computer systems of the [organization] are a vital part of its existence and must only be operated by those appointed and authorized to do so.

2. Employees may only operate within the areas of their own departmental operations and service areas.

3. Access to the systems of the [organization], particularly, but not exclusively, the computer systems, is reserved to authorized personnel only.

4. Unauthorized access to, or in any way tampering with, any computer system or software, or computer installation (including but not restricted to the items in this policy) will be regarded as gross miscon-

duct and will render the offender liable to dismissal and possible prosecution under the Computer Misuse Act 1990.

5. All computer records must be backed up daily with such back-up stored in [specify – a remote location].

6. Data files altered during daily working will also be backed up daily.

7. In no instance should any computer owned or leased by the [organization] be used for playing games or any purpose other than the legitimate work of the [organization].

8. No software and/or discs etc other than those owned or leased by the [organizations] may be used in its computers. All software and discs must be purchased new from recognized and reputable suppliers, backed by a confirmation that all such items are free from viruses etc and/or with a guarantee/liability acceptance in the event that virus(es) which have caused damage, were present on purchase.

9. Anti-virus programs should be used regularly [specify intervals]. Any item found infected must be immediately separated from any networking arrangement, and steps taken to eliminate the virus.

10. Since it may be possible to access data, formerly stored on the hard disk of a computer and then deleted, suitable protection (or destruction) must be considered for such disks if the disk or the whole computer is to be dispensed with.

Energy

Introduction

It has been suggested than many businesses are quite capable of saving between 4% and 5% of their turnover by employing WASTE minimization techniques (in some cases this would result in them doubling their profits). However, that reflects an acceptance of waste-creation, whereas ideally it should be prevented. Many organizations are inherently wasteful in their energy consumption. It has been estimated that implementing cost-effective energy efficiency measures could save UK industry as a whole, nearly £2 billion a year. Energy costs will inevitably rise – worldwide demand alone is expected to double or triple by 2050. Energy demands from China and India (whose economies are expected to overtake the existing top five in the immediate future) are rapidly increasing. Greater demand will inevitably lead to greater cost.

Scope

The Carbon Trust (an independent organization established by the UK Government with the task of cutting carbon emissions which are partly responsible for damage to the environment, global warming etc) estimates that most organizations fritter away 20% and many waste as much as 50%, of their energy. As the need to reduce energy consumption becomes more widely understood, those perceived to be economical energy users may be able to steal a march on their competitors – not least in recruiting the most responsible employees.

Those who are not responsible should be trained. Inevitably some will never learn whilst others, when under pressure, may forget to save. The facility organizer should consider ways in which their assistance can be harnessed in order to help achieve savings.

Reduction ideas

1. Report annually to the Board the costs of all energy being used reflecting not only the current year's cost but also comparative costs over the previous five years. Expressing these costs as a percentage of the sale price of goods or services may help concentrate attention.

2. Check all bills and readings for accuracy. Compartmentalize charges so that the cost to each department/process can be identified. Communicate the results to those using the energy. It might even be feasible to share savings achieved with the employee users.

3. Many employees leave computers on stand-by believing there is no cost. All electrical items left on standby use electricity and the slight extra cost of starting up will usually be more than saved by switching off. Some computers now have energy-saving devices.

4. Leaving a photocopier on overnight means using energy sufficient to generate 1500 copies – often more than a day's use. Since copiers create heat, if they are sited in a separate office there may not be a need to heat it. Alternatively siting equipment within a general office might help reduce the cost of heating that area.

5. Implement a process whereby each time electric bulbs, strip lights and appliances need to be changed, consumption figures are considered so that low use replacements are installed. It is claimed that although energy-saving light bulbs are slightly more expensive than standard bulbs, they consume over 70% less electricity and last up to ten times as long. Modern slimline fluorescent tubes are not only cheaper than the thicker tubes, they also consume 10% less power.

6. Photoelectric cells can be used to ensure lights are only on when someone needs them to be on (for example, in toilets, cloakrooms, hardly-used passageways etc). Similar cells can be used for hand driers in toilets.

7. When refitting large offices or other areas, consider installing separate switching systems to break the overall area into smaller sections so that not all lights have to be on simultaneously.

8. Check heating/air conditioning systems. One very common situation is where the central heating is on fully and the hot radiators are immediately below open windows. Reducing the level of a thermostat of a heating system by 1°C can save around 8% of the cost. Alternatively the effectiveness of radiators is often impaired by placing desks, cupboards etc against them.

9. Water may be heated to too high a temperature. It is common to find that the water supplied must be cooled before it can be used (e.g. for washing hands). If so, this is extremely wasteful (unless there are hygiene requirements) – apart from being dangerous to the unwary.

10. Motors use electricity and a badly adjusted motor uses electricity inefficiently. Variable Speed Drives can be fitted to pumps to reduce speed of operation (if this is not essential) and can considerably reduce running costs. All equipment regardless of energy source should be checked for efficiency.

11. Compressed air facilities are often subject to leakages which means the compressor is working inefficiently.

12. Do we really need to heat the whole facility? Remove heating from areas where employees do not work – or provide localized heating only where necessary. Providing materials stored in such areas will not deteriorate if cold, why heat such areas?

Case study

The Zodiac toy chain acquired a new purpose-built warehouse in Bedford. At 40,000 sq ft and with an eaves height of 22ft, the projected cost of heating was considerable. Since most product was not temperature-sensitive, rather than heat the whole, picking areas surrounded by plastic sheeting were created. Those (mainly using fork lift trucks) required to visit the unheated areas were issued with appropriate clothing – and high quality vending machines were made available so hot drinks were always available.

13. Warehouses need to open their main doors for deliveries and issues. The cost of opening main doors as well as the loss of heat whilst open can be considerable. Using plastic strip curtains can insulate the interior whilst still providing access to the exterior – particularly if a double 'air-lock' system is used.

14. For added security many organizations use exterior lighting although much of the time it is simply consuming power. Increasingly powerful solar-powered lights are available. Most operate on an 'activity' generated basis – that is, they light up when there is any activity – and thus their effect on security may be minimal. However, if half the lights

could be supplied on a traditional basis with the other half powered by the sun – considerable savings can be made.

15. Solar panels can also be installed in roofs to generate an additional energy source – mainly as a supplement to traditional sources but every supplement reduces costs.

Windpower

There is considerable investment now in windfarms such that organizations can invest in the 'windmills' and not only use the electricity thereby generated but can sell any surplus to the National Grid. There are grants to assist organizations wishing to invest in this alternative power source (see USEFUL CONTACTS).

Case study

For £250 a subscriber can become part of co-operative operating wind farms in Lincolnshire, Cumbria, Oxfordshire, Scotland and Wales. All members will have an equal say in how the co-op is run. (www.energy4all .co.uk or 01229 821028)

Environmental obligations

Introduction

All property occupiers operate within an environment and use scarce resources. Demand for resources is increased by both useful and wasteful usage which increases the price to every user. Many processes not only use resources but also create by-products harmful to the environment. Increasingly operations and operators are legally required to take account of environmental matters and the potential and detrimental effect of their actions.

Survey

An NOP survey for the Institute of Directors discovered that:

- in roughly 50% of the 500 organizations contacted, the Board discussed social responsibility (66% of large companies)

- 60% discussed environmental issues (66% in large companies and 85% of those engaged in manufacturing)

- 36% had a Board member whose responsibilities included social issues

- 48% had a Board member whose responsibilities included environmental issues.

The duty to care for the environment is not new – legal requirements to protect the environment stretch back to the early years of the 20th century. For example, the Alkali Works Regulation Act 1906 required registration of industries creating pollution and established the principle of 'best practical means of avoiding pollution'. That phrase perhaps summarizes the problem, since almost by definition industry (indeed most economic activity) 'damages' the environment and the emphasis is to minimize the effect rather than eradicate it. The same phrase re-appears in modern protective laws: the Environment Protection Act 1990 (EPA90) and the Environment Act 1995 (EA95).

Environment Protection Act 1990

This Act established:

a) Integrated Pollution Control

Those organizations whose activities have a potentially or actual harmful effect on the environment must assess the manner by which their activities pollute and control emissions (for example) into the air by using alternative measures if practical (e.g. emission into water). This part of the EPA90 was strengthened following the passing of the Pollution, Prevention and Control Act 1999, the obligations under which are being introduced over a transitional period lasting until 2007. All organizations whose activities have potentially polluting results are required to try to prevent pollution in its many forms – air, water, gas, fume, smoke and solid emissions, waste (there are now target levels of reduction of waste set by the EU and incumbent on those industries that create it) – both toxic and radioactive, dust, noise, litter etc. Those responsible for uncontrolled harmful emissions can be fined up to £20,000.

EPA90 coined a derivative of the phrase referred to above – the 'batneec' principle – *best available treatment not entailing excessive cost*. Additional pressure came from UK membership of the European Union. The concept of 'not entailing excessive cost' was not however in accordance with EU principles.

b) The Environment Agency (EA)

The EA was set up under EPA 1990 as the monitoring and regulatory body responsible for overseeing compliance with the Act. The EA has rights of entry and can bring prosecution of those in breach of the law with penalties including fines of up to £20,000 on summary conviction or unlimited fines on indictment. Inspectors have an advisory role trying, for example, to ensure that where there is pollution it is dealt with. The 'batneec' principle has to some extent now been dropped in favour of a stricter regime which has no 'cost alleviator' – *'best practical environmental option'* (BPEO). The change to 'providing advice' reflects the experience of the USA where the regulatory bodies have altered their approach from 'charging for pollution at the end of the pipe' to providing advice and suggestions for reducing pollution.

The EA also oversees the environmental aspects of accidents at work, under the Control of Major Accident Hazard Regulations 1999, which aim to prevent major accidents and limit the consequences of accidents to both people and the environment. The schedule to the regulations lists various substances and two threshold quantities. They require any establishment which keeps such substances in excess of the thresholds to comply with the regulations. If the establishment has substance(s) in excess of the lower threshold they must notify the appropriate 'competent authority' (CA) (i.e. in England the HSE and the Environment Agency) of

- their name and address
- the address where the substance(s) is/are if different
- the characteristics of the substance(s)
- details of the activities in the establishment and
- details of the environment which could cause or aggravate an accident.

Operators must also prepare a Major Accident Prevention Policy and must consult their employees or representatives about the preparation of on-site emergency plans.

If the establishment has substance(s) in excess of the higher threshold they must comply with all the above requirements and in addition must – prepare safety reports and emergency plans which must show that all necessary measures have been taken to limit the consequences of an accident to people and the environment – in conjunction with the local authority, prepare an off-site emergency plan.

c) Registers of Contaminated Land

These are maintained by local authorities to record uses and users of land who may, as a result of their activities, have polluted it. Since the occupier/user responsible for the contamination may have moved on, without such a record a future purchaser could, in all innocence, become responsible for cleansing the land. When acquiring land, its former use and possible pollution (which could affect its value) should be questioned. If it is not known if the land is polluted, the vendor should guarantee to cover costs (possibly by insuring this risk), if it is later discovered that there is pollution.

Environment Act 1995

This Act granted local authorities power to monitor and improve air quality. This was first a requirement in 1956 brought about by the 'smogs' (fogs accentuated by smoke from coal fires) that then so badly affected the UK. Similar and renewed requirements in EA95 received added emphasis by the passing of the Air Quality Regulations 2000 which require local authorities to reach set target levels for air quality by 2005. Advice is available to those that create a challenge to these aims. All aspects of the environment – water, air and land

– are thus protected by these and other enactments and those in charge of organizations, the activities of which create waste or pollute, must be aware of the requirements to ensure full compliance including assessing levels of pollution and waste created. As well as ensuring that levels of waste are within the required targets, Boards must also ensure that whoever is removing the waste is properly licensed and should inspect their licence and all renewals. Increasingly it is expected that companies should include an environmental report within their Annual Report highlighting their

- declining waste levels
- increasing recycling of materials (e.g. toner cartridges)
- energy savings
- extended usage of recycled materials.

* *

Example

The UK Hilton hotel chain, as part of its provision of materials for seminar delegates, issues pens made entirely from recycled paper.

* *

Generally:

- where there is contaminated land, remedial action is required where there is 'significant harm' or 'pollution of controlled waters' and there are cost-effective methods of cleansing

- local authorities must identify land within their boundaries which is contaminated. Following a three month 'consultation period' the local authority can serve a remediation notice on the 'appropriate person'. If this notice is not complied with then the authority can enter the land and cleanse it – recovering the costs from the 'appropriate person'. It can create a charge in its favour on the land if these costs are not reimbursed. Heavily contaminated land is classified as a 'special site' requiring special provisions overseen by the Environment Agency rather than the local authority.

- the 'appropriate person' is the person who caused the contamination. This may not be the owner although if the polluter cannot be found it may be the current owner who has to pay.

Air pollution

The Secretary of State can set standards, reduction targets and timetables on a national basis. Local authorities have similar powers related to the areas under their control.

Water pollution

When water has been (or could be) polluted, the Environment Agency can serve a notice requiring anti-pollution action. The defendant no longer has the right to a sample of the water being used as evidence of the pollution so that they can have it independently analyzed. Companies having emissions into water might be well advised to sample the target water regularly and to keep the dated samples.

Asbestos surveys

Regulation 4 of the Control of Asbestos at Work Act requires those occupying/owning commercial (non-domestic) premises, which thus covers most employers, to:

a) determine the location and condition of materials in premises likely to contain asbestos ('asbestos containing materials' – ACM)

b) where materials could contain asbestos assume they do and treat them as ACM

c) compile a record of the location and condition of all ACM

d) consider and set down the risk of anyone being exposed to the fibres in the known or suspected ACM

e) compile and implement a plan for dealing with the risks arising from the materials

f) review and, if necessary, update the plan regularly (annually?)

g) provide data re. the above to anyone who could disturb the ACM and, if ACM are to be disturbed ensure those doing so are qualified to deal with the matter.

This needs to be conducted for every non-domestic building for which the employer is responsible. Inevitably there may be a duplication of effort (or a disagreement between parties) where more than one may be responsible (e.g. between landlord and lessee).

Note: Current draft EU proposals require companies in 58 industries to produce annual audits of their environmental performance at every site.

F

Fire precautions   101

First aid   111

Freehold ownership   117

Fire precautions

Introduction

Fire is no respecter of rank or person. History is littered with fire disasters – each of which have tended to create subsequent reactions aimed at minimizing a repetition. Such reactions are not new: the fire in Rome in 64AD resulted in a requirement to provide greater space between buildings to prevent fire spread. Similar requirements followed the Great Fire of London in 1666, although iron- ically the Mayor's consultation document published in late 2005 regarding new planning advice for London allows buildings to be built closer together. Commer- cial buildings are subject to ever-increasing regulations to try and minimize fire risk and to protect human beings using such buildings. Not that such people necessarily concern themselves too much about their safety. Indeed, many people on hearing a fire alarm are affected only by inertia. This dangerous inactivity needs to be overcome, which itself needs practice so that everyone moves rather than freezes. Such movement may need to be hastened by employees acting as fire marshals (and deputies, to cover absences). Regular fire alarm tests and fire drills (which are now mandatory in some cases) should be conducted.

Setting the scene

The 'morning after the fire before' is obviously far too late to try to consider how to deal with such a problem resulting from a fire. Contingency, emergency, disaster recovery planning is essential so that alternative actions can be consid- ered without the pressure of the aftermath of the incident. To put this in perspective it has been demonstrated that 80% of businesses who do not have recovery or continuity plans fail within a year of a major dislocation such as a serious fire, whilst 33% of all businesses will not survive a serious fire at all. This is not a scenario that always happens to 'someone else'. Statistically, around 20% of all organizations suffer some kind of major dislocation or disruption every five years.

Legal obligations

The Fire Precautions (Places of Work) Regulations 1997 required employers to be pro-active regarding:

- carrying out assessments related to fire risks

- ensuring there is appropriate fire-fighting equipment and, if manual equipment is provided, indicating its location clearly

- training employees in fire-fighting procedures and techniques

- ensuring all emergency exits are kept clear, are well-indicated and accessible and, when dark, are lighted, and

- adequately maintaining all fire-fighting equipment.

Fire authorities are responsible for ensuring compliance with these regulations.

Failure to comply will not only lead to the issue of enforcement certificates but is also a criminal offence, punishable by fines and/or imprisonment.

The Building Regulations 2000 require a business, when constructing new buildings, making material alterations to a building or materially changing its use, to:

- have means of early warning of a fire to assist a speedy escape

- use appropriate materials to reduce the spread of fire

- improve facilities to enable firefighters to save/protect life and

- make suitable provision at the building for the easy access of fire appliances.

For non-domestic premises developers are required to:

- introduce measures regarding inclusive design

- design compartment walls to take account of inflexions during a fire

- introduce a national maximum 'unsprinkled' compartment size for warehouses

- provide for fire protection of corridors in 'self-storage' warehouses

- provide additional dry rising mains for tall buildings

- provide phased evacuation procedures for staircases and escape passages

  and so on.

The Regulatory Reform (Fire Safety) Order 2005

This Order simplifies fire safety law for non-domestic occupiers. It restates or initiates measures to:

- reduce the risk of fire – and risk of fire-spread

- ensure means of escape ('moe') and that these can be safely and effectively used

- fight fire

- ensure fire detection and warnings are provided

- provide instruction and training on fire

- mitigate the effects of fire.

Although the 2005 Regulations revoke the 1997 regulations referred to above, most of the requirements are restated with the very important change that Fire Certificates will no longer be issued. Thus the previous requirement to react to the advice of the fire officer, and obtaining guidance and clearance by the issue of such a certificate has now been replaced by a requirement to be completely proactive particularly regarding the preparation of (and regularly updating of) risk assessments. Such assessments must be carried out by a 'responsible person' (RP), If the workplace is under the control of the employer, the RP is the employer; but if the workplace is under another person's control, the RP could be the owner. Thus where a property is in multi-occupation, in each of the 'suites' or areas occupied by individual employers, they are the RP for their own area. However, the RP for 'common areas' would probably be the landlord. RPs have 'duties' as set out in the following checklist.

RPs must

- take general fire precautions in respect of their employees (and others lawfully present) on the premises or in its immediate vicinity

- make assessment of all risks to which those present may be subject – with special attention paid where those persons are aged 18 or under

    (**Note:** it would be best if these were in writing and dated, made available to all involved and regularly updated. Everyone should be encouraged to report hazards – see FIRST AID and FIRE PRECAUTIONS.)

- not permit a new work activity involving a risk to commence unless a risk assessment has been made and measures have been implemented

- implement the preventative and protective measures set out in the 1997 regulations (see above)

- eliminate (where it is reasonable to do so) or reduce the risks from dangerous substances

- ensure there is fire fighting equipment, detectors and alarms

- comply with emergency routes and exit provisions

- follow procedures for serious and imminent danger

- ensure there is a suitable system of maintenance of premises and safety equipment

- appoint competent persons to assist in conducting these preventative and protective measures

- provide information and training to employees (and others present)

- co-operate with other RPs (in neighbouring premises etc).

Enforcement is normally carried out by Fire Safety Inspectors (appointed by the local fire and rescue authority) although in some circumstances (e.g. where the subject location is a construction site) enforcement will be under the control of the Health & Safety Executive, or (where the location is a sports centre) the local authority. Failure to comply with requirements issued by an enforcement authority could lead to a fine of £20,000 or, on conviction, to an unlimited fine and/or two years imprisonment.

* *

Arson

Fire statistics demonstrate that nearly half of all fires (45%) are started deliberately – there were 18,500 arson attacks on businesses in 2005. The property must be protected not only from TRESPASSERS but also from arsonists. Proactivity is required from Facility Managers.

* *

Providing defences

- deter unauthorized entry to the facility in general and the buildings in particular (ensure boundaries are sound with fencing, shutters, security lighting and/or CCTV, thief resistant locks, intruder alarms)

- ensure vision of neighbours and passers-by is not obscured (so that they may spot unauthorized entrants etc and hopefully raise the alarm)

- reduce the ability to start a fire (refuse should be held in secure containers)

- waste bins should be surrounded by a 'cordon sanitaire' (i.e. to ensure the bins are kept away from buildings)

- mobile and temporary buildings should have 'skirts' to prevent intruders getting underneath

- oil and fuels must be kept secure and in bunds not only to prevent spoilage but also to restrict fire spread.

Good housekeeping

Fire needs three 'ingredients' – material, time and ignition – and if one or more is absent, it cannot start, or, if it does it is unlikely to last and/or should be able to be brought under control swiftly. Of the 55% of fires that are 'accidental' 23% are caused by a misuse of equipment, 48% by defective equipment and 29% by careless actions.

If a workplace is untidy, with waste improperly stored, and/or electrical sockets and/or equipment are poorly maintained and/or overloaded, this is not only bad housekeeping but can also increase the incidence of accidents and loss of materials through theft and damage. Highlighting the dangers may, at least to employees, act as some kind of pro-active precautionary preparation. Notification such as the following may be helpful.

Fire precautions

Fire is dangerous to individuals and to your continued employment. All employees (and their visitors) are expected to adhere to the following precautions at all times:

- smoking is only permitted in the designated areas

  (**Note:** Until legislation is implemented to cover all workplaces – proposed to become effective by 2007 – it would be preferable for an employer to ban smoking altogether. No-one has any right to smoke at work.)

- ash, matches, lighters and all smoking residue must be deposited in metal waste containers

- no other material should be placed in the metal waste containers provided for smoking residue

- inflammable material (e.g. lighter fuel, petrol, paint, spray cans, etc) must not be brought on to the organization's premises without prior written approval from [name]

- personal electrical equipment should not be brought into the organization's premises without prior written approval from [name]

- waste and waste materials must only be placed in appropriate containers and these must be cleared to the designated areas every day

- all workplaces must be kept tidy at all times, with papers and all other materials safely stored outside working hours

- supervisors and managers are responsible for ensuring their team members adhere to these precautions at all times

- anyone in breach of these requirements will be made subject to the disciplinary procedure.

The premises should be subject to a practice evacuation at least once a year with those subject to particularly hazardous risks practising more often. Evacuation practices should be monitored and any required improvements communicated to all. Records should be kept of each evacuation to prove that the organization took its obligations seriously and was endeavouring to provide as safe a place of work as possible.

Policy

The organization's fire and risk procedure (and/or instructions to be followed in the event of fire) should be disseminated to all employees (with regular updating reminders) as well as to all recruits as part of their familiarization (or induction) process.

❋ ❋

Example

1. Procedure and advice

The alarm is tested every week/month at [Time] a.m./p.m. Familiarize yourself with the alarm and, should it ring other than at these times, follow the evacuation procedure IMMEDIATELY.

Details of the primary and back-up evacuation routes of each department are posted within the department. You MUST familiarize yourself with such routes.

Each department has a fire marshal and deputy, to oversee all evacuations. All employees must comply with instructions issued by fire marshals or deputies.

2. Drills

Fire drills are held [monthly]. When the alarm sounds for a drill or at an unexpected time (i.e. other than on a previously advised test):

a)   if it is safe to do so, switch off your machine, if any, and close any windows in the immediate vicinity

b)   proceed to the department's primary evacuation route, or, if the primary route is blocked, to the secondary route

c)   after evacuation, assemble in the designated assembly point for your department and ensure your name is checked by the fire marshal (or deputy) – follow the marshal's (or deputy's) instructions

d)   do NOT return to the building or attempt to move a car from the car park unless instructed to do so

e)   DON'T RUN. DON'T PANIC. DON'T USE LIFTS. DON'T VISIT CLOAK-ROOMS or collect bags, etc.

3. Discovery

If you discover a fire:

a)   operate the nearest fire alarm call point

b)   if there is no immediate danger to life, attack the fire with the appliances supplied

c)   if the fire seems to be gaining a hold, or life is threatened in any way, abandon such fire-fighting activities and evacuate

d)   make any knowledge of the fire, its origins, seat, etc known to the Fire Brigade

e)   assess all risks in the workplace.

Pro-activity

Fire certificates issued under the previous legislation specified the means of escape and fire fighting appliances required, including that:

- appliances must be supplied with adequate notices and appropriate markings of fire escape routes etc

- fire fighting appliances and equipment must be regularly maintained

and so on. Most of the requirements are little more than common sense – regular safety checks to ensure escape routes are kept clear, there is no obstruction of fire exits, or of safety signs, or any reduction in the effectiveness of (for example) sprinkler systems and so on.

These obligations are now placed on the RP who needs to be pro-active – possibly needing to take advice from experts etc – and to communicate (and update) and advise those affected.

Fire safety checklist

Inspection carried out on _____ by _____

If any answer is no, indicate when corrective action is required to take place and subsequently ensure such action is taken by the date stated.

PAPERWORK

1. Do all notice boards bear an updated fire evacuation procedure (see SAFETY COMMUNICATION) within the Workplace Safety folder?

2. Have all hazards reported since last inspection been dealt with?

3. Have all defect reports issued after last inspection been properly dealt with?

MONITORING

1. Are there fire marshals and deputies for all areas?

2. Have all marshals and deputies been trained?

3. Have changes in layout and/or procedures been brought to the attention of the marshals?

4. Have supervisors and/or marshals made all newcomers familiar with action required in the event of a fire?

ESCAPE ROUTES

1. Are all fire doors and exits etc checked each morning?

2. Are all escape routes clear with no goods, furniture etc obstructing such routes?

3. Are all escape routes well signposted?

4. Are directions to all escape routes clear from all departments?

5. Do all exit doors open easily?

6. Are all exit signs visible and legible?

7. Are fire-resisting doors operative and undamaged?

8. Do fire resisting doors shut properly?

EQUIPMENT

1. Are all extinguishers, hoses etc in place?

2. Is all such equipment within its time limit for checking?

3. Are all fire alarm call points in good condition?

4. Are all fire alarm call points clearly marked and not obstructed?

5. If smoking is allowed on the premises, are all departments supplied with well-maintained metal waste containers?

6. Is emergency lighting operative?

ASSEMBLY AREAS

1. Are all assembly areas clear and well signposted/identifiable?

2. Is protective clothing available?

Action as a result of such checks should be initiated by written Defect Report with an action date. Checking to ensure that defects noted at the previous inspection then themselves (as shown above) form part of the checklist at the next following fire safety check.

Case study

I was impressed by preparedness of the Hilton Hotel at Edinburgh Airport when there was a fire evacuation at 1.30am one cold December morning. Many guests had not stopped to grab a coat and the hotel staff were issuing foil wraps similar to those used by mountain rescue teams and given to runners at the end of marathons to retain body heat of those who had evacuated only in their night garments.

Being pro-active makes sound business sense. Inevitably there are risks in business and sometimes a simple reaction to the risk could save considerable loss.

Case study

A retailer operated a number of units; some being very small. In a few cases the unit was little more than a lock-up (that is one where the only entrance was through the customer access). During the fire-fighters' dispute it was suggested to shop managers and franchisees, that, as well as checking fire extinguishers, they should fill two buckets of water for instant availability. The retail areas of some shops were remote from a water supply (or in the case of lock-ups did not have a water supply) and instant access to water might snuff out a fire that could take a hold if left even for a very short period.

First aid

Introduction

First Aid is 'instant action carried out (normally) by 'not medically qualified' persons in order to preserve life, pending attendance by a trained medical practitioner'. Such assistance is vital since it may sustain life which otherwise would be lost. However, it should be stressed to those so acting, not least to avoid possible liability claims, that First Aiders should limit their input to emergency assistance.

Notification

Employers are obliged to provide emergency assistance in the event of injury, etc and under the Reporting of Injury, Death and Dangerous Occurrences Regulations (RIDDOR) are also required to notify appropriate authorities of all reportable incidents affecting everyone on their sites whether employed or visiting. Under the 1995 RIDDOR revisions, employers must also report acts of non-consensual physical violence (e.g. 'sky-larking' or pranks of a physical nature) to a person at work.

Requirements

The Health & Safety (First Aid) Regulations (and the revised code of practice issued in 1997) requires an employer to provide First Aid facilities and the following checklist sets out what might usually be expected.

Checklist

1. Provide suitable First Aid staff and services in accordance with the nature of the business, the degree of danger or hazard in the operations, the number of employees, and the proximity to medical assistance. A 'First Aider' is defined as someone who holds a current certificate in First Aid.

2. The number of First Aiders required is not stipulated but generally it is expected that there should be one person who holds a current certificate in First Aid per 50 employees in a low-risk environment. If there are fewer than 50 employees and no qualified person, then someone responsible should be appointed to act in the event of an incident. In a 'high-risk' environment there should be a First Aider for the first 50 employees plus one for every additional 50 employees.

3. If there are 400 or more employed at a single site, an employer will normally be required to provide a First Aid room. Again its provision will depend on the assessment of the hazards.

   A First Aid room would normally be equipped as follows:
   - hand basin with running hot and cold water
   - supply of drinking water
   - lockable medical supplies store
   - disposable towels
   - couch or medical trolley and a chair (both waterproof)
   - stocked First Aid box
   - disposable protective aprons or similar
   - bowls, disposable beakers, etc
   - table or work surface with a smooth (for ease of cleaning) plastic or similar surface
   - waste bin with plastic bags or bin-liners

4. Provide properly stocked First Aid boxes. It is usual to provide a First Aid box per First Aider and to make the him/her responsible for the contents of the box (and re-ordering) which should be kept locked when not in use.

A First Aid box will normally contain:

- guidance card (stressing that First Aid is only preservation pending the arrival of trained medical attention)

- 20 sterile adhesive dressings (assorted sizes)

- six safety pins (if food preparation and/or catering is being conducted, detectable pins and dressings may be required)

- two sterile eye pads

- a large sterile unmedicated dressing

- a supply of moist cleaning wipes with a protective dispenser

- six medium, two large and three extra large wound dressings

- disposable plastic gloves

- airway (to facilitate mouth-to-mouth resuscitation without direct contact)

- re-order sheets.

Obviously there may be a need to add specific items depending upon the work being conducted.

Policy

A First Aid policy and procedure should be adopted, reflecting the organization's commitment to and administration of First Aid. Employers are legally required to enter details of all accidents at work in an Accident Book. Since this means personal details of employees are included in such a record, the provisions of the Data Protection Act must be observed and revised editions of such a book which conceal such personal data are now available from HSE Books on 01787 881165.

Example

1. The [name] provides a workplace and processes in compliance with health and safety regulations to ensure a safe location for its employees and visitors.

2. When First Aid is needed [employees' names] have volunteered to provide such assistance.

3. The organization sponsors its First Aiders by:

    i)   funding their training to acquire a certificate of competence, and any updating required

    ii) giving each First Aider an annual honorarium of [£50] in recognition of their assistance

4. The First Aid room is available for all employees who need rest after injury etc. Such use must be authorized in advance by a manager or a First Aider.

5. The duty of First Aiders is to preserve life until the attendance of a paramedic or qualified medical practitioner, to reassure the patient, and to ensure the speedy removal of the patient to hospital in the event of a serious accident. First Aiders are not permitted to issue drugs of any description or to offer medical advice. No liability can be accepted by the organization, or individual First Aiders, for attending and helping in a situation requiring First Aid.

6. In the event of an accident or an employee feeling unwell, a supervisor should call a First Aider who will treat the patient (as above) and enter in the Accident Book, the patient's name, the nature of the accident or incident, the patient's condition and details of any treatment given, with a note of the time, date and place.

7. If it is a simple cut or abrasion, the First Aider, or the patient, can clean the wound and apply an adhesive dressing. If the patient feels unwell, they should be taken to the First Aid room and allowed to sit or lie quietly for 30 minutes. If the feeling continues, the patient should either be taken home, or to their, or the organization's doctor, or to hospital. Organization transport should used rather than the employee's own vehicle. No liability will be accepted as a result of the organization trying to assist in these ways. In the event that the employee's vehicle is left on organization premises, efforts will be made to protect it, but no liability can be accepted for it.

8. If a First Aider considers an incident is serious, and that emergency treatment is required, they will be responsible for summoning an ambulance. The First Aider will brief the ambulance staff and, should the circumstances require, either the First Aider, or [a Personnel Department] representative, should accompany the employee to hospital, and either remain there until completion of treatment, or until the family of the employee has arrived, depending upon the circumstances.

9. First Aiders are expected to set an example by maintaining a high level of personal hygiene, e.g. washing their hands and removing overalls

before administering treatment of any kind. A First Aider needing to deal with bleeding, burns, sickness or risk of contact with bodily fluids should wear the protective gloves provided in every First Aid box. Such gloves should be disposed of safely after treatment. Any clothing which becomes soiled should be removed as soon as appropriate and carefully cleaned or disposed of hygienically, as should any treatment dressings or swabs, etc.

10. If artificial resuscitation is required, an airway (provided in each First Aid box) should be used rather than direct, mouth to mouth, contact.

11. Any First Aider required to provide treatment, whilst suffering from a cut or abrasion, should ensure such cuts, etc are adequately protected.

12. Each First Aider will be responsible for a First Aid box, and for the re-ordering of dressings so that the minimum contents are always available. Only a First Aider should have access to a First Aid box.

Hazard reporting

Prevention being better than cure, a system whereby employees are encouraged to report hazards or potentially hazardous occurrences or incidents should be considered utilizing a hazard report form such as is shown in SAFETY COMMUNICATION.

Freehold ownership

Introduction

Making the decision between buying or leasing a property may not only depend on individual preference but also on the availability of capital, timing etc. At one stage in an organization's life it may be preferable to buy – at other times leasing may be more appropriate and affordable.

Speculation

Although there may be a temptation to use property for speculative purposes rather than simply as a means of housing the business, this may be best resisted unless there is a clear strategy and considerable and well-founded confidence concerning the long-term strength of property demand both generally and in the particular area. Property can be used as a commodity and thus traded profitably, although in this book the emphasis is on its use within the business. Although one purpose which might come under this heading is the opportunity for organizations operating an occupational pension fund to use a property to reduce their levy to the Pension Protection Fund. If they pledge freehold property/ies to the fund, the levy can be reduced.

Case study

Maynards owned a number of valuable freehold properties. Since the company had no borrowings, its credit rating was very high. In the mid-1980s one small retail property, in the centre of Worthing, Sussex, became the subject of interest for several institutional investors and a bidding war broke out. As a result of playing one interested party against another the offers were advanced from around £200,000 to approaching £700,000. The company still wished to trade from the premises so was interested in a sale and lease-back rather than a complete disposal. An investment of £700,000 would, however, have resulted in too high a rent for profitable trading, so a lower offer (with lower rent) was accepted.

Long-term lock in

Buying a freehold should be actively contemplated when:

- the long-term business plan calls for it to remain in the same location for a considerable time

- the nature of the business is such that the means of production cannot be easily moved

- the business has funds which it can afford to invest long-term in property assets

- there is confidence that the underlying value of property in the area chosen will, at least, not depreciate

- the organization wishes to control the cost of property occupation. This is difficult with leasehold property as it is virtually impossible to predict rental increases.

- the organization wants to be able to control the internal layout of the property to accommodate changing processes and practices. Whilst not impossible with leased property, the approval of the landlord to such changes may be needed, as well as REINSTATEMENT leading to further costs on lease termination.

Using the investment

A freehold property is a fixed asset and its value can be used to support the balance sheet or even used to generate cash at some time in the future by means of a sale and lease-back arrangement (a freehold property is sold but subject to a lease the former owner has already created in its favour). Property values tend to appreciate and VALUATION of such assets on a regular basis may not only support the asset value in the balance sheet but also provide security for borrowings to be used within the business.

Alternatively the value can be left out of the balance sheet, thus being available as a hidden reserve. Some companies (particularly listed PLCs) include the purchase value but not the market value of their properties, from their balance sheets. Some (e.g. the Bank of England) do not include any value of their valuable properties. Having available such 'hidden' assets may be advantageous at times of (for example) hostile takeover bids.

Opportunistic actions

Monitoring the property market may enable a freehold owner to maximize their investment. Whilst dabbling in the property market may be a dilution of management attention from its core business, it may be possible to obtain additional profits as a result of such awareness. For example, acquiring adjoining properties may grant flexibility of use of the existing premises, but also the value of the two buildings in one ownership may be greater than their individual values. The potential of such MARRIAGES OF INTERESTS should not be overlooked.

Position

Property is a unique asset in that unlike any other it cannot be moved. Whereas the original location may have been ideal for the business, circumstances tend to change and the original reasons for a particular site may disappear – or be replaced by pressure for a relocation. Whilst all property occupation, other than a short-term licence, tends to lock the occupier into a location, a freehold can act as a greater 'anchor'. If property demand in the area has reduced, the value of the asset may have decreased. Few businesses will wish to take too great a loss on a disposing of a freehold investment since the loss on sale could severely impact the balance sheet.

Use

Whilst to some extent the uses to which a freehold property can be put is greater than those allowed by a lease (particularly if a lease contains a restricted user clause) the requirements of local planners may constrain the widest use of the premises.

Inelastic supply

Property assets are in inelastic supply. If considering an investment for a growing business the possibility of acquiring neighbouring land and/or buildings (even if not used initially) might be considered. If the original building erected upon the land is such that extension or additional bays can be added at will, this may help overcome the 'inelastic supply' nature of the location.

Upkeep

The maintenance in a good state of repair and redecoration of premises occupied under a lease can be ensured by the landlord requiring that the lessee adhere to the 'repair and redecoration' covenants set out in the lease. Since there is no similar 'external force' in relation to freehold properties there may not be the same level of commitment to the upkeep of these properties resulting in damage to their value.

Internal rents

Those departments or divisions or parts of a business that are occupying properties that are owned either by themselves or an associated organization (e.g. a parent company) gain a benefit not enjoyed by other occupiers within the same organization occupying leasehold premises – that is they do not pay rent to an external body. Where divisions or subsidiaries results are required to be comparable, the concept of the 'owner' of the freehold charging a nominal or INTERNAL RENT could be considered.

G

Guarantees 123

Guarantees

Introduction

Smaller companies and/or those without a history of reasonable trading results may be requested, on entering into a property commitment (lease or licence), to supply the names of persons and/or organizations to guarantee performance of the organization's financial obligations under the lease.

Directors as guarantors

The protection of 'Limited liability' means that if a company becomes insolvent, unless guilty of wrongful trading, no liability attaches to the directors. A landlord with a limited company as a lessee knows therefore that should that company become insolvent, there will be no one from whom to obtain monies due. Accordingly the landlord may request the directors of the company personally guarantee the company's financial obligations. A guarantee is a legally enforceable personal undertaking and, if called upon, the guarantor must provide any shortfall – to the limit of the guarantee. If the organization cannot pay rent and other outgoings, this undertaking could prove very costly and meeting the liability very difficult, not least since if the organization is in trouble, the director may already be having difficulty obtaining his/her salary. Too often guarantees are given with insufficient consideration of the onerous liability being entered into.

Security

This situation can become far more serious personally if the guarantor is required to provide security, for example, their home. If unable to meet the debts they have guaranteed, the security pledged could then be seized by the creditor and sold as payment. If the organization needs the premises, there may be no option but to agree. However, a guarantee should be limited either in amount, or in time or both. Thus a director providing a guarantee might stipulate that the guarantee should be restricted to:

- (say) £10,000

- the first three years of the term of the [lease]

- the payment of rent (only)

and be payable only provided the creditor has given official notice of their intent to call in the guarantee and allowed the guarantor(s) sufficient time to try to raise alternative funds to settle the outstanding payments. In addition the guarantor should endeavour to gain agreement to their guarantee ceasing on assignment (in which case the landlord will almost certainly require replacement guarantors for or from any assignee).

Option to break

Whilst there may be an understandable wish to minimize the effect of the guarantor, the interests of the landlord are diametrically opposed to this and there will need to be some negotiation to achieve a compromise acceptable to both parties. If, however, open-ended guarantees are insisted on (that is they are not protected by any of the limitations set out above) it may be advisable to try to insert an OPTION to break the lease or licence after say five years. Providing this is agreed, then should the organization get into difficulties, once again the effect is to limit the effect. If there is an option, it is essential to ensure that not only are the requirements to effect its exercise strictly adhered to but also all covenants are complied with.

Authorized Guarantee Agreements (AGAs)

Until January 1996 when the Landlord and Tenant (Covenants) Act 1995 came into force, even if a lessee sold their lease, if their purchaser defaulted, the original lessee was still liable for rent and other outgoings under the PRIVITY OF CONTRACT rule. Under the new arrangements, privity of contract is abolished but landlords can require lessee to enter into an AGA. Under an AGA the lessee agrees to reimburse the landlord for rent and service charges for a maximum of six months should the purchaser of their lease fail to pay those outgoings. Legal advice should be taken.

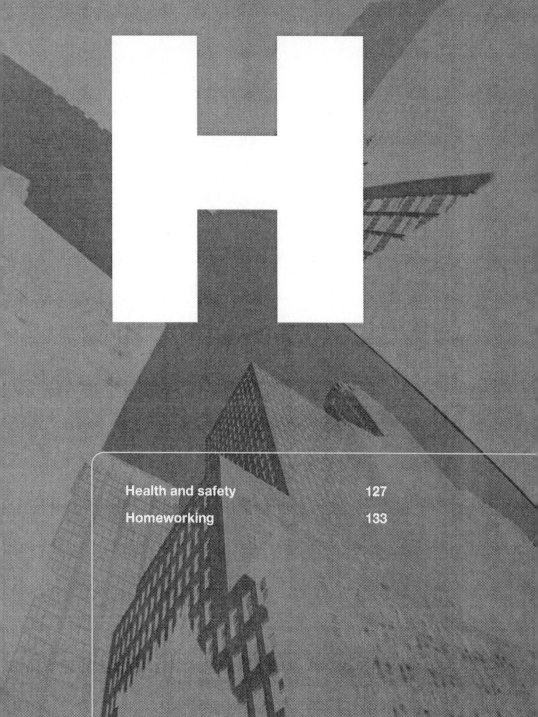

H

Health and safety   127

Homeworking   133

Health and safety

Introduction

Many accidents happen in industrial and commercial premises: most are minor but in 2004/5 alone there were 220 deaths. Some accidents, however, are not 'accidental' – many are caused by negligence or carelessness, poor systems and/or precautions or lack of perception. 'Accidents do not happen – they are caused' was the thought-provoking punch line of a former advertisement advocating greater care. Employers are required to take reasonable precautions to ensure the safety of those for whom they are responsible – their employees and visitors (including contractors) – and can be held liable for compensation to those injured at, or as a result of their work or activities. Although there are a considerable number of later regulations covering, for example, display screens, manual handling etc the current legal framework derives from the implementation of the Health & Safety at Work, etc Act 1974 (HASAWA).

Responsibilities

Under HASAWA:

1. Employers must provide a safe place of work for their employees which these days is taken to mean the protection, as far as reasonably practical, from harassment, bullying and discrimination as well as from physical harm, and

2. Employees must take reasonable care of themselves and their colleagues. The legislation places a wide-ranging and onerous responsibility on every property occupier/employer, and its implementation should be made the responsibility of a senior, even board level, manager. A competent person should carry out safety and risk assessments (see FIRE PRECAUTIONS). This does not necessarily mean that an 'expert' should be used, as competency is judged on training, experience, and knowledge of the workplace/process. Such assessments are individual to each location and require detailed, and ongoing attention throughout the business. All organizations with five or more employees are

required to prepare and display in the place of work their policy statement regarding Health and Safety matters and company-employers are also required to appoint one of their directors as their Safety Director. The Health and Safety Commission Executive (HSC) Code on Health and Safety Responsibilities of Directors suggests that directors should:

- Ensure they understand their personal legal liability and responsibility. Boards should consider the requirements to report publicly on their organization's record on health and safety, including accident and enforcement data. They should also consider if there are breaches of the requirements and, if so, identify action to be taken – and ensure it is taken.

- Collectively and individually accept 'publicly' their collective role in providing health and safety leadership in their company. This might entail directors and senior executives undergoing training in safety management and risk assessment, containment and prevention.

- Ensure board decisions reflect these health and safety intentions as set out in their company's Health and Safety Policy. This could include not simply analyzing the effect and eradication of occurrences that caused accidents, but also identifying and recording details of 'near misses' (see INSURANCE), and learning from them by making adjustments to try to prevent a repetition.

- Consult employees on matters of health and safety. Encouraging employees to report hazards should assist not only in eradicating or minimizing such hazards but also comply with this requirement – at least in part.

  However, a formal process of such consultation should also be set up – possibly using elected safety representatives and a safety committee. (See example of Hazard Report form in SAFETY COMMUNICATION.)

- Appoint one of their number to be responsible for health and safety and the promotion of such matters. Successful prosecutions usually result in fines but may increasingly result in imprisonment of those responsible. The Company Directors' (Health and Safety) Act requires boards to appoint one of their number to be the 'safety director' and stresses that directors have a duty to consider matters of health and safety in all company operations.

This obligation might be met by the board requiring that at all its meetings there should be a health and safety report and that whenever a new product or procedure, or a revision of an existing product or procedure, is considered, or a location is acquired or altered, and so on, the safety aspects of those innovations and/or changes should be investigated and again a report submitted to the board. This is evidenced by the report and discussion being minuted. Obviously the nominated Health and Safety Director should lead the discussion. The advantage of adopting this course of action is that should there ever be a liability claim against the board it can be shown that the body took their obligations to provide a 'safe place of work' seriously. The legal maxim 'in litigation the person with the best paperwork stands a better chance of winning' is apposite.

HSC enforcement policy

The revised Enforcement Policy setting out the principles and practice, now expected by the HSC to be followed by those policing this area, includes criteria to be used to decide which injury or other complaints should be investigated and detailed guidelines regarding initiating prosecutions where:

i) death resulted from a legislative breach

ii) the situation is grave or the general record of the offender requires it

iii) there has been a repetition of breaches

iv) non-compliant work has been carried out without a licence

v) there has been a failure to comply with an improvement or prohibition order

vi) a breach subject to a caution has been repeated

v) false information has been provided and/or there has been an intent to deceive

vi) inspectors have been deliberately obstructed.

In future, prosecutions are to be recommended (*inter alia*) where:

i) it is appropriate in order to draw attention to the need for legal compliance

ii) a breach has continued despite repeated warnings.

Generally, this version differs from its predecessors in that it places an increased emphasis on managerial responsibility. For example it states that enforcing authorities should:

> 'prosecute individuals … if they consider that (it) is warranted. In particular (the authority) should consider the management chain and the role paid by individual directors and managers, and should take action against them where the inspection or investigation reveals that the offence was committed with

their consent or connivance or (is) attributable to neglect on their part... Where possible, enforcing authorities should seek the disqualification of directors under the Company Directors Disqualification Act (CDDA).'

A number of directors have already been disqualified under the CDDA for safety offences (maximum disqualification period: 15 years).

Case study

In *Rainham Waste Recycling and O' Sullivan*, an employee lost an arm using an unguarded waste recycling machine. The company and its director were both successfully prosecuted. Whilst the company was fined £25,000 plus £4,000 costs, the director was personally fined £5,000 and also disqualified from being a director for five years under the CDDA.

New legislation enhancing the effectiveness of the old 'corporate manslaughter' legislation has created the offence of 'Corporate killing' where the defendant is the corporate body. This could give rise to fines of over £1,000,000 on the corporate body. Officers of companies found liable could face personal fines and/or prosecution under the CDDA which could lead to their disqualification from acting as directors.

The Government has stated that employers should have no fear of prosecution under the new law, where they have 'conscientiously':

- ensured safe working practices (e.g. workers are trained and their knowledge is regularly) and equipment is safely maintained)

- safely maintained premises (e.g. adequate fire precautions etc are set up), and

- complied with health and safety legislation.

Case study

In *R v F Howe & Sons (Engineers) Ltd* the company was held liable for the electrocution of one of its employees. The company was fined £55,000 but appealed to the Court of Appeal stating that if it paid the fine it would be liquidated. The Court of Appeal reduced the fine but warned 'some safety offences could be so serious that they could lead to fines being levied at a rate which would bankrupt the company'. Basically the Court does not need to take 'ability to pay' into account when levying a fine. The Court went on to comment that generally the fines for safety offences were too low. Courts were urged to consider how far defendants fell below the 'reasonably practical' test.

The thrust of this anticipated legislation is to make those ultimately responsible for death and/or injury accountable for their actions (or inactions). This reiterates the requirement in safety matters that has been developing since the early 1990s i.e. that employers/occupiers must take positive steps to create as safe as possible an environment within which they require their employees to work.

Control of Major Accidents Regulations 1999

These regulations seek to prevent major accidents and to limit their consequences to people and the environment. A schedule in the regulations lists various substances and two thresholds requiring any establishment that keeps substances in excess of these thresholds to comply with the requirements of the regulations.

1. For establishments with substances in excess of the lower threshold the appropriate competent authority (the HSE and Environment Agency) must be advised of:

   - their name and address

   - the address housing the substances if different

   - the characteristics of the substances

   - details of the activities carried on in the establishment

   - details of the environment which could cause or aggravate an accident

2.   If the establishment has substances in excess of the higher threshold they:

   • must comply with all the above and in addition must show that all necessary measures have been taken to limit the consequences of an accident to people and the environment, and

   • prepare an off-site emergency plan in conjunction with the local authority.

The HSE, Environment Agency and local authorities can charge for applying their regulatory functions.

Performance indicator

The HSC has launched a web-based Corporate Health & Safety Performance Indicator (CHaSPI) to help highlight the important role required to be played by directors. By giving case studies and a scoring technique, the aim is to enable directors to:

   • measure the effectiveness of their internal controls over health and safety

   • benchmark their performance against their own targets and the performance of their peers.

Since the results can be made public, one would expect organizations to ensure before using it that they would score well.

Homeworking

Introduction

In recent years there has been a considerable increase in the number of workers (employees and self-employed) using their homes as their main places of work – a trend which continues. The Office of National Statistics (ONS) calculate that there are approaching 3 million home or 'tele' workers in the UK (although other research claims a higher figure). It has been estimated that the ONS figure (which itself represents an increase of 65% over the past 4 years) could grow to over 8 million (roughly 25% of the workforce) by 2010. The greater requirement for consideration of flexible working from those with parental and carer responsibilities will almost inevitably increase the numbers of homeworkers. The result could have major implications for facility and property managers – after all, if 25% of an organization's workers no longer need full-time accommodation this will generate surplus commercial space.

Advantages and disadvantages

It is claimed that homeworkers have a lower incidence of absence and higher morale than those commuting to work, and a greater number of productive hours (mainly since they avoid the costs and stresses of travelling and can concentrate without workplace distractions). It may also be an attractive proposition to those with domestic and family commitments. Conversely, the social aspects of working are absent which some may find unacceptable. In addition, the normal flow of information through which workplace-based employees acquire knowledge can be lacking.

Employers may gain since they may be able to reduce the space they need and (since travel costs are minimized) may be able to pay less for the duties undertaken in the home. (In December 2005, a report in 'The Times' indicated that every month employees spend over £200 at work – £120 on food, £35 on work clothes, and £50 on travelling. Obviously a homeworker would not spend at least part of this which would need to be reflected in the rate even for comparable jobs.) Conversely, supervision/control may become more difficult, and the costs of both supervision and communication with homeworkers may rise.

Administration

Whilst those responsible for Personnel or Human Resources will need to draw up contracts etc for homeworkers, facilities managers should also be involved since a person's home is now a place of work and must be treated as such. Normally the homeworker, where they have a dedicated room for the employer's business, will expect to receive payment for such use although the equipment they need may be provided by the employer. However, questions of liability, insurance, recovery etc must be addressed. It is advisable to devise a policy which determines all such matters.

Draft policy

1. The [organization] is committed to the growth of homeworking where this is both feasible and welcomed by those concerned.

2. Those wishing to be considered for this type of work should register this interest with [specify].

3. Homeworkers need to be able to make a room in their house (the homebase) available for use as an office/workshop for the [organization] on a dedicated basis. To compensate for this use the [organization] will make a payment of [sum].

4. In the event that a homebase can only be made available on a dedicated basis after some works and/or expenditure, the [organization] will consider making an advance (recoverable by agreed deductions from subsequent payments to the homeworker) to fund such works.

5. The employee will be required to commit to working a set number of hours per [day/week/ month] for an agreed sum although the hours can be varied to suit the requirements of home and office. The employee, however, must be available for core hours which are [specify].

6. The homeworker will be required to sign an agreement which will cover the items set out in this policy and any further items specific to the individual.

7. To set up the homebase the [organization] will provide the following equipment [specify] and pay for the cost of installing renting and using dedicated telephone line(s).

   [Details of equipment]

   The employee is required to add the value of this equipment [specify] to their home contents insurance policy, notifying the insurers that their house is being used for restricted business purposes. The insurers should be required to note the interest of the [organization] as owner of the equipment on the policy. Any additional insurance premium can be re-charged to the organization on the first timesheet. This should be accompanied by evidence that the value of the items has been added to the policy and the insurers are aware of the business use.

8. The homeworker will be required to agree a schedule of work from time to time and to report on the work done. Such reports should accompany timesheets which should be submitted on a weekly basis. These reports will include details of all [calls made] and a précis of the response.

9. The [organization] reserves the right to visit the premises from time to time to allocate and collect work, assess the performance of the homeworker etc.

10. Other than necessary changes to hours, place of work etc the provisions of the employee's contract of employment will continue in force until termination in accordance with that contract.

11. The homeworker will be required to report personally to the organization premises on a [weekly/monthly] basis. Costs of such travel and time can be claimed on the next subsequent timesheet.

12. If work/material/goods are given to the homeworker for transport to the homebase (or elsewhere), they will be provided with a letter of authority to ensure Security allow them to pass with such goods.

13. The homebase will be subject to the [organization's] SAFETY Policy and Procedure and the homeworker will be expected to undertake any works required to meet these obligations (at the employer's expense). Visual display and computer workstations will be checked initially [and at six monthly intervals] for ease of use and compliance with legal requirements.

14. On termination of the homeworking arrangement, the homeworker will return all equipment and material provided by the [organization] within seven days of the termination. The [organization] will deal with the cancellation of any telephone line(s), Internet connection etc. Should return of the equipment not be effected within the above period the homeworker expressly grants to the employer by this agreement a right of access (subject to three hours notice between 9.00am and 6.30pm Monday to Friday) to the homebase, in order to recover such equipment.

Since the employee's home is now a workplace, Employers Liability (EL) insurance may need to be extended to cover the location, and there may be a requirement to post a copy of the certificate in the house. In addition, a risk assessment should be compiled.

Agreement

The advantage of delineating a policy is that those interested in the possibility of homeworking can immediately gain an outline of what the requirements will be. An agreement should be concluded and, if the homeworker is an employee, they should also have a contract of employment.

* *

Example of agreement

This Agreement is made this [date] between [parties – 'homeworker' and 'employer' or 'client'] with the purpose of controlling the arrangement by which the homeworker undertakes to carry out work and duties for the [organization – 'the organization'] at [address of homeworking base] with effect from [commencing date] and is additional to and does not infringe in any way the Contract of Employment between the parties dated [date].

The homeworker agrees that they will:

a) provide a room (the 'homebase') at the above address which will be [solely] used for the work of the employer. If the property is not owned by the homeworker, the homeworker will obtain permission of the owner to the arrangement and produce this to the employer before commencement. Failure to do so may negate this agreement. Should such permission be withdrawn subsequently, the employer must be notified within seven working days.

b) carry out the duties set out in the schedule hereto for a minimum of [hours per week/month] on the terms set out in the [contract of employment]

c) allow reasonable access to the homebase during normal business hours to the employer and their staff for the purposes of supervision, training etc.

d) staff the homebase for the express purposes of [taking orders, sourcing customers, etc] for at least [number] hours per working day including between [specified times which will be regarded as core times when the homebase should always be staffed] and when not present ensure the fax and answerphone are available to callers. All messages left by answerphone, fax or e-mail must be acknowledged personally by the homeworker within three working hours

e) not use the equipment provided by the employer for any purpose other than for the services covered by this agreement and not use any computer disks in that equipment other than those supplied by the employer

f)   ensure the equipment (as confirmed in the attached schedule) is added to the domestic contents insurance policy at the premises and provide evidence to the employer that this has been done and that the interest of the employer has been noted and of each renewal of the cover

g)   provide a weekly time and expense account (a draft of which is included in the attached schedule)

h)   keep the homebase tidy and in a safe condition, complying with any safety requirements imposed by the employer

i)   within seven days of the termination of this agreement either return all the employer's equipment, files, papers etc, or, subject to receipt of three working hours notice, allow access to the employer to recover such items. It is expressly agreed by the parties that failure to allow access for such purpose will generate a County Court action by the employer to recover the equivalent value of the equipment as set out in the Schedule hereto

j)   keep the homebase decorated to a reasonable standard so that this is appropriate for regular supervision, as well as occasional customer visits. The costs of such work (since it enhances their domestic property) will be met by the employee and deemed to be included within the [weekly fee].

The homeworker hereby also undertakes that they do not know of any reason why they should not be able to work from the premises using the homebase for these purposes.

The employer agrees that it will:

a)   provide suitable equipment (as set out in the attached Schedule) for the homeworker to arrange installation, the costs of which (to a maximum of £X) it agrees to meet

b)   refund the cost of insuring the equipment

c)   refund the costs of additional telephone lines and internet access required for the employer's work

d)   pay the homeworker the sum of [£Z] each [week/month] for the use of the homebase

e)   extend Employer's Liability insurance to cover the homebase.

The parties agree that this agreement will last for [six months] and thereafter it will be subject to one party giving to the other of not less than four clear weeks notice in writing by recorded delivery using the addresses stated in the introduction to this agreement for this purpose.

SCHEDULE

1. Duties: The duties to be carried out by the homeworker are [specify].

2. Equipment and services to be provided by the employer are: [For example: desk, chair, footstool, computer, printer, fax machine and ancillary telephone line, modem connection and telephone line, access to Internet].

3. For the purpose of insurance the value of the equipment set out in 2 immediately above is [£Y]

Signed [by both parties, dated and witnessed]

* *

Legal implications

1. If the homeworker provides their own computer (or operates a computer not linked to the employer's computer) they may need to register under the Data Protection Act and advice should be sought from the Information Commissioner.

2. Draft EU legislation suggests those who work away from the 'main place of work' (e.g. homeworkers) may become entitled to the same employment rights and conditions as those who work (doing the same or broadly similar work) in the main place of work unless the difference can be objectively justified (the comparability principle). Those carrying out such work in their home must do so voluntarily and will be given the right to transfer back to the traditional workplace.

3. In the 2003 Budget, employers were given the right to pay their homeworkers £2 per week tax free without supporting documentation to provide 'recompense' for the additional costs of working at home. Larger amounts can be paid tax free but only if there are supporting invoices.

4. Ms Tully won a recent case against her employer – the Inland Revenue – the dual effect of which is that:

    *   no business rates will be charged against people using part of their houses to work at home provided they do not employ people to work at the house on their business and the house does not lose its 'domestic character', and

    *   capital gains tax will not be sought on any 'profit' (made on selling the house) related to the proportion of the house that was used as a business.

Type of work

It should not be assumed that only lower grade work can be conducted by tele-working.

Case studies

1. The UK Probationary Service has moved to homeworking providing those undertaking such work with access to local Inland Revenue offices for administrative support.

2. In running around 100 seminars each year throughout the UK, I have increasingly found occupations such as solicitors, architects and surveyors who have their main 'office' and place of work in their own home, attending the traditional office infrequently.

3. Travel Counsellors uses 570 self-employed counsellors to sell travel bookings etc. They all work from home on a commission only basis. Each year they generate £150 million worth of business.

Insurance and incident reporting   143

Internal rents   153

Insurance and incident reporting

Introduction

Whilst, within the same organization, 'insurance' and 'property' may be separately administered, their functions need to work in close harmony since many insurance risks are related to, or result from, property occupation. With leasehold property, a range of covers may be stipulated in the lease with the lessee's interests restricted to reimbursing the landlord for premiums, ensuring the cover is accurate and that the sum demanded is fair. Where freehold property is owned, however, a more proactive attitude needs to be adopted.

Freehold portfolio

From exchange of contracts, on freehold acquisition, the organization should ensure that adequate insurance cover is effected e.g. against fire and an associated range of covers – impact, explosion, riot etc. Thereafter these 'sums insured' should be re-assessed annually to ensure adequacy. If the organization has underinsured, the insurer may apply 'average' (i.e. if the organization has only valued the item at 75% of its value, the insurer will only pay 75% of the claim). The basis of insurance (e.g. reinstatement or 'new for old') should be determined. If the facilities administrator is not experienced in insurance it may be helpful to retain a broker who has experience of the industry in which the organization is engaged. Such appointment should be made on a fee basis with the broker remitting any commission earned to the organization so that performance can be compared with cost.

Leasehold occupation

With leases, the landlord normally insures and recharges the lessee for the stipulated range of covers. This places the lessee in a somewhat invidious position since they may have little say over the costs involved.

Case study

In *Havenbridge v Boston Dyers Ltd* the Court stated that a landlord is under no obligation to shop around to obtain the lowest premium.

With a full repairing lease it is prudent to request that the lessee's interest is noted on the policy. In the event of any under insurance the landlord should then be precluded from trying to pass onto the lessee the responsibility for any shortfall. The following draft letter to the landlord (or their agent) could be used:

Example

Dear

Address of property   *Details of lease*

As you are aware we are your lessees [lessees of your clients] at the above property under the lease details of which are given above.

Included in your covenants is an obligation to insure the property, whilst included in our covenants is an obligation to refund the premium to the landlord.

I should be obliged if you would confirm that this company's interest as tenant (lessee) under the above lease is included on the policy.

If this is not the case please take this as our request to ensure that our interest is noted immediately. Your acknowledgement of this request and confirmation that this has been effected would be appreciated, but if we do not hear from you [or your client] we will assume our interest is noted

Yours faithfully,

Note: Such a letter could be sent stapled to the cheque in payment of rent and/or premium – or else sent by recorded delivery – so its receipt can be proven.

Advice of incidents

Not all incidents that occur at working premises will be covered by insurance. However, the property administrator should know of all incidents whether claimable or not (particularly if adopting a process of Risk Management). This is a challenge, particularly where there are several units geographically separated. Sometimes simply collating such data centrally can demonstrate a problem.

Case study

A manufacturing company operated a number of sites with delegated authority for minor expenditure. Centralization of an incident reporting procedure disclosed that one factory had a disproportionately high number of 'routine' payouts in respect of 'minor' accidents. On investigation it was discovered that the fact that 'you could win a bit of cash' (as one claimant put it) by claiming that you had suffered a minor injury at work was widely known and some employees, if they injured themselves elsewhere (or even if they did not), would pretend their injury occurred at work in order to gain such a payout.

Whilst the facilities manager may be aware of incidents in his or her immediate locale, unless there is a process by which incidents can be logged, the facilities manager (for example) on the 3rd floor could be totally unaware of an incident on the 5th floor. Often those involved may not realize the potential danger of incidents and that a similar scenario could have resulted in losses affecting the property, personnel or products. A procedure is needed not only to record such incidents but also to provide data from which risks can be assessed or re-assessed so that preventative measures can be taken. Risk assessments are legally required in any event and these could need to be updated as a result of incidents. Hazard reporting forms could be utilized for this purpose although the thrust here is not only to ensure the safety of the occupants and visitors but also to try to prevent damage that can be caused to the building and products. Since some incidents may not fit the pattern envisaged in the hazard report form however, a separate Incident Form may be helpful. For organizations that do not have a procedure manual, a General Incident Folder may provide the essential aide-memoire to line/local management for the reporting of both safety hazards and incidents.

Example: General incident folder

Concept

An A4 plastic folder containing a number of forms for immediate use in the event of an incident, held by the local manager/employee appointed to report all incidents to the property/insurance administrator.

Contents

  i.   Procedures to be followed

  ii.   Incident forms

  iii. Hazard forms (if reporting of safety hazards is to be made via the same procedure – see example in SAFETY COMMUNICATION)

  iv.   Panic numbers (for management contacts to be advised out of office hours)

  v.   Telephone hotline procedure

  vi.   Incident checklists

  vii. Pre-addressed internal/external envelopes

  viii. Contents re-order slip

  ix.   Check sheet for 'correspondent' to note action taken and dates etc.

Note: It may also be prudent for each correspondent to be instructed to take photos of every incident.

Procedure

  1.   Note date, time and report source on Incident form.

  2.   Visit site of incident and record as much information as possible.

  3.   If you have access to a camera or mobile phone/camera, take several photos particularly endeavouring to obtain views from different angles. If no camera is available, make a sketch of the scene of the incidents and include all relevant data.

  4.   Collate the names of all present and involved.

  5.   Should the incident involve physical injury to any person, or be such that it appears to involve loss or damage to company property in excess of [e.g. £5000], use the telephone hotline to advise (contact). If the incident occurs out of normal office hours, use the Panic Number List to advise [contact].

6. Follow any instructions issued by the [contact].

7. Request statements from willing eye witnesses and any others involved.

   WARNING: Advice should be taken before witness statements are compiled as they could be subject to legal disclosure requirements.

8. Complete the other information required on the Incident Form

9. Review the information obtained and witness statements taken to ensure that there is a realistic précis of the incident, such that a third party reviewing it at a later date will be able to gain an accurate insight into the occurrence.

10. If the incident is such that a claims checklist is applicable, advise those included on the checklist to commence sourcing the information required.

11. Send the Incident Form with all ancillary items, including jottings, witness statements, sketches etc within 12 hours of the incident to the (contact). Follow this initial notification with any supplementary information, photos, claim checklists data, etc as soon as possible.

12. React to, and obtain further information requested by the (contact) and the insurers as requested, assisting with any subsequent investigation.

Note: It is good policy, even if the telephone hotline is used, to obtain some written record from the correspondent – initial jottings may be of assistance to an incident investigator and should be preserved.

Incident form

An Incident Form could be used to ensure prompt notification of incidents.

URGENT

Please complete as soon as possible and send IMMEDIATELY to (contact) in the event of any injury to personnel, or (contact) – in the event of any damage or loss to property, or products etc.

Dept/Shop/Site _____ Date _____

Report completed by _____ Position _____

Telephone _____

Details of occurrence _____

_____

_____

Time of incident _____Police informed _____

If police informed, details of station/officer_____

_____

Witness details _____

_____

Organization contact for further details _____

_____

Other back-up documentation (attached/to follow) Specify _____

_____

_____

OFFICE USE ONLY

Claimable? YES/NO If YES, which policy _____

Reportable? YES/NO If YES, entered in Accident Book? _____

Date claim/report made _____

Contact numbers

Large or multi-facility organizations may need to develop a list of names and telephone numbers for each site, or division etc. If contingency/disaster planning is in operation this list could form the initial part of such planning i.e. swift reporting of the incident.

Out of hours contacts

In all cases of loss, fire or other serious incident out of normal hours where there is injury to an individual or the potential loss seems likely to exceed £5000, telephone:

MANUFACTURING

Works Director	Tel: _____
Property Administrator	Tel: _____
Works Manager	Tel: _____
Chief Engineer	Tel: _____
Company Secretary ⎫ (for insurers)	Tel: _____
Insurance Manager ⎭	Tel: _____
Chief Executive	Tel: _____
Safety Officer	Tel: _____
Personnel Officer	Tel: _____
Shift Managers	Tel: _____
Transport Manager	Tel: _____
Purchasing	Tel: _____

RETAILING

Area Controller	Tel: _____
Property Administrator	Tel: _____
Area Manager	Tel: _____
Company Secretary ⎫ (for insurers)	Tel: _____
Insurance Manager ⎭	Tel: _____
Chief Executive	Tel: _____
Personnel Officer	Tel: _____
Transport Manager	Tel: _____
Warehouse Manager	Tel: _____
Buyer	Tel: _____

Telephone hotline

A 'hotline' can be used (linked for out-of-hours calls to an answerphone) if there is difficulty obtaining written information from correspondents. Using this facility they can 'notify' by means of a swift telephone call. Correspondents should be prepared when the message ends to provide the following data in this set order.

1. Date

2. Time

3. Name of correspondent

4. Site of incident

5. Brief description of incident

6. Injury caused (names and apparent injuries sustained)

7. Damage caused (details of damage with approximate value)

8. Likely length of interruption to production (if any)

9. Action being taken (including using the Panic Number system)

10. Telephone number of correspondent or person dealing

To ensure record is complete each item should be prefaced by stating its reference number as above e.g. state 'One – 28th March 1997, Two – 19.45, Three – Frank Jones, Four – Paint works, Birmingham ....' and so on. If an item is not applicable its number should be stated followed by the words 'Not applicable'.

Note: An internal e-mail system provides a further alternative means of notification.

Claim checklists

Claim checklists are lists of the information and data that will be required by the insurers before they can start processing a claim. The list should be agreed for each cover at renewal. Each correspondent can then be advised what will be required in each instance. In this way without reference to, or being chased by, the contact (s)he knows what information needs to be sourced and submitted. For example:

1. Retail stock and/or cash loss

Item required	Person responsible
Incident form	Shop manager
Till check and cross check	Area staff
Stock check	Area staff
Shop staff statement	Area staff
Manager's statement	Area staff
Police details	Area manager
Description of suspect	Area manager
Prior till/stock checks	Office manager
Any disciplinary letters issued	Office/personnel manager
Staff records	Office/personnel manager
Shop incident history (if any)	Office/personnel manager

   and so on.

2. Fire

Incident form	Manager
Stock/Product/Machinery/ Plant loss	Manager/Accounts
Valuation of stock, etc., loss	Accounts/auditors
Con. Loss estimate	Accounts/auditors
General information	Insurance manager
Photos	Insurance manager
Builder's repair estimate	Manager/engineer
Incident history	Office manager
Replacement lead times	Purchasing dept.

Internal rents

Introduction

Where an organization occupies a number of properties on a 'mixed owner-ship' basis – that is owning the freehold of some and leasing others – those departments or divisions that are occupying properties that are owned either by themselves or an associated organization (e.g. a parent company) gain a benefit not shared by other occupiers within the same organization who occupy leasehold premises, in that they do not pay rent to an external body. Where the financial results of divisions or subsidiaries are required to be made compa-rable the concept of the 'owner' of the freehold charging a nominal or 'internal rent' could be considered.

Principle

Using the capital value of freehold properties and a notional return, an annual 'value' can be calculated (e.g. as a return on capital employed – ROCE). This figure can then be 'charged' against the part of the business occupying the free-hold, with the income going to a reserve. This means the 'occupier' will bear a similar charge to parts of the business occupying leased premises. As an alter-native to using 'ROCE', the charge could be related to rents charged commercially on similar properties in the area.

Case study

The Maynards property portfolio consisted of around 120 freeholds mainly CTN shops and a further 260 leased premises – mainly CTN and Zodiac Toy shops. To maximize profit figures, insufficient resources had been invested in the freeholds. As a result, many were in urgent need of maintenance. Where a shop occupied a freehold, although this fact was noted in its results, no financial adjustment was made. To deal with both problems, the freehold shops were professionally valued (1/3rd of the portfolio each year) and figures of around 7% of the values so determined were charged to each shop. This not only put the results of leased and freehold on a more comparable basis but also created a fund which was used for the upkeep of the freehold portfolio (so that freeholds were redecorated and repaired periodically – as would happen with the leaseholds as a result of landlords invoking lease redecoration covenants).

Example

Organization owns property valued at £450,000. It uses an internal rent process and applies (say) 7% of the capital value (that is £31,500) against the occupying part of the business. If the freeholds are regularly revalued (e.g. every five years) then using the latest value as a base for the re-calculation of the re-charge has virtually the same effect as a rent review in leased premises.

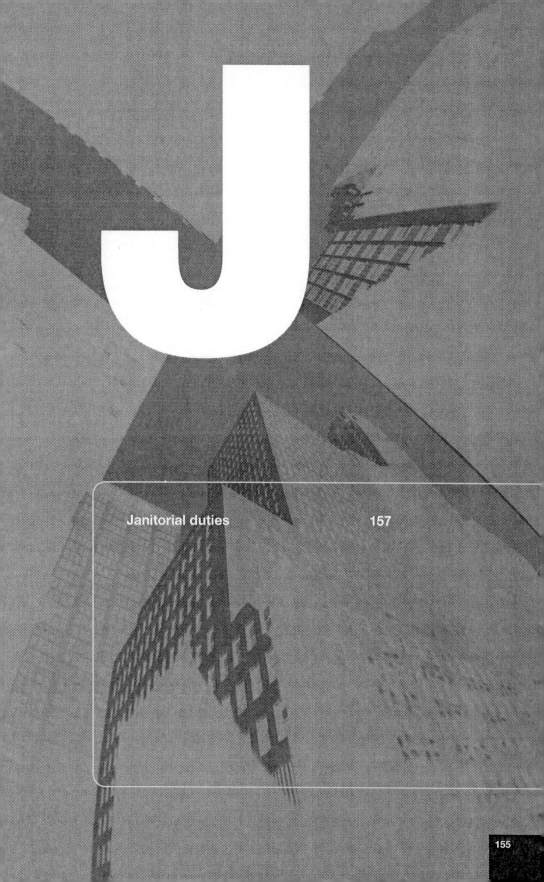

J

Janitorial duties 157

Janitorial duties

Introduction

Janitorial requirements are unobtrusive when effected properly but notable, and noted, when they do not exist – or are carried out poorly. Whilst in most cases this is a matter of ensuring the premises are unlocked and locked at appropriate times, kept clean (particularly cloakrooms), secure etc sadly in the current climate there are more serious aspects to even these mundane matters, not least keeping people aware of the dangers of terrorism and the need to protect both the premises and the occupants.

Exterior

To visitors, job applicants etc the exterior presentation of a building can have a considerable impact on their impression of the organization as a whole. If the exterior is uncared for and untidy, almost certainly the same careless attitude may be evinced within its 'internal relationships'. The roof, walls, windows and frames, doors and frames etc should all be kept in good repair. Name, logo and notice boards should be kept fresh and tidy. Flowerbeds or patio areas should similarly be tidy with plants pruned following flowering and fallen leaves and other debris removed. Car parking bays and access should be clean and well-marked.

In our current social environment, spoiling exterior (and sometimes interior) surfaces with spray paint to create 'tagging' or graffiti images is on the increase. If swift action is not taken, the creation of these images can proliferate. Not only is the result unsightly, but also it can encourage a feeling of unease that this may be a 'crime-ridden' location. Areas targeted by graffiti 'artists' can reduce the value of nearby properties which could then be avoided by potential purchasers, so that not only are prices reduced, but also disposal of the property may be difficult. Unfortunately some spray paints penetrate the top of the surface onto which they are sprayed and their removal can cause more damage than the paint itself. It should be removed as quickly as possible, however, and it may be best to start with the mildest removal agents, moving to stronger means in turn e.g.

1. Soap and water – and elbow grease!

2. Warm water

3. High pressure washer

4. Solvent or paint stripper.

Unfortunately, although cleaning may remove the 'message' or 'image', sometimes a kind of shadow (or 'graffiti ghost') may remain and its removal may require specialist treatment.

Conversely, there are now available 'anti-graffiti' treatments (see DATA) which can be applied to most surfaces. If a treated surface is then subject to graffiti, usually it can be washed off with water.

Reception

Except for the exterior, reception facilities are the first indication to a visitor of the ethos of the occupant. A tidy well-ordered area, with fresh flowers and clean chairs and tables for those waiting to be seen, conveys a 'message', to be endorsed by a friendly welcoming receptionist. 'You only have one chance to make a first impression' runs the saying. Sadly it must be said that in many cases reception and receptionists get the least attention and, as a result, visitors can feel unwelcome and unwanted.

Case study

As someone who gives around 100 UK seminars each year, I visit and stay in hotels and conference facilities. Relatively few have Receptions that are really welcoming and portray their organization in a positive light. There is a conference facility near Swindon where the attitude of some of the reception staff is arrogant to the point of rudeness. Treatment like this is hardly a good start for any visitor. Needless to say we no longer use that location.

Often the receptionist also operates the switchboard. This can mean that visitors can be kept waiting whilst calls are dealt with. Whilst economics may dictate this, it is hardly ideal, the hidden message to visitors being 'you are not as important as this caller' which is not exactly the warmest greeting. If information-seeking calls are received regularly, technology is available which can provide such information automatically rather than the receptionist having to recite the details.

Whilst the invention of e-mail led to some reduction of telephone calls the invention of mobile phones has probably resulted in there being greater telephone use than ever. Telecommunications may be so high-tech in some organizations that the responsibility for it may be better left to the IT department. Whether it is with IT or is under the control of the 'janitorial department' any switchboard must be properly and securely sited and whoever is responsible should be known to – or at least easily contacted by – all internal users so that faults can be reported easily. The person responsible should also regularly update any telephone list or directory.

Searches

Theft is on the increase – much perpetrated by employees. Random searches of employees leaving the premises, either on foot (requiring them to open bags etc) or by transport (requiring them to allow the boot and interior of their car or van to be inspected) may be required. Searching should only be introduced after consultation with those affected – itemizing the need, giving time for objections to be considered and explanations offered and so on. Once in operation it should be made clear that refusing to submit to a search is 'gross misconduct'. Reception or security staff should be trained in conducting searches or, perhaps preferably, an outside body could be used. Searches should be conducted with tact and confidentiality – a private room may be needed. Anyone required to remove material etc from the premises (e.g. to work on it externally) should be provided with a 'pass' or 'explanatory letter' to avoid embarrassment if stopped for a search.

Cleaning

Cleaners tend to be the 'Cinderellas' of the workforce despite their work being vital for the cleanliness of the building, not only so that employees and visitors feel they are in clean facilities, but also and particularly that toilets and kitchen facilities are kept in a hygienic state. Sadly often as little as possible is spent on cleaners and the cleaning contract and as a result standards are low. Standards, as well as items in the cleaning specification, must be checked regularly to ensure they are being met – and rectified if not.

Case study

In an East London hospital, the cleaners are issued with a new mop head every month. During that month they must each use that sole issue mop head to 'clean' every floor and spillage, constantly rinsing it in water changed so infrequently that it seems they may be putting more dirt on the mop than removing it. After rinsing, the mops are stored, but not otherwise cleaned, in a cupboard where the ingrained dirt (which could consist of remnants all manner of waste) can fester happily. It is hardly any wonder that MRSA and other 'bugs' can proliferate. Surely in the 21st century it should not be impossible for a 'mop-sized' electric cleaning device to be invented simultaneously sucking up liquid dirt whilst simultaneously laying down disinfectant?

There is a telling argument for ensuring cleaners are paid a decent wage. They have access to all areas and thus can, if dishonest, breach security and leak confidential material.

Case study

In the mid 1980s a national paper scanned 300 properties in London and in 100 of them found electronic bugging devices – a proportion which reflects the national average of there being bugging devices in one in every three locations. The placing of bugs is often carried out by cleaners acting for competitors etc.

Parking

Finding sufficient space for employees and visitors to park is an increasing problem, particularly if the premises are open to the public and the situation is aggravated by those without any right to be there using part of the available space. Ideally there should be some 'barrier' to entry and use – either a physical barrier – or a 'barrier of determent' using large notices warning of (for example) clamping of unauthorized vehicles. Clamping organizations are subject to firmer control than hitherto, but providing they do their work efficiently and politely – and with prior warning – this may be a method of controlling 'fly parking'. Posting notes on windscreens may also be effective although great care needs to be taken to ensure there is no damage caused to the vehicles.

Alternatively, registration numbers of unauthorized vehicles can be taken and DVLA asked for details of addresses so that the owners can be written to (using recorded delivery) requesting that they cease trespassing in this way. If they ignore this, a threat of legal action may be effective.

Toilets

Toilet facilities are not only an obvious requirement but are also subject to legal obligations. Under the Workplace (Health Safety and Welfare) Regulations 1992 employers are required to provide the facilities stated depending on the numbers employed in each location.

Employees	Water closets	Wash stations
1 – 5	1	1
6 – 25	2	2
26 – 50	3	3
51 – 75	4	4
76 -100	5	5
thereafter for every additional 25 employees	1	1

Note: These facilities are required for each sex and once the number of employees breaks a threshold (e.g. 101, 126), the requirement is for the next higher number of facilities.

For toilet facilities provided solely for men, the employer can provide (in addition to the wash stations as stated above) either the water closet facilities set out above or the following:

Male employees	Water closets	Urinals
1 – 15	1	1
16 – 45	2	2
46 – 75	3	3
76 – 100	4	4
thereafter for every additional 25 people one more WC, but every 4th additional WC can be replaced by a urinal.		

The approved code of practice (sanitary and washing facilities) re Workplace (Health, Safety and Welfare) Regulations is available from HMSO and should be referred to.

Whether due to coincidence or to perceived 'global warming', even the UK, with what most would consider is a wet climate, is subject to periods where drought orders are given. Water needs to be used wisely not least since increasingly it is metered and charged by usage. All users should be encouraged to save water and to try to ensure this, washing basins can be fitted with floor-operated 'taps' which only supply a measured amount of water thus avoiding the situation where taps are left running. The standard domestic WC uses 7.5 litres of water per flush whereas dual standard cisterns use only 4.5 litres when a 'reduced' flush is utilized. However, in many commercial facilities, urinals are flushed by an automatic system regardless of use (including at night). Urinals tend to use 6 -10 litres per flush. There is an inherent wastage of water and cost here which needs to be addressed – either 'flush on demand' buttons or sensor devices which operate when the basin has been used can be fitted, or even the latest 'waterless' urinals can be used. For cistern-operated flushes, the 2004 British Invention Show's top prize for a device which allows flushing only whilst the handle is pressed could be considered. There is also available a Swedish invention (Ifo Cera ES4) which uses 4.5 litres per flush.

Obviously, toilets must be kept clean and may best be kept this way by regular inspections being made during working time. Although it must be said that in some hotels that use this system – despite the 'inspection chart' being regularly updated – the toilets are not as clean as one would have thought would be the case had they been properly inspected so regularly and recently.

K

Keeping property records   165

Keeping property records

Introduction

Regardless of portfolio size, property administration needs a reliable database. Since conveyances and leases tend to be bulky documents not normally presented in a user-friendly format, a means of converting such verbose legalese into a short user-friendly data sheet containing only succinct details is necessary. A précis of both documents should be created, showing:

a) basic ownership/occupation details

b) timing of costs and/or alterations (e.g. on review or where redecorations/ repairs must be carried out) and

c) details of ending/variation of commitments etc to assist planning.

Taking this one stage further, the information can be used for budgeting and forecasting as well as for providing planning and historical information. Not only is salient information available incorporating warnings of potential forthcoming expenditure, but also an instant visual picture can be created of the portfolio as it will appear at any one time in the period covered.

The précis concept

Most leases and conveyances are complex documents where both size and language are hardly user-friendly. These factors can combine to make it difficult to find the required reference with any ease – even with an index that many leases now incorporate. For a property administrator under pressure, instant guidance to the salient features of both documents (and any others that affect the use of the property) is essential. This can be achieved by completing a précis for each property. This can provide not only details of the item being checked but also, if a standard format is used for all leases, provide a 'guide within a guide' since the same information will always be found in the same place. Having a précis for each individual property provides a data bank from which can be drawn the information essential to produce a property register.

Freehold property précis

Organization name   Freehold précis sheet

Address of property _____ Internal ref. number _____

Date of purchase _____ Price _____

Finance details _____

Land Charge Certificate data _____

Conveyance data _____

Ground rent (if applicable specify review terms etc) _____

_____

Third party rights over the premises (if any) (e.g. those of a mortgagor, in which case, a synopsis of the terms of the mortgage, repayments, terms etc could be incorporated).

_____

Details of any shared rights of access over land/premises (that is use of land retained to a neighbour, shared facilities etc including details of anyone holding and/or administering such rights). _____

_____

Any charge registered on the property (in which case it may be convenient to attach a copy of the documentation). _____

_____

Details of all consents, wayleaves, advertising sign agreements etc with names and addresses of the parties involved, and synopsis of the terms. _____

_____

Details of all obligations required as a term of the sale/acquisition, with a dated entry made once the work has been completed, the cost involved and any guarantee given in respect of the work. _____

_____

Use within business (specify) _____

_____

Revaluation data _____

INTERNAL RENT (if any) _____

Future requirements (see ACCOMMODATION PLANNING) _____

_____

Special features or restrictions _____

_____

Areas (Zoning and Zone A equivalents for retail premises, net internal for offices, gross internal for industrial premises, and so on). _____

_____

Lease précis

Compiling a freehold précis (summarizing the contents of the conveyance plus data from the organization's own records) is likely to be a relatively simple task. Performing the same task for a modern lease however may be anything but simple. It may be preferable to give the following pro forma précis sheet to solicitors and require them to complete it as part of their service on acquisition.

Organization name   **Leasehold précis sheet**

Address of property _____ Internal ref. number_____

Landlord (name and address) _____

_____

Agent (name and address) _____

_____

Guarantor _____

Date of acquisition _____ Price_____

Unit data: _____

Rent £ _____ p.a. payable _____ to _____

Days grace? _____VAT payable? _____

Interest on late payment? _____

Date of lease _____

Date of commencement _____and termination_____

User (and any variation) _____

Assignment (details and restrictions) _____

Subletting (details and restrictions) _____

Reviews _____Dates_____

Procedure on review _____

Covenants   Repair (due dates) _____

                       Redecoration (due dates) _____

Insurance (basis of covers, and responsibility) _____

Service charge (details and basis)_____

Other (specify)_____

Does Privity of Contract apply? _____

Option to break (if any) _____

Procedure re option _____

Floor area (retail)   Zone A sq ft. _____

                      Zone B sq ft._____

                      Zone C sq ft. Storage _____Other _____

Net internal area (offices) _____

Gross area (industrial premises) _____

Parking arrangements/costs _____

Special features or restrictions _____

Comments_____

_____

A worked example

It may be helpful to demonstrate the above concept in practice by showing the following worked example:

LEASE PRECIS SHEET

44 Kings Rd, Buckingham, Sussex (Ground floor shop and garden only)

Landlord: Widgets Ltd, 101 Manor Way, Manchesterford

Tenant: J Bloggs   **Acquired**: 13th August 04   **Price**: £10.000

Rent: £23,500 p.a. payable on usual quarter days to A N Agent [address]

Days grace? No   **VAT payable?** Yes

Interest on late payment? Yes   **Rate?** 4% over Barclays base rate

Lease commenced? 13th August 2004   **Terminates?** 12th August 2019

User?: Sale of tea, coffee and light refreshments, delicatessen, tapas bar, sale of fine art, fancy goods, electrical goods, culinary equipment, preparation of food for outside catering. Such other use as landlord may approve, such consent not to be unreasonably withheld or delayed

Assignment and Underletting: Can only assign/underlet whole, must get Landlords consent and must (for assignment) complete Authorized Guarantee Agreement

Reviews: Five yearly   **Dates**: 13th August 2009, 13th August 2014

Redecoration: Exterior every 3rd [and LAST] year (2007, 2010, 2013, 2016, 2019)
Interior every 4th [and LAST] year (2008, 2012, 2016, 2019)
Clean windows monthly

Insurance: Fire, lightning, explosion, aircraft, riot, civil commotion, terrorism, earthquake, storm, tempest, flood, bursting and overflowing of water pipes etc. Landlord arranges and recharges

Option to break: Not less than six months written notice expiring not earlier than 8th August 2009 **(Option to be exercised by (for safety) 1st February 2009.)**

Floor area (retail) Zone A   sq ft.   Zone B   sq ft.
Zone C   sq ft.   Storage & Garden
(ITZA stated on lease as 554 giving £42 p s f)

Note: The interior redecoration requirements in this lease mean that the process is required to take place twice in three years. It may be possible to gain the landlords consent to redecorate once during that three year period.

Subletting

In both types of occupation there may be sublets and thus a subletting précis (i.e. an amended Leasehold précis), completed with details of the sublet(s) which could accompany the main précis sheet. Using coloured paper for a précis of a sublet can help differentiation from units occupied for the organization's own business.

Property register

The data generated as above can also be used to produce a full property register. Illustrated is a grid which can be used in hard copy and/or computerized format. The advantage of the computerized record is that it can be updated easily.

Where updated information is to be provided, the system should allow previous information, whilst crossed through, to remain visible. Most rents of leased premises are subject to review, and those inspecting the record may want to know not only the latest rent but also what the pre-review rent was.

Computerization not only facilitates updating, but also allows the whole record to be 'shrunk' to the required size.

Case study

During the 1970s and 1980s, Maynards had around 400 properties. About 270 confectionery, tobacco and news (CTN) shops, up to 90 toy shops and a range of factories, warehouses, offices and even residential properties. Lease and freehold précis sheets were prepared for each property giving around 400 sheets – replacing perhaps over 10,000 pages of information. The salient information for those units was then carried forward into a register. Since the skeletal data on around ten units could be fitted on each page, this reduced the bulk to 40 pages which could have been further reduced to 20 had we wished to print on both sides of each page. The register was slim and easily carried to board meetings etc providing users with fingertip access.

Property register

In the example of a property register sheet that follows, the following apply:

1. Premises (both leased and one freehold) have been summarized. The freehold is shown with both internal rent and valuation.

2. The salient features of the units together with contact names and telephone numbers are shown. These details could include:

   - for owned and occupied premises – the name of the senior person present

   - for owned and sublet premises – the name of the lessee

   - for leased and occupied premises – the name of the landlord or agent

   - for leased and subleased premises – the name of the landlord or agent and the lessee

3. Key: R: rent review, I: Internal redecoration covenant, E: External redecoration covenant, O: Option to break lease, T: Termination date, IR: Internal rent.

4. All primary obligations – rent, redecoration internal, options, termination dates are shown. As each item is passed it can be crossed through (but not deleted) in order to provide a history of occupation.

5. Using the calendar not only highlights timings for action but concentrates attention on facts. For instance, if their leases are not renewed occupation of no less than five units might be lost within two years.

6. The calendar representation shows that whereas in 2014 there are only two internal redecoration cost, in most years there are several obligations to be budgeted.

7. Most leases will be renewed so the schedule allows for continuation past present termination dates. If the record is computerized it might be better to revise it at least annually – deleting past, and adding later, years, to the planning calendar.

8. Where leases expire later than the calendar extends to, this can be indicated as shown.

9. Where leases are due to terminate, this is highlighted by a solid vertical line. Where there is an option which might terminate a dotted vertical line is used.

Property	Term	Rent	R.R.s	Decoration Years		Insure	Sq ft	User
				Interior	Exterior			
13, Aclam Rd London (Office)	20yrs 1/00 1/20	£40000 £42500	5 yrly 05, 10, 15	7+ last	5+ last	L'lord + recharge	950	Office
17, Tong Rd Doncaster (Warehouse)	25yrs 12/90 12/15	£17000 £23000 £26000	5yrly 00, 05, 10	7+ last	5+ last	L'lord + recharge	22000	W/H (Office ancill.)
17 Highgate Lane, London Contact [Name]	25yrs 6/90 6/15	£10000 £16500 £17500	5 yrly 95, 00 05, 10	5 last	7+ last	Comp.	1350	Class 1 retail
24, Broadway Manchester Contact [Name]	20yrs 9/93 9/13	£11500 £17000	7yrly 00, 07	5	3	L'lord + recharge	1000	See précis
62, Haymarket Bristol Contact [Name]	17yrs 3/97 3/14	£12500 £17800 £17800	4yrly 01, 05 09, 13	3+ last	3+ last	Comp	1450	Class 1 retail
1a, West St Norwich Contact [Name]	20yrs 6/95 6/15	£6000 £9000 £10000	5yrly 00, 05, 10	5+ last	5+ last	Comp	950	Class 1 retail
26, Parade York Contact [Name]	21yrs 8/99 8/20	£30000 £32500	4 yrly 03, 07, 11, 15, 19	7+ last	5+ last	L'lord + recharge	625	Class 1 retail
137, High St Scarboro' FREEHOLD Contact [Name]		IR £12600						

	2005	2006	2007	2008	2009	2010	2011	2012	2013	2014	2015	Valuation
	R̶ E		I			R E				I	R E	▷ 2020
	R̶ E					R E	I				T I E	
	R̶ I					R I	E				T I E	
	E		R O	I E			E		T I			
	R̶	I E			R I E			I E	R	T I E		
	R̶ I E					R I E					T I E	
		I	R O E				R E		I		R E	▷ 2020
		R E		I	R E			R E	I		R E	£210000

L

Landlord's rights and duties 177

Leasehold commitment 181

Lessee's Works 187

Licence 193

Landlord's rights and duties

Introduction

There are more lessees than landlords. Whereas lessees are mainly persons or organizations operating on their own, the majority of commercial property landlords are individuals or, more likely, organizations, in both cases controlling property portfolios which can comprise many units. Lease terms are biased in favour of landlords since they have many rights and relatively few duties; lessees have many duties and relatively few rights.

Acting as landlord

Some lessees are also landlords requiring them to view the challenge from both angles. Thus in terms of payment for occupation, a lessee should not pay until the final date allowed by the lease before interest could be charged. For a landlord, however, there is an understandable need to ensure prompt payment of rent and other charges. There is nothing to stop rent being payable in advance and in some cases (for example with a lessee whose financial strength is suspect) a landlord might insist on being paid a year's rent in advance and holding this as a deposit during the whole term, with subsequent rent payments being demanded in the normal way. Conversely, during the recession a number of businesses successfully negotiated payment of rent monthly in arrears to assist with cash flow. There is no obligation on a landlord to allow any such variation of the lease terms, but obviously rent being paid on a delayed basis is preferable to it not being paid at all.

For landlords, prompt payment of rent is not only a basic requirement of the contract set out in the lease but is also a commercial necessity. Accordingly, the fact that 'rent is due on a certain date (whether demanded or not) and delays are unacceptable and treated seriously' is a philosophy which should be understood by every lessee. Other than setting out the requirements (and the penalties) in the lease itself (where it may be overlooked not least because of the legal terminology) lessees may need to have their attention drawn to this point at a more appropriate time – that is each time rent is due!

Getting paid

Although most leases state that rent is payable 'whether demanded or not' and thus a lessee has no right to 'wait for the demand' before paying, it is prudent to issue a demand in advance of each quarter day – warning that late payment could lead to penalties.

Case study

An organization with 100 lessees had a rent collection problem. Credit control had been so lax that only two were paying on time, and thus the organization was losing the interest on the value of the late payments. A new system was adopted whereby rent was invoiced 14 days in advance of the due date, with written advice to lessees that no reminder would be issued, and that if rent was not paid on the due date the matter would be passed to its solicitors for Court action. All fees incurred as well as interest on the late payment would be due from the lessee. Within a year all lessees were paying on the due date.

New leases granted by the organization stipulated that rent had to be paid by direct debit, allowing the landlord to collect the amounts due on the quarter day without chasing.

Rent demand

A rent demand such as the following could be used:

Name and address of organization

Name, (address, if different from above) and telephone number of person responsible for property rental collection.

RENT DEMAND _____

Date _____

To (name and address of tenant) _____

_____

Property (address) _____

_____

THE FOLLOWING AMOUNTS IS/ARE DUE IN RESPECT OF THE ITEM(S) SHOWN

Rent for period [dates] _____[amount]

Service charge [date – may also need supporting schedule
– check lease requirements] _____[amount]

Insurance_____ [data] _____[amount]

Other (e.g. interest due re. late agreement of rent review, late payment
of previous rent, although this would be better collected at the time, etc.] _____[amount]

TOTAL DUE ON BEFORE [DATE] _____

PLEASE NOTE:

1. Under the terms of your lease, rent is due whether demanded or not.

2. This rent demand is issued as a courtesy. No reminder will be issued.

3. Please ensure your cheque/money transfer/cash is received by us no later than the due date.

4. Should rent not be received on or before the due date, our solicitors will be instructed to take action to collect it immediately. Their charges (and any charges incurred as a result of any court action), will then also need to be met by you.

5. Interest at [state rate in lease] will be added in respect of any late payment. Such interest payments are due within seven days of notification and again no reminder to pay will be issued. Any charges arising in respect of the collection of such payments will also be due from you.

Yours etc.

NOTES:

a. If rent is to be collected by credit to a bank account, details of the account will need to be supplied.

b. This form facilitates the collection of other charges due under the lease at the same time as the rent.

c. Request for payment must accord with the terms of the lease. Any days of grace must be allowed for.

Other rights

a) Landlords also have the right to expect the lessee to comply with the various COVENANTS in the lease and can take action where there is non-compliance. If a lessee breaches a covenant the landlord's ultimate right is to forfeit the lease – the lessee then loses occupation but may still be liable for all the financial obligations remaining. A breach of covenant may also mean that a lessee's right to exercise an OPTION to break the lease is lost and the lease continues.

b) Usually the landlord has an obligation to effect insurance and to recharge the premium to the lessee.

c) Any dates on which the rent can be reviewed are specified in the lease and to institute the process the landlord must serve notice as set out in the lease.

d) If at the end of the term the landlord wants to take back the property for his own use or to redevelop the property, they can legitimately refuse to permit a lease renewal, in which event the lessee is usually entitled to compensation equivalent to twice the rateable value of the premises. Otherwise, not more than 12 months and not less than six months before the termination date, the landlord must issue a Landlord and Tenant Act (LTA) notice on the lessee bringing the term to an end and stating that he will not object to the issue of a new lease, specifying the suggested terms. The lessee no longer has to serve a counter-notice but still needs to apply to the Court or risk losing their right to security of tenure. If the parties cannot agree terms for a new lease, both parties have the right to apply to the Court to decide such terms – mainly the rent.

If the landlord fails to serve a valid notice expiring on the lease termination date, the lease continues until the expiry of six months from the date of any late notice – the lessee meanwhile pays the existing rent.

e) The lease usually gives the landlord a right of entry in a number of instances – to inspect generally, for insurance valuation, and to prepare a schedule of dilapidations and so on.

Leasehold commitment

Introduction

A lease exposes a lessee to many obligations – and potential liabilities. Before agreeing these obligations and commitments, someone who knows the business and can appreciate the effect of these covenants on the day-to-day operation of the property needs to check to ensure they do not impede the business.

A considerable commitment

The bias to the landlord should not be under-estimated, for example, at RENT REVIEW if the lessee is faced with a large increase the one thing he cannot do is walk away from the lease since he is committed to it for the balance of the term. In addition, some or all of the value of his business may be related to its location – which in turn is dependant on the right to occupy. Hence the full impact of COVENANTS and other terms should be examined before the lease is signed – the only time the parties interface on something approaching equal terms.

No lease should even be considered unless the rent is roughly in line with rents in the area. Whilst special features may support a higher rent, care needs to be taken to avoid creating a precedent for increased rent which could affect all neighbours.

Checklist

1. Resist a lease term exceeding (say) ten years unless the business can plan that far ahead. If a short-term is resisted – request an option to break it either half way through or on an ongoing basis. Options should ideally be operative after a review has been agreed since the lessee will then know their future commitment and if the terms of trade in the locale have moved against them can bring their commitment to an end via the option.

2. Fully understand and comply with all covenants to protect any option to break, since this may usually only be validly exercised provided the lessee has complied with them.

3. Resist any requirement for sureties and personal GUARANTEES. If these are inevitable keep their time span short e.g. terminate after two years or at least at first rent review

4. Commission a full structural survey. Insert a schedule of condition in the lease and seek to restrict repairing and redecoration to the level shown.

5. Itemize any inherent defects in the property and clarify obligations. Many landlords will refuse to exclude such items from a repairing obligation but it is worth at least asking.

6. If the premises are not in a state suitable for the lessee's occupation, try to agree a rent free period during which work customizing the premises can be undertaken.

7. If lessee's works (to customize the unit to suit its occupation and operation) are required, seek permission of the landlord. If the lease is already signed, a deed of variation may be required. However, it may be possible to gain agreement by sending two copies of the plans asking the landlord to sign and return one copy as consent. The signed plan should be kept safely with the lease – since it amends it.

8. Try to avoid any obligation to remove lessee's works by the end of the lease and particularly to reinstate the property (if not, three sets of costs could be involved: the works themselves, removing the works and then making good and reinstating the property to the original layout).

9. Some landlords may wish to carry out the fitting out works themselves (particularly if they enhance the value of the property generally) or where the lessee cannot afford the works. If so, the landlord may wish to rentalise the cost of the improvements. The extra payment should be separately determined and charged from the rent and, at review, only the rent should be re-assessed.

10. If the lessee funds the works, ensure any enhancing value of such works are excluded from the valuation of rent at review. This agreement should always be specific and recorded in writing.

11. Resist rent reviews being required at a greater frequency than five years – this period is usually fair to both parties.

12. Resist upwards only rent reviews (UORR). That rents will always rise is a fallacy – they are a product of demand and supply and an UORR unfairly denies the effect of market forces.

13. Constantly seek evidence of other rents in the locale. Reviewing the rent is not purely a matter of negotiation and arbitration.

14. Resist penal interest charges on late payment of additional rent when under review.

15. Stipulate the wording and format of a memorandum for recording a rent review (see RENT REVIEW) in the lease – to avoid being charged for its preparation.

16. Stipulate that in the event of a lack of agreement re. rent review it will be determined by an expert rather than an arbitrator. It should be preferable that someone – an 'expert' – knowledgeable about the property market makes the decision having listened to such arguments.

17. Resist any requirement to keep an agreement to review the rent confidential. It is in the interests of lessees that everyone knows what rents are being charged in the neighbourhood.

18. Consider whether to ask for a restricted use clause. Whilst this could suit the subject lessee (and possibly hold the rent down at review) this could be a problem should the lessee wish to assign the lease.

19. Resist any suggestion that a restricted use should be ignored in review calculations. Restricted use will normally reduce the value of the lease and hence the rent. Conversely a restricted use may militate against ease of selling the lease.

20. Resist the imposition of time limits for the agreement of a rent review – deadlines can place a greater pressure on the lessee than on the landlord.

21. Repairing clauses can be very onerous. Resist any wording which requires the lessee to 'put and keep' the premises in a proper state of repair. The word 'put' imposes a wide duty which could involve the lessee being responsible for improving the state of repair over and above the level when the lease was granted. 'Keep repaired' is fair to both parties.

22. Check the landlord's right to serve a 'wants of repair' (DILAPIDATIONS) schedule and resist the lessee paying for its preparation. Such a schedule should always be checked to ensure only items properly demanded are included.

23. Stipulate there should be no contingent liability on assignment for the failure of a subsequent lessee – the Privity of Contract (PoC) rule. For post 1996 leases, landlords will usually require an Authorized GUARANTEE Agreement (AGA) to be entered into by an assigning lessee, which to some extent reinstates the PoC liability.

24. If contingent liability or an AGA is required, insist on the right to underlet the whole property. If an assignee fails, the original lessee has liability for losses but no right to re-enter the premises. However if the lessee underlets and their tenant fails, they should be able to re-enter the premises and use it themselves – or find a new sub-tenant.

25. Creating an underlease and/or assigning the lease requires the landlord's consent. Insist that the basis of the landlord's consent is 'not to be unreasonably withheld' and this wording is in the lease.

26. Check who is responsible for INSURING – and what are the covers required. If the landlord insures, insist that the lessee's interest be noted on the policy.

27. Rent is due on the dates specified in the lease – and must be paid on that date whether demanded or not. Check calculations particularly following a review and to ensure the benefit of any rent free period.

28. Ensure the method of calculation of apportionment of any shared services is stipulated, that such services are provided (and applicable to the subject premises) and that charges are not payable for services not provided.

29. In premises with multiple occupation ensure that should other units be empty any costs for shared services are not borne by lessees in occupation. It is the landlord's problem if there are empty units.

30. Check all lease COVENANTS to be given by the lessee, not only for legal reasons, but also for their practical impact on the lessee's business. This is best done by the lessee themselves rather than advisors.

* *

Term

Landlords will normally prefer to have a longer rather than a shorter lease since, providing the current lessee complies with covenants, the cost of finding a new lessee is minimized. Lessees probably have the reverse preference and, if pressed to take a longer term than they wish, lessees should insist on an option to break. Thus, if the term is 15 years, the lessee might require an option to break the lease after (say), five and ten years. If that option is exercised then the lessee can walk away from the lease without further commitment. However, if the lessee has not complied with all the covenants, the landlord may be able to resist the operation of the break option, thus requiring the lessee to assume the obligations under the lease for the remainder of the term, or until assigned.

Notes:

1. Often the exercise of an option is tied to the rent review. It is in the interests of the lessee to try to arrange the timing so that the review is agreed before the time limit for giving notice to exercise the option. In that way they will know their financial commitment before they have to exercise the option.

2. Since June 2006 under the Land Registration (Amendment) (No 2) Rules 2005, leases must contact certain standard clauses including date, landlord's title number, parties' names, full description of the property, term, any premium paid, prohibitions or restrictions on disposing of the lease, rights to renew or surrender, restrictive covenants, easements etc. Details from Land Registry (see DATA).

Lessee's Works

Introduction

Lessees may carry out work to the premises they occupy because they are required to do so:

a) by Statute or regulation,

b) to customize the premises for their own occupation,

c) by the landlord in order to bring the premises to the level of repair and redecoration required under the lease (See DILAPIDATIONS).

Statutory requirements

If work is legally required to be carried out in order for premises to be fit places for work (i.e. where employees can work safely, etc) most leases make it the lessee's responsibility to carry out such works – and to pay for them. If the lease is silent on this point then the landlord may be liable although it may be more convenient for the lessee to arrange for the works to be carried out (ideally at the landlord's expense) so that the works can be planned around working require-ments. There are extensive and recently revised obligations on occupiers to be proactive in developing appropriate FIRE PRECAUTIONS in the workplace, whilst under the Construction (Design and Management) Regulations 1994, if any building work:

- is to last longer than 30 days and involve more than four people or

- is to boiler/heating plant or

- is to be carried on inside offices or shops without interrupting normal activities,

a safety planning supervisor must be appointed and a suitable health and safety plan must be compiled.

The plan itself must address various phases in the process:

- the tender period (when details of health and safety requirements must be given to those submitting tenders)

- the design period (when the designer needs to consider health and safety requirements in planning the design and to advise the client of these and their implications)

- the construction phase (when health and safety becomes the responsibility of a planning supervisor who is required to coordinate and manage health and safety matters in liaison with the principal contractor).

The safety plan must be complied with at all times and made available to interested parties including members of the public.

Customizing premises

Carrying out building works or alterations in order to make them more appropriate to the purpose of occupation generates a number of requirements to be addressed:

i)   permissions from landlord and Building Regulation officials

ii) FIRE PRECAUTIONS, training and communication

iii) funding the works

iv) the relationship of such works with the rest of the premises.

Virtually all works may require the landlord's permission. This may be obtained by the landlord simply signing the plans and specification for the alteration or it may require a full legal Licence for Alterations or Deed of Variation. The landlord may be content for the works to be carried out as they enhance the value of the property, however, it is more likely that the landlord will insist (as part of the granting of permission) that the lessee reinstates (that is puts the premises back to the state they were before the works were carried out) the premises on or before the lease expires.

Payment

It may be simpler for the landlord to fund the works (which then pass into the landlord's ownership) and to recover their investment by increasing the rent – or by making a separate charge for these items. This may avoid the lessee having to remove the works and reinstate the premises to their original state.

Rentalising lessee works (i.e. adding an annual charge to the rent to fund the works) may be feasible but this can cause difficulties where the rent (inflated by the cost of the additions) is substantially more than the rent being paid in respect of similar properties in the area. One way of achieving this is to leave the rent unchanged but for the lessee to pay a further sum in respect of the added investment made on their behalf. Alternatively, the works may be funded by the lessee. If so, any enhancing value of the works should be excluded from following rent reviews otherwise the lessee will be in the position of paying for the works and then paying additional rent for the benefit of an extension or renovation etc that he has funded. Not only does there need to be a form of words stating that the effect of the works will be ignored at the next [number] reviews, but also any clause in the RENT REVIEW arrangements which enables the landlord to bring such works into the calculation must be specifically excluded.

Whilst minor works may be effected without formal permission, if these result in items being fixed to the structure then they are usually regarded as becoming part of the landlord's fixtures. If, however, if they are demountable or not fixtures, they usually remain the lessee's property. The question of responsibility for insuring such items should be addressed.

Range of works – and required permissions

The following permissions/consents may be required:

- Public Health and/or Environmental Health (depending on the use of the building).

- Insurers (whose stipulations regarding security often run counter to requirements under fire risk assessments).

- Landlord's consent – carrying out alterations to leased premises without the consent of the landlord (and any superior landlord) will usually be a breach of one or more of the lease covenants, so permission will need to be obtained – usually by means of a LICENCE specifying the works.

- Planning consent and Building Regulations.

- Petroleum officer – if petroleum spirit or diesel is to be stored on the premises.

- A safety plan and person responsible under the Construction (Design and Management) Regulations 1994. This plan must be made available to anyone wishing to inspect it.

Services

- **Electricity**. The correct phase supply and amperage need to be assessed, utilizing power factor correction equipment if necessary. Computer systems normally require a clean level circuit and/or an uninterrupted power supply. Battery or generator back-up power source equipment may be needed. (Generators normally need a large area, can be noisy and create vibrations, and should be operated at least once a week.) The power supply should be capable of coping with the demand at levels anticipated for at least three years.

- **Gas**. Suppliers will require estimates of annual and shorter period consumptions and for a contract to be entered into. There are a number of alternative tariffs, and demand estimating needs to be as accurate as possible.

- **Compressed air**. It will be more economical to make the original layout as comprehensive as possible to minimize disruption from later alteration/installation.

- **Water**. The water supply needs to be adequate for the demands of the business. New supplies will almost certainly have to be metered. If a sprinkler system is to be installed it may be necessary to install a header tank to provide sufficient pressure. The installation of a tank may require planning consent.

- **Heating, air conditioning and cooling equipment**. The exact requirements need identifying and alternative methods should be costed.

Fitting out – building works

Alternative quotes for full contract; part contract (a number of suppliers taking responsibility for part of the contract under the control of the main contractor); or direct management works (where the occupier or a project manager employs a number of contractors to carry out the works on an individual project basis), should be obtained. If time is short, contractors should be subject to penalties for late completion – and/or offered a bonus for early completion. If a main contractor employs sub-contractors, any contract should make it clear that responsibility for such sub-contractors, and their payment, rests with the main contractor.

Although the direct management works may seem to be the cheapest alternative, the time challenge of scheduling and overseeing different trades whilst ensuring the work progresses should not be underestimated.

Occupiers have a responsibility to ensure that contractors and sub-contractors adopt and maintain safe working practices and do not breach Health and Safety legislation (including compiling fire risk assessments). The safety rules and requirements must be given to, and explained to the contractors and their staff, with a stipulation that they must work subject to, and always comply with, such rules. The occupier cannot simply assume the contractors will work safely – they must ensure this is so. Failure to do so can bring personal penalties.

Insurance cover

The contract under which building contractors carry out works will specify the amount of cover required and whether the name of the occupier needs to be endorsed on the policy. If a building is erected on a green field site the builder will be responsible for the building insurance cover until Practical Completion. When alterations to an existing building are being effected the owner (if freehold) or occupier or landlord (if leasehold) will usually be responsible for the cover and for advising insurers that contractors are working in the building. If the insurer loads the premium because of the works, the additional cost is usually passed to the builder who will usually also insure the works being carried out and be responsible for that premium. Confirmation of the builder's insurance cover(s) should be obtained before the contract is signed.

Security protection

Fire and/or intruder alarm systems should be commissioned and appropriate automatic telephone links arranged. Assessing fire precautions, as well as the requirements of the building insurers may generate a need for extensive work, for example, the installation of smoke detectors. The number and type of fire extinguishers required must be assessed and installed. It may also be advisable to install card access systems and/or closed circuit television systems to assist with the protection of the property (see SECURITY and NEIGHBOURS).

Administrative checklist

- Ensure everyone involved knows the Project Manager and his/her mobile phone number.

- Arrange refuse/waste disposal by authorized contractor.

- Assess equipment, furniture, fittings required: check delivery delays and order appropriately.

- Prepare data on building and works including any reinstatement requirements.

- Carry out a fire drill as soon as possible after works completed.

- Change locks once all fitting out work is completed.

- Preserve three sets of building and fitting out plans safely.

- Re-assess insurance cover.

- Check rating valuation.

- Once Practical Completion of fitting out works is certified by the building surveyor or architect arrange for the preparation of a snagging list which the builder should complete within 14 or 21 days.

- Fix a date for the expiry of the Defects Liability period (usually six months for building works – 12 months for mechanical and electrical services – after completion of the works).

Licence

Introduction

Licences related to property occupation and subsidiary permissions exist in a variety of formats. A licence to occupy property is similar to a lease but without the formal and legal ramifications – and protections – granted by a lease. Unlike a lease, a licence gives no guarantee of continuation of tenure after expiry. Other licences can be granted on an ad hoc basis. This section addresses both.

Licence to occupy

Particularly where there is a delay between the vacation of a property by a lessee and (for example) its redevelopment (or the grant of a full lease to a new lessee), a landlord may be prepared to grant a licensee a right to occupy the premises without the protection of the Landlord and Tenant Act. Licence occupation might also be useful for an operation which has committed to a new location which is not ready even though they must vacate their existing premises. A licensee takes occupation of the premises normally without a lessee's level of commitment (e.g. for repairs etc) and is often simply required to pay the rent and any other outgoings – rates, services etc. Although requirements can vary, a licence term will always be stipulated and the licensee must vacate on or before the date stated. This arrangement is usually only of interest to organizations where the 'assets disappear down the stairs at night' i.e. 'people based' operations with few fixed assets. It can suit small office-based operations who will normally gain from lower occupation costs than they would otherwise bear. Conversely they incur increased charges for removal and advising everyone of their new location.

Although the arrangement is outside the protection of the Landlord and Tenant legislation (meaning particularly that on termination the occupier has no right to a new lease), legal advice should be taken to ensure full occupation rights are preserved for the period agreed.

Other arrangements

Lessees and others may wish to come to a semi-formal arrangement regarding use of their premises without applying for the landlord's permission. Care has to be taken with this arrangement, since if the lessee parts with possession this could void the lease or breach a covenant thereby imperilling the exercise of a valid option to break the lease.

Example

This Licence is made this _____ day of _____ 20XX between

_____[name]

operating in _____[location]

('the premises') and [name and address] ('the operator')

It is hereby agreed between the above two parties that the retailer will allow the operator to sell [specify] ('the goods') within its retail premises at the above address on the following basis:

1. The operator will pay the retailer £XXX per week ('the weekly fee') for the right to sell the goods from a table he will set up in the shop in such a position as may from time to time be dictated by the retailer.

2. This Licence commences on [Monday _____ date _____] and will continue until one party gives notice to the other as follows :

   • From the retailer to the operator: One week

   • From the operator to the retailer: Four weeks

   • Notice of termination must be given in writing by one party to the other in person or sent by recorded delivery to the last known address of the operator or the premises of the retailer.

3. Rent will be paid four weeks in advance by the operator to the retailer in cash by 9.00 a.m. each Monday. For the purpose of clarity, on commencement of this Licence the operator will pay the retailer four weeks rent and each following Monday will pay the retailer the weekly fee.

4. The area to be used by the operator is not to exceed one square metre.

5. A notice no bigger than paper size A3 or 12" x 17" can, subject to approval by the retailer, be displayed immediately adjacent to the area being used from time to time by the operator.

6. The operator hereby confirms to the retailer that this is a legitimate business and he will do nothing whatever to damage the business and reputation of the retailer. He also confirms that he is entirely responsible for all legal requirements placed on his business which is entirely separate to that of the retailer. He will account to his own tax etc authorities for earnings derived from this trade.

7. The operator undertakes to comply with all obligations of the retailer under the terms of its occupation of the premises and all statutory and other obligations applicable to both the retailer and himself. He will abide by all requirements of the retailer with regard to the location and manner of trade of his business.

8. The operator undertakes to adhere to and comply with all instructions issued by the retailer and its staff.

9. The operator undertakes not to interfere with the trade of the retailer or its goods either on display or in storage, not to take money for the retailer's goods and always and at all times to refer customers for such goods to the assistants employed by the retailer.

10. The operator will be permitted to use the toilet facilities of the premises having first requested access from the retailer's manager.

Signed on behalf of the retailer by [name] _____

Date _____

Signed by the operator _____

Date _____

WARNING: In granting such a right, the lessee should always be aware of the lease obligations – if in doubt, take advice.

M

Maintenance   199

Marriages of interests   207

Maintenance

Introduction

Other than if occupying under licence, property occupation entails a long-term commitment to maintenance, redecoration and repair. If leasehold, despite the sale of that interest by assignment, certain commitment to the lease covenants will not only apply during the term but may well continue after the sale. Freehold properties must also be maintained, although since there is no external party, as there is in leased premises, to enforce such obligation, it is all too easy to overlook or ignore the need to keep such properties in good condition. Failure to maintain property however tends to result in large, and often unbudgeted, expenditure occurring when it is least expected or wanted. There is a philosophical choice here – some organizations subscribe to 'preventative maintenance' (actioning repairs now to prevent greater expenditure later), others to the concept of 'repair only when broken'.

Usage

Regular maintenance can pose a severe problem when there is high usage of the asset. Whilst from the 'work performed' perspective, high usage is beneficial, it creates a dual problem to facility administration. Not only do buildings with high usage suffer greater damage and deterioration of decoration, but also the fact that they are well-used may cause repairs and redecoration to be postponed until 'a more convenient time' or creates a disproportionate disruption and then, possibly being rushed, poor execution. If routine maintenance is neglected or deferred, however, defects are aggravated and items that could have been dealt with at relative low cost can deteriorate and create more serious and costly repairs. With leasehold property this can culminate in the service of a schedule of DILAPIDATIONS.

Budgetary control

Resources are almost always limited and since 'property investment' often has a low profile it is all too easy for other demands to take priority. It may sound odd to say so but despite their obvious presence property assets are often 'overlooked'. This 'failure to see' a valuable asset should be avoided and a budget should be allocated for the purpose of keeping buildings in a fair state of repair and redecoration. There is often a temptation, when under financial pressure, for such budgets to be cut – and for property repairs to be 'delayed' – which can sometimes means 'cancelled'. Almost inevitably these costs will need to be met by the organization sooner or later. Indeed, cutting a current maintenance budget can mortgage future income, since failure to repair a small problem today may incur greater expenditure later. Most budgets are prepared on an annualized basis which may be inappropriate for long-term investments like property. A longer term budget with the ability to move the timing of expenditure around may be preferable.

Condition planning

Adopting a commitment to property maintenance achieves greater awareness of the true costs of occupation which may be invaluable when considering future space utilization and comparing costs of alternative facilities (see ACCOMMODATION PLANNING). A full survey of the properties and plant should be prepared. If the organization is felt to be a potential TERRORIST target, requirements for protection might also be built into such a survey.

Condition checklist

Answers are needed to the following with, where applicable, estimates for and the timing of repairs. This checklist is not meant to be exhaustive. It is simply a base from which an individual plan can be customized.

Condition checklist

If an answer is 'no' specify what is required and when

ROOF

If pitched, is it waterproof with tiles/other covering sound? _____

How old is covering and what is expected life? _____

Are timbers or other supports sound? _____

Check eaves, guttering and fascia boards – are these worn? _____

Chimneys and vents – are they in good repair or in need of repointing?_____

Are chimney-pot caps in position and sound? _____

If flat, what is life and when was it last treated?_____

Are gutters cleared regularly?_____

Is asbestos present? _____

If yes, has it been contained? _____

WALLS

Are they sound with good quality material? _____

Are they damp protected – do they need such protection? _____

Is any rendering sound and in good repair? _____

Is mortar sound or does it require repointing? _____

Is asbestos present? _____

If yes, has it been contained? _____

WINDOWS AND DOORS

Life of frames – is this reasonable or is earlier replacement likely? _____

Is glass shatterproof – or if not, is it worth implementing this protection? _____

FOUNDATIONS

Any problems with construction indicating required repair? _____

Likelihood of incidence of subsidence and consequential costs? _____

Are drains and sewers sound? _____

(For relatively low costs specialist contractors can survey this using mobile underground cameras.)

Have major trees been removed from nearby the property? _____

(Advice may need to be taken before removing trees, as this could impact subsidence. In addition some trees may be safeguarded under a tree preservation order – check with local authority.)

ENERGY

What steps are being taken to reduce consumption of energy?

_____

_____

NEIGHBOURHOOD PROBLEMS

Are there any problems experienced by neighbours which could impact own property?

_____

_____

Likelihood of flooding, damage to foundations from trees and so on?

_____

_____

PLANNING REQUIREMENTS

Are there any requirements likely to be imposed which could impact the property a) during the life of the plan and b) subsequently?

_____

_____

NOTE: Local authorities are required to have prepared plans showing all anticipated usages. Although the fact that there is a requirement of alteration in the middle future may not impact the plan itself, it might condition consideration of the future use/retention of the property.

PLANT AND MACHINERY

Expected life/replacement/reconditioning/repair of hot water system, lifts, central heating, boilers, air conditioning, and all other items. _____

_____

Investigate compressed air/compressor system and life. _____

Check gas supply system _____

Note: Since October 1994 all commercial gas installations have been required to have an emergency cut off switch. Expert assistance should be sought.

Similar enquiries regarding own installation e.g. kitchen equipment (compliance with Food Safety Act) sports and other facilities. _____

ELECTRICAL INSTALLATION

Expected life/replacement/reconditioning/repair of supply/wiring and sockets.

_____

Expert assistance may be required. Possibly link with insurance surveys.

_____

Such work will identify a range of items needing work – some more urgent than others. The ideal timing for maintenance/repair of each item can also be arrived at and form the basis for a long term plotting of the required dates.

WARNING: To discover the condition of certain aspects of the above it may be necessary to use access equipment or ladders. The Work at Height Regulations 2005 require all those working at height to take suitable precautions, for example, securing a ladder needed to gain access to a roof. A risk assessment should be completed on each occasion with dangers thereby identified and risks minimized as far as possible.

Creating the plan

1. As well as identifying items needing attention a property maintenance cycle should be established. This could run for between five and ten years. All expenditure anticipated in respect of all properties during this period should be estimated and plotted on an 'expected time of incidence' basis.

If there is a property register, this can provide both a base and a means of recording the process. The organization needs to determine whether maintenance is to be on an 'as required' or 'preventative' basis. 'Preventative' maintenance entails projecting the life of various items of plant, or time before redecoration and repair etc and then carrying out such work according to the time projection – that is before it fails. This is as much a question of philosophy as anything else – the organization must decide whether to repair and replace in advance of failure or to wait for failure. If the latter, a fund to cover such emergencies should be created.

2. Regardless of whether buildings are leasehold or freehold, all should be allocated a repair/redecoration programme. Leasehold properties will normally have such a programme set out as one of the lease COVENANTS but a similar programme is needed for freehold properties.

3. Where there is a mixed portfolio (i.e. both freehold and leasehold properties are owned/used) there may be scope for staging requirements for freehold properties between those for leasehold premises so that the cost implications of both sets of obligations is evened out.

4. If it is required to develop or extend properties during the period, such costs could also be built into the plan.

5. To ensure adequate costing, surveys of the state of the building, plant and equipment need to be conducted and estimates put on the life/investment required – and revised regularly.

6. Once the budget is finalized, commitment should be sought to expenditure of all items on the understanding, subject to cash flow constraints, that items may be able to be brought forward or deferred for, say, six months either side of the planned date. For example, if the building industry is slack, it may be possible to obtain a keen price for work otherwise not due for some months when the industry might be busier and prices harden. This 'time refining' (or 'opportunistic' repair) is cost effective but can only be used if there is a maintenance demands projection.

7. It may be preferable to use Day 1 prices and at the time of each subsequent budget agree an inflation factor for items still outstanding. Investigation should only be necessary when estimates vary by (say) 5% of inflation-adjusted figures.

Case study

Davenant Foundation School was founded in 1680 and is now a 1100 pupil (11-18) secondary school in Loughton Essex. It opted out of full State funding, one effect being that it is responsible for its own facilities etc and needs to contribute 10%-15% of the capital cost of new projects. When the facilities were transferred into the responsibility of the governors and school, the buildings had not been well-maintained by the local authority. A condition survey was undertaken, estimating when building mainte-nance would be required as well as estimating the life of plant such as boilers etc over a seven year period. All items were slotted into a schedule using the same 'at a glance' design as used in KEEPING PROPERTY RECORDS. This enabled regular updating as new items were identified or projects etc were completed. Obviously money was restricted, even though the school has access to certain of its own funds built up over its lifetime, and projects were often delayed pending obtaining grants etc from a variety of sources. Initially many entries in the 'required main-tenance' category had to be timed for the later years, but as items were dealt with it was possible to space such items out. An example of the plan generated whilst the author was a governor in charge of the school's estate management committee is attached.

Key:

a) The first part of the plan deals with new builds and projects giving ideal timings and identifying sources of funding – special grants, the school's own budget and funds made available from its private trusts (the Whitechapel and Reynolds funds) – including contributions from parents, past pupils etc. Between 1994 and 2005 over £5 million worth of new builds/renovations were completed.

b) The lower half of the plan covers the maintenance programme – again demonstrating the sources of funding for each.

Davenant Foundation School
Seven year building development and maintenance plan

Yr ended 31 March	2003	2004	2005	2006	2007	2008	2009	Suggested Source of Funding	Notes
MEDIUM TERM PLAN									
Refurbish Rms 29/30	93,000							LCVAP grant	
Stage to Drama Rm	115,000							) Basic Need, fundraising,	
6th Form block		265,000	500,000					) Formula Capital grants	
Rm 34 to Music Rm	24,000							) and contributions from	
I.T. Office	11,500							) Reynolds and	
Reynolds Suite	30,000							) Whitechapel	
Art Room 26		14,000						School budget	
Additional offices	10,000							School budget	
Refurbish ch rooms		17,000						School budget	
New PE Office		17,000						School budget	
Hall			100,000					Fundraising	
Kitchen				72,000				Fundraising	
Drainage of field		30,000	30,000	30,000				LEA liability	
Tennis Courts		10,000						School	Additional to LTA & NOF
Sub-total 1	**283,500**	**353,000**	**630,000**	**102,000**					grants
Grant	147,500	268,500							
Trust's commitment	96,000	36,500							
School commitment	40,000	48,000							
PREVENTIVE MAINTENANCE									
Decorations	PROGRAMME TO BE DETERMINED IN LINE WITH AREA DEVELOPMENT PLAN								
Hall Related									
Re-wire			MTP Hall						
Kitchen									
Kitchen essentials	13,000							School budget	
Hall ventilation									
Main boilers							120,000	School/Trust	
Roof			MTP Hall						
Windows			MTP Hall						
Kitchen car park			MTP Hall						
Non-Hall Related									
Boiler chimney/reroof		1,200						School budget	
Air handling		75,000						DfES (excepted buildings)	
Block A									
- electrical	500							School budget	
- heaters				16,750				School budget	
- HE heating			9,000					School budget	
Block C									
- elect. lighting			4,000					School budget	
- elect. power			4,000					School budget	
- heating		10,000	10,000	10,000				School/Trust	
Block F									
- re-wire	2,000		40,000					School/Trust	
- boiler			33,500					School/Trust	
- heating		7,500	7,500					School budget	
External									
- drive/car park	3,500	45,000						School budget/LEA	
Sub-total 2	**19,000**	**138,700**	**108,000**	**26,750**	**0**	**0**	**120,000**	**412,450**	
TOTAL	**302,500**	**491,700**	**738,000**	**128,750**	**0**	**0**	**120,000**	**1,780,950**	
Trust's commitment	96,000	36,500						132,500	
School commitment	59,000	111,700						170,700	
Fundraising			100,000	72,000				172,000	

Marriages of interests

Introduction

In the simplest form of occupation – an organization occupying and owning a property – there is a single interest in the facility. In most other instances there are at least two interests – those of the owner and of the occupier. In a lease there will be at least two interests – landlord and lessee, but there may be many more. Often a lessee's immediate landlord may themselves hold the lease of the property as an underlease from a superior landlord who may themselves have further superior landlord(s). To each of these parties the lease of the facility may have a value, which potential value may be enhanced by merging with (or 'marrying') another interest.

Effect

In the simplest 'vertical marriage' instance, a lessee could buy the freehold from their landlord or alternatively the landlord could 'buy in' the lease from the lessee. The effect is that a sole organization gains control of the rights of both owner-ship and occupation which combined and sole interest could then be sold as a freehold with vacant possession. Being able to offer the property on this basis should, in most cases, enable a greater value to be obtained than would be possible by selling the separate interests. Thus 'marrying' the interests may have a value itself.

To gain this value, obviously one party needs to purchase the other party's interest. Occupiers and owners do not always realize the potential value of their property rights, and thus if such an offer is made, not only should a realistic value of one's own interest be obtained but also an indication of the likely poten-tial marriage value since, with such knowledge a better offer may be negotiated – any alternative could result in selling the business short.

Proactive strategy

Such transaction profits can only be achieved if there is an awareness of:

- the value of the property(ies)
- trends in property values (nationally and locally), and
- opportunities on a local basis.

In addition there needs to be a willingness

- to be prepared to deal, and
- to interface with other property occupiers and owners.

Expert advice may be essential to ensure the maximum value is achieved. The secret is always to be aware of potential. This is not a recommendation for property trading but simply a suggestion that if there is a deal it may be worth exploiting.

Case study

Maynards had both a freehold factory in North London (with some surplus capacity), and a leasehold factory in Crawley (on a site owned by the Commission for the New Towns – CNT). The Crawley factory had been built by the company in the early 1950s when the CNT had granted the company a 99 year lease of the land at a fairly nominal rent to encourage manufacturing to take space in the area. Prior to the rent review in the mid 1980s, however, the Government instructed CNT to divest themselves of their freehold ownership. The company was able to purchase the freehold interest for £75,000. Following a rationalization of output, production was transferred to the North London factory. The company now owned the freehold as well as its former leasehold interest of the Crawley factory and offered the whole site with vacant possession. The site was then sold for £1.25 million.

Neighbourhood marriages

As well as the above 'vertical marriage', 'horizontal' marriages can also be effected. To an organization with insufficient space, the opportunity value of the adjoining property may be higher than that of another prospective purchaser. Even if the occupier does not wish to use the premises, a larger plot may command a greater value than selling two properties separately. The difficulty here, however, is that the owner of the neighbouring land will perceive that to their neighbour the property may have an enhanced value and attempt to inflate the price accordingly. It may be advisable to acquire via a nominee without disclosing the identity of the principal. Property administrators need to be aware of the values of their properties at all times.

N

Neighbours	213
Notice Boards	219
Notice serving	223

Neighbours

Introduction

Of all property occupation problems, those relating to neighbours may more than outnumber all others. Further, of problems with neighbours, that of authorized and illegal parking and denial of, and the creation of difficulties in gaining access to one's own premises is probably the greatest. However, there are several other aspects that need to be addressed.

Assessing problems

In contemplating an acquisition, means of access to and egress from the property as well as facilities for parking both the organization's vehicles and those of its employees and visitors must be considered. Valued employees can be lost if they find they are unable to park within a reasonable distance of their workplace, or their vehicles are damaged whilst so parked. Enquiries should be made of existing occupiers as well as of the local police. If premises are being obtained with the intent that the organization may expand whilst at the site, an assessment of all projected requirements (including parking) should also be made. Whilst an isolated site may pose problems of its own (e.g. SECURITY) at least access and parking difficulties should be fewer.

Employment demand

The close proximity of a competing employer may also militate against the choice of a particular property. If rates of pay are not competitive (and the organization is not prepared – or even able – to keep them competitive) then moving near a competing employer could result in losing more valued employees. Conversely, provided the employer's conditions and rates of pay are at least competitive, the move might be advantageous as it may enable the best skills to be drawn from an existing labour pool.

Shared resources

Where there are a number of neighbouring trading organizations e.g. a retail shopping centre, office complex, manufacturing industrial estate, there can be advantages in such occupation. Many such entities operate their own security forces, janitorial services, pressure groups etc. Since the costs involved are shared, the service is likely to be provided for a fraction of the cost of setting up individual arrangements. Further, the fact that such services are known to be available may make the site somewhat more secure and attractive to prospective occupiers thus enhancing the value of the interest – both on acquisition and when selling – a valuable marketing point.

Joint action

Where a number of similar facilities are available on lease, they may have a common landlord. If neighbouring lessees are in contact it may be possible to ensure that action on common areas of concern is effected quickly and even that by concerted action (for example, to resist too great an increase in rent at review) some advantage can be obtained. Similar action may be able to be orchestrated in dealing with local authorities over planning or other proposals. The pressure that can be brought to bear by everyone acting in harmony will often result in a decision difficult to achieve by an occupier acting independently. Indeed, landlords' strategy could well be to try and conclude a 'one-off' deal to act as a benchmark for the others.

Case study

Capital Newsagents occupied one of five units in a small parade on the outskirts of High Wycombe. The reviews were timed at roughly the same time and the landlord attempted to conclude a deal with one lessee who knew little about the normal rent review process. Pre-empting such an agreement, the person acting for Capital contacted all the lessees and suggested that it might be better if they acted in concert. This was agreed and rents around 20% lower than had been virtually concluded between the landlord and Capital's neighbour were agreed. Had the original deal gone through, the landlord could then have used that as evidence against the other four units.

Trespass

Trespass is a civil wrong and a trespasser is defined as someone who:

- enters premises or land (or parts thereof) where he or she has no permission or invitation to be, or

- remains on premises of land (or part thereof) after the permission to be so present has expired, or

- leaves or delivers goods (or waste) on premises or land without authorization.

Whilst trespass may be a matter for each individual occupier, an arrangement with neighbours who are working outside 'normal' hours, or simply an arrangement for the exchange of information and ideas for combating the nuisance (particularly from children) may help contain or prevent these incursions (see TRESPASSERS).

Effluent, noise and nuisance

Increasingly, control over the creation of noxious fumes, smells, smoke etc – even intrusive light – is subject to statutory control, and problems in these areas should be referred initially at least to the local authority. Currently the Department for Environment, Food and Rural Affairs (DEFRA) is working on two initiatives:

- the Noise and Nuisance team is devising a policy to try to curb unacceptable neighbourhood noise (an initiative not presumably divorced from the anticipated problems associated with the relaxation of the opening hours of licensed premises) and

- proposals for a National Ambient Noise Strategy (NANS), whose first task is to chart noise levels in 20 of England's major towns under its Noise Mapping England project.

However, legal procedures to prevent noise and other nuisances can take some time to become effective and an on-site relationship may result in greater control and provide a swifter remedy than legal measures. Noise caused by, for example, building works, can be very disruptive to business, yet legal action could take some weeks to become effective, by which time the works may have been completed. If a relationship has been built it may be possible to reach a compromise whereby (for example) noisy work is only undertaken outside specified hours, or for short bursts at pre-determined intervals (before commencement, during lunch breaks) etc.

NOTE: If informal or good natured requests fail, it may be necessary to take legal action in which case advice should be sought. Generally the courts may be sympathetic to plaintiffs and, as stated above, new controls are being introduced. The legal authority in this area is very old.

Case study

In *Ryland v Fletcher* (which dates from 1866!) it was laid down that 'a person who for his own purposes brings on his lands ... and keeps there anything likely to do mischief if it escapes, must keep it at his peril and, if he does not do so, is prima facie answerable for all the damage which is the natural consequence of its escape'.

Under the Control of Noise at Work Regulations 2005 the maximum levels of noise at work were reduced by five decibels. Employers must take action to limit employees to excessive noise and provide protection against hearing damage (see DATA).

Boundary disputes

As always, if there is a problem, an informal approach may be the best initial tactic. Some problems arise simply because the extremities of the building are actually on or very near the boundary line. This can render access to the exterior somewhat difficult and although there is now a legal right to enter neighbouring land to gain such access (the Access to Neighbouring Land Act 1993) subject to application to Court, recourse to legal action may be best avoided. The question of ownership or, and responsibility for fences, party walls etc should also be determined using expert advice – matters that should have been checked on acquisition.

Party Wall Act 1997

This Act extended the previous rights existing in London to all England and Wales. Where there is a wall which provides a boundary between two adjacent properties each party has ownership up to the boundary and statutory rights over the other side of the wall. Each party can:

- repair, rebuild and increase the load capacity of the wall

- construct a wall that straddles the boundary

- carry out works to the wall from the neighbour's building.

The owner must serve notice on the other party who may object to the works. Each party must reinstate any damage caused by the works.

There are alternative systems for resolving disputes using either:

- a single 'agreed surveyor' who will act as an arbitrator or

- a 'triple surveyor' procedure whereby each party appoints their own surveyor and then the two appointees jointly appoint a third.

Access to Neighbouring Land Act 1993

This grants to neighbours the right, subject to notice, to gain entry to land adjacent to their property so that they can carry out work to their own premises which cannot be carried out on their side of the boundary (e.g. due to lack of access space). Notice must be given and the neighbour can object to entry. Any damage must be made good.

Hedge boundaries

The height of hedges comprised of (for example) the fast growing conifer, Leylandii, as well as holly and laurel trees, is now subject to legal controls. Hedges comprising such plants (but not those comprised of deciduous trees, such as beech, or those that are ivy clad) are limited in height to two metres under the Anti-Social Behaviour Act 2003. Those believing a hedge is in breach of this requirement can apply to the local council for adjudication and, if successful, it results in the person responsible being required to reduce the plants to the required height. Adjudication (which is subject to the complainant paying for the process – and fees vary from around £100 to £650 depending on the council involved – average around £350) can take several months.

Excess height is not the only problem with hedges and trees – their roots can spread widely and cause damage to walls, drainage pipes etc (although many thousands of trees were killed as a result of the excavations of roads and pavements conducted on behalf of Cable TV). In addition, falling branches can also cause damage and claims for loss caused by such damage, can be lodged in the small claims court. Overhanging branches can be cut back to the boundary line and can be returned to the owner – although care should be taken if simply dropping them over the boundary as they could cause damage.

Summary

Ideally there should be a reasonable relationship between neighbours. Although creating such a relationship will take time and resources, it can result in long-term savings. Increasingly there are legal protections, but using these may be expensive and will almost certainly damage what may be required to be a long-term relationship. In this, 'jaw jaw' may be better than 'war war'. In other words, making informal contact with the neighbours before there are problems may stand you in good stead when problems arise.

Case study

At the height of its rapid expansion in the 1980s, Filofax, the personal organizer company, acquired a warehouse facility by means of an under-lease from Polygram Records who continued to operate eight of the ten bays of a warehouse of which Filofax now had occupation rights to two bays. The Polygram employees as well as employees of other units on the industrial estate had become accustomed to parking on an area that was now designated as Filofax' parking area. There was concern that there could be arguments once Filofax occupied the bays – and their employees occupied 'their' car parking area. In the period during which the bays were being fitted out for Filofax, the owners of cars parked in the area, were regularly reminded by Filofax' property personnel (including having handbills placed on their cars), that although they were welcome to use the land during the building works, once these were completed, the space would be needed for Filofax' own staff and they would have to park elsewhere.

Note: Most councils operate a mediation scheme for neighbours, whilst Hedgeline can also advise (see DATA).

Notice Boards

Introduction

Most organizations use notice boards to convey information to their employees – but often without sufficient control over the posting of notices. As a result, many boards become swamped with old notices often well past their effective date, impairing the impact and effectiveness of new material. The challenge is to keep notice boards fresh and uncluttered so that boards – and the notices – are read rather than passed by. This may be easier with electronic notice boards operated via an intranet but research indicates that most people prefer not to have to read substantial amounts of text on-screen.

Location

Notice boards should be located where people are likely to stop to read the content. This does not mean a place where many people pass – since they may be conditioned to do just that – pass, rather than to stop and read. Locations where people pause – by the drinks machine, in the lift lobby (even in the lift), in cloakrooms – may be more suitable. Notices should also be numbered to aid control. If exactly the same number of copies as there are boards are run off, the person posting the notices should have only the master left having visited the last board. Similarly when removing out of date notices, if the person returns with the same number of old notices as boards, all should have been removed.

Procedure

Whether traditional or electronic notice boards are used the following check-list is apposite.

Suggested checklist

1. Data for display must be written in the language and for the understanding of the recipient and be presented in a manner that will attract and retain attention. Posting an item on the [organization's] notice board, implies that the [organization] has approved the content. All notices should therefore be approved for posting by [specify name].

2. All notices should bear dates of origination and destruction (the date on or following which the notice should be withdrawn). To avoid notice boards becoming overburdened no notice will remain posted after its destruct date unless the data requires an extension in which case it will be given a new 'destruct date'.

3. [Specify] will act as notice board administrator and will keep a register of all notices with origination and destruct dates together with a master notice board (showing all notices on display at any one time). (S)he is responsible for posting all new notices and for ensuring notices past their destruct (or extension) date are removed.

4. All notice boards are numbered and numbered copies of each notice will be generated to ensure a copy of every notice is posted on every board.

5. Each week the administrator will post any required new notices and remove any notices which have passed their destruct date.

6. To aid employee recognition, notices will be colour-coded by content (e.g. red for safety matters, green for disciplinary items, yellow for benefit related topics, blue for social events and white for management initiated items).

7. Notices for employees and/or their representatives will be displayed on the section of each board reserved for [non-organizational] matters. Such notices will be expected to conform to the foregoing rules and must be controlled by this procedure. They will be required to bear a destruct date etc. No notice will be posted which is poorly presented, is in poor taste or is in any way against the interests of the [organization]. In this respect the decision of [specify] to whom every notice must be shown before posting, will be final

8. Managers and those responsible for conducting team briefings etc are expected to check that notices are seen and read as part of the management or cascade briefing system and to this end will be supplied with a copy of each notice posted.

Permanent notices

Notices required to be displayed permanently by law may preferably be posted on separate boards.

Checklist: Permanent notices

i) Certificate of employer's liability insurance (renewed annually). Since 1st January 1999 each certificate has been required to be kept for 40 years (in order, should there be a claim in respect of an illness or injury which has taken many years to surface, that the person responsible for the liability, if proven, is known).

ii) Corporate name and address where documents may be served. This is a requirement for the benefit of third parties rather than employees.

iii) Health and safety policy.

iv) Such notices as are required to be posted under FIRE PRECAUTION risk assessments covering the premises.

v) Details of how FIRST AID can be obtained/is administered.

vi) Factories Act 1961 notice (for factories only.)

vii) Offices shops and railway premises guide and thermometer (for facilities covered by the guide only).

viii) Wages council notices (where applicable).

ix) (If a leaflet covering the item is not given to each employee) a notice under Health & Safety at Work Act 1974, *What you should know*.

WARNING: This list is for example and should be used as a base only. Individual industries may have additional notices which must be displayed.

* *

Composition

When committing ideas, instructions or guidance to paper, authors should always try to compose the item to meet the needs of the target audience. Basically, if the reader does not understand the item written then it is the writer's responsibility since they have probably not presented the information in a format capable of being easily understood by their target audience. Authors of notices should review them and possibly even check them for ease of comprehension with a member of the target audience. For my book, *How to be a great communicator* (Pitman 1995), the following guidance was provided on the presentation of written material derived from research within a number of organizations.

Written information should

- be well spaced with good use of headlines, sub-headlines and visual impact; that is, leaving plenty of white paper to attract attention and make the whole 'accessible' to the target audience

- use bite-sized chunks of text (say not more than 100 words in the average paragraph) so the content is easy to digest and the page does not look 'cramped'

- be written in language that is easy to understand at first glance – since only if initial attention is retained may the item be read at all. This indicates a need to use simple rather than complex sentences which cause the reader's brain less activity to aid comprehension that the latter

- be presented using lines of type with on average no more than 65 characters (including letters and punctuation marks). This echoes the old printing rule that no line of type should be more than 2.5 alphabets long. The problem with repeated lines of dense type is that, without a straight edge under the type, the human eye may wander to the lines above and below. (As an example the average number of characters in the lines in this book is 60.)

- written in ordinary everyday English avoiding jargon or if this is unavoidable explaining any jargon used. (The dictionary definition of 'jargon' is 'the meaningless babble of an infant'. If jargon users are told this it might encourage them to cease using it, to the benefit of ease of comprehension by all!)

- avoid presenting data in a way that makes the written page look dense. If it is, it will almost certain repel the reader rather than attract them, whereas the whole rationale of a notice is to attract attention – to convey the message swiftly without the reader needing to re-read the item.

In short, in writing anything the aim should not so much be to make the item easy to understand as to make it impossible for it to be misunderstood.

Notice serving

Introduction

Limited liability (LTDs, PLCs etc) companies are required to have a 'Registered Office' and to display this address on every sheet of notepaper, bill of exchange, order, statement etc. This is required so that those dealing with the company know where to serve legal and official notices. Dealing promptly with such notices is important as often they require action (sometimes within a set period) and failure to respond could result in liabilities and/or penalties being borne by the company. Organizations other than companies should similarly nominate an 'administrative office' to which such correspondence should be sent. Ideally the location of the executive charged with actioning a response to such notices should be the designated office.

Location

In every lease or licence the designated address should be nominated as the place to which all notices should be sent. Where an organization occupies only one location, this may not cause too much of a problem as it can when there are additional sites. Landlords usually prefer a lease provision that notices will be served at the facility to which the lease relates, and if they are unwilling to agree to change this, then a requirement to serve an additional copy on the administrative office should be inserted. It is also good practice to advise those in satellite locations that all such notices must immediately be passed to [a nominated person].

Note: The term 'administrative office' has been used deliberately to draw attention to the location where notices must be sent. If the words 'Registered Office' are used then notices can be sent there. Using 'Registered Office' may be inconvenient if that is not where the property or facility administrator is based.

Change of administrative office

If the administrative office is changed, landlords (and agents) of all leases and licences which specify that address, should be notified by recorded delivery with a covering letter in duplicate. They should be asked to sign and return the covering letter confirming they have altered their records accordingly. It may assist if no receipt has been obtained, for a copy of the letter to be attached to the next rent payment. If a notice is subsequently served on the incorrect address, at least the receipt is available as evidence of the change and its acceptance.

Procedure

Most leases and licences specify in exact terms how notices are to be served, and on receipt of a notice the appropriate clause should be referred to. The following should be checked:

a) the address is that which the lease states is the one where notice is to be served and that it has been so served

b) the time limit within which the lease states it must be served and that it has been served in accordance with such time limit

c) that the notice is issued by the person authorized to do so by the lease terms

d) that the wording is in accordance with that set out in the lease (if any)

e) that any specific method of serving is as stipulated.

If any aspect of the notice is not in accordance with one or more of these require-ments, it may be possible to reject it and for it to be returned to the sender with the advice that it is considered that the notice is invalid. Advice should be taken as minor irregularities may not invalidate it.

Timing

If the notice is out of time, it may be possible to reject it which would mean that either the action the notice was intended to start (e.g. a rent review) cannot commence, or that the action must be delayed until the serving of a fresh notice. Whilst late serving may not normally invalidate the notice, should the termi-nology state that 'time is of the essence' then it may be that the action required is lost. Late serving of a notice of TERMINATION of a lease has the effect of extending the lease term until the expiry of six months from the date of the notice.

Action

Very often the notice will require the recipient to acknowledge receipt with a duplicate notice enclosed for return, and if the lease requires this, it should be complied with. Otherwise the requirements of the lease as to the lessee's action should be checked and carried out to the letter. In replying to the notice of a rent review, the lease may require lessees (if they dispute the figure quoted) not only to object to any figure proposed by the landlord but also to state their valuation of the rent at the review date. If so, a figure should be inserted. Failure to do so may mean that the landlords figure will prevail. The assessment of any counter-offer needs some thought:

- with a lease that has an upwards only rent review (UORR) clause, the current rent should be inserted (since the reviewed rent cannot be less than that figure in any case),

- with a lease where there is no UORR clause, lessees should check local rental levels and insert a figure around (say) 80% of that figure in case rents decline between the date of the notice and of the review itself. In stating a figure, the words 'Without prejudice' should be inserted on the letter or counter-notice. This means that the figure cannot be produced in Court and is a protection in case, during negotiations, the lessee realized their assessment was too high.

Case study

The lease stipulated time limits within which a landlord had to serve notice of a rent review but went on to state that unless the lessee objected within a time limit, the level of rent demanded in the landlord's notice would apply from the review date of six months after the serving of the notice. The notice had to be served on the address set out in the lease which was the unit's address. Unfortunately for the lessee property administration was dealt with in an office some miles from the unit. The notice was served later than the landlord was entitled to serve it, but since it was served on the unit, it was simply filed rather than actioned. Six months later when the quarter's rent at the increased figure was demanded, the lessee, unable to understand the amount required discovered that the landlord had implemented the review at the figure stated in the notice which had not been queried.

Note: In some new leases it is stated that if the review process is not completed within [say] two months of the review date itself, the matter will be referred to a third party. This should be resisted since it puts the lessee under unfair time pressure. If the requirement remains it should be suggested at review that the effect of the clause is waived.

O

Option to break 229

Outsourcing 233

Option to break

Introduction

Generally leases run for a fixed term of years with their original terms punctuated only by regular reviews of the rent. In some instances, however, it may be in the interests of the lessee or the landlord, or even both, to be able to bring the relationship to an end before the natural term by means of an option to break the term.

Grant

Except where both parties agree to vary the term of a lease by agreeing to bring it to a premature end – perhaps because there is the possibility of both acquiring value from a third party by means of a MARRIAGE OF INTERESTS – a lease normally runs until its termination date. However, for a variety of reasons either or both parties might wish to insert in the lease (when negotiating its terms) an option to determine it earlier than its stated expiry date. As far as the lessee is concerned, the operative date of an option to break should follow (rather than precede) a rent review, since in this way the occupancy cost for the period until the next review will be known before the option must be exercised.

Rationale

A break clause could be required to be incorporated for several reasons:

- the lessee does not want to be committed to a lengthy term, particularly where there are upwards only rent reviews

- the lessee (for example, being in a new business) is unsure of the viability of the business and whether it will survive for the full-term of the lease,

- the landlord may want to redevelop the site (for example most of the station-based leases issued by London Transport contain a six month break clause at the landlord's discretion in case they wish to redevelop the station), or

- both parties want to try the relationship which if it works in the short-term can continue but, if it does not, can be terminated.

Implementation

a) Lessee's option

The procedure for generating the break clause is set out in the lease and it is essential that, not only is the exact procedure followed, but also that all other COVENANTS are complied with. The exercise of a lessee's option may not be welcomed by the landlord (since it could result in a loss of rent whilst the property is vacant). Landlords sometimes attempt to resist the exercise of an option by suggesting that, since the lessee has not complied with the lease covenants, they are in breach and cannot exercise the option validly. Thus rent should always be paid on time, the repair and redecoration timetable should be kept up to date and so on.

Note: Sufficient time should be left to allow for any queries to be resolved prior to crucial dates. For example if the lease does not state on whom a notice exercising an option is to be served, clarification should be sought well in advance, with any letter requesting clarification being sent recorded delivery and requesting a reply within (say) 14 days. In the event of any ambiguity advice should be sought.

b) Landlord's option

Again the means and method by which the landlord can exercise the option to break should be laid down in the lease and the exact procedure must be observed.

Termination

The exact way in which termination is effected following the exercise of an option should be laid down in the lease. If the landlord accepts a lessee's option, it is prudent to expect service of a DILAPIDATIONS schedule, and prompt execution of its requirements will be needed to ensure the work is completed prior to vacation. Where the landlord exercises the option, compliance with the requirements will be expected of the lessee although again a Dilapidations schedule may be served.

Awareness

The fact that there is an option should be noted in the property précis and suitable reminders inserted so that if notice is required, preparations can take place in sufficient time to allow all necessary checks to be made. Notices to exercise the option must be served exactly as the lease dictates and a receipt should be obtained in case of challenge.

The fact that there is an option affects the value of the lease. A ten year lease with a five year option is effectively a five year lease and would be valued as such.

Outsourcing

Introduction

Whilst larger organizations may be able to afford to employ a facilities and/or property executive, smaller organizations may need to 'buy in' services in this area from specialist organizations. Obviously this must be paid for and the essential decision to use or not requires analysis of costs – and potential outcome – against the benefit of expertise.

Commissioning third parties

Advantages

- Gaining expertise which may not be available in-house. Specialists should be aware of the latest developments, equipment, processes etc.

- Improving the quality of service. It is unlikely unless an executive is employed solely to concentrate on facilities management that they will be able to spend as much time on the matters as specialists.

- Reducing the in-house work burden particularly if has to be handled by a manager already fully committed in other areas. Although if outsourced, there will still be some residual overseeing and checking compliance with requirements.

- If the bought-in service is to cover all areas, other specific contractors can be released – possibly reducing total costs. Specialists should have access to – and possibly have gained concessionary prices from – contractors to provide such services.

- Availability of input regardless of other considerations or pressure. Having external third parties available at the other end of a phone means a call should be sufficient to gain input releasing the internal executive to concentrate on other matters.

- Predicting and controlling costs. If necessary, suppliers can be substituted. Terms should be set for at least a year ahead, enabling the client to 'buy certainty' not only of cost but also of support.

Disadvantages

- Additional costs. Inevitably a third party will levy a charge to recover their expenses plus a contribution to their profit. Such a price will almost certainly be reviewed each year.

- Loss of immediate control. Placing an additional interface between client and operatives may prevent swift and effective control.

- Difficulty of gaining required attention reflecting the ethos of the organization. This may be a problem when outsourcing to a smaller organization.

- Input will be required to check that the service and quality bought in, is being delivered and thus the internal contact will not be relieved of all their obligations. He or she may need to conduct regular checks to ensure initial and required motivation has not been lost.

- Security and confidentiality may be compromised. Cleaners are very often those who can breach security. Documentation may need to be shredded or otherwise defaced before being collected for disposal. Cleaners are believed to be responsible for the placing of a large proportion of electronic eavesdropping devices.

- Possible breaching of 'Chinese walls'. Chinese walls is the name given to confidential 'barriers' within a third party whereby one branch (or department) of that third party does not release to another branch (or dept.), details of their client or its business. Such protections against knowledge being passed to those in like businesses may not be present. If an organization provides services for a number of competing clients, a confidentiality undertaking should be signed so that details during 'careless talk' let alone deliberate leaking of information does not take place.

Alternative services

The choice is not simply between running the whole internally and handing it over to a specialist. There are several types of 'outsourcing' services:

- a managing agent who can provide all services to the client
- a managing contractor who will oversee the provision of such services which they buy in

- a 'total facilities management' organization whose service-provision can be tailored to the requirements of the client organization and be much wider than the service normally provided by the above two alternatives

- 'property transfer' where the property itself is transferred to an entity which then charges the client occupier an annual charge for using the property including the provision of services which it oversees

- occupying the premises on a basis akin to that of a licensee for a charge which can include the provision of all facility services even including photocopying, reception services etc.

The actual wording of the contract needs careful attention and should not only include the normal terms (e.g. names of parties, date of commencement and termination, notice required, payment etc) but also the following must be delineated: the exact scope of the services being provided, the level to which such services must be delivered (and details of corrective action and timetable where the required level is not achieved), as well as provision for regular reviews, penalties for non- or poor- performance, and so on.

Searching for the provider

Unless the organization has been told of an excellent provider of such services, a 'beauty parade' (inviting a number of providers to quote for the work) should be used. Items to be considered in trying to source the best provider could include:

- references – particularly regarding deliverance, reliability etc

- whether the provider acts for competitors

- how important would this contract be to the supplier?

- size of organization – are there key people and how much time will they have to deal with requests and problems?

- how do they obtain staff (and can the client ensure anyone they do not wish them to continue to use will be replaced?)?

- how will senior staff monitor activities on day-to-day basis?

- payment terms

- contract term, penalties etc

- cost and period of commitment to stated level of cost.

It may be preferable to keep the commitment relatively short, at least initially.

P

Planning 239

Privity of contract 243

Planning

Introduction

Although freehold property owners have wider scope for the use of their properties than do occupiers of leased property (who may need the landlord's consent to vary its USE), both types of property are subject to local planning requirements, and alterations (particularly to the use and/or exterior of the premises) will very often require consent from local officials. On occasion the extent of their powers may come as a surprise. In December 2005, farmers using plastic tunnels to encourage the growth of products in as disease-free environment as possible were astonished when an appeal against the use of such tunnels by a farm in Surrey was upheld. The use of such tunnels is widespread in the UK and it was assumed they did not need planning consent. This decision states that they do.

Scope

The scope of planning authorities (usually the local authorities) is wide and has grown rapidly over a relatively short time. The main principle is that alterations to the use and fabric of commercial properties will almost certainly require planning approval. This could mean that although a design was approved – the material to be used might not be e.g. the white plastic in the tunnels referred to above was one of the bases of the objections to their use. Perhaps using a coloured fabric more empathetic to the countryside would avoid objections to the use. The simplicity of this intent, however, can be contrasted with the complexity of the planning laws and regulations. The following checklist (the first part of which is drawn from the Department of the Environment's own advice) may be a useful guide, however, with anything other than the most routine alteration, expert advice should be obtained, not least since proceeding without consent could incur substantial costs including the requirement to remove and/or demolish any structure or works. The Office of Deputy Prime Minister (ODPM) has on at least two occasions issued somewhat contradictory advice to planning authorities.

Action plan

1. Visit the planning officer. Describe what the organization wishes to do, showing the outline plans.

2. Ask for assessment of whether there seems a reasonable chance of obtaining consent to the current proposals.

3. If not, enquire whether there is any way of modifying plans which would help obtain consent. Sometimes quite minor alterations can ensure approval, whilst if major alterations are necessary, or the entire proposal is unacceptable, knowing this before excessive time and resources are wasted is sensible.

4. Ask advice on various matters: roads, footpaths, power cables, water courses, sewers, telephone lines, toxicity etc.

   Note: Under developing ENVIRONMENT PROTECTION legislation, local authorities have wide powers to prevent land contamination and to require the cleansing of land that is contaminated.

5. Discuss problems re. noise, traffic etc.

6. Discuss whether the authority is likely to apply any conditions and consider the effect of these on the proposals.

7. Query whether publicity of intentions is required.

8. Ask for timetable of planning committee meetings. Since these meetings only tend to be held every four/six weeks, timing, particularly with a complex building operation, could be vital.

9. Check the costs involved. Authorities are allowed to charge for planning considerations up to a maximum of £5500, or even more if the subject is related to the use of land for the disposal of waste etc.

10. Leave plenty of time for the whole process. Informal discussions such as the above can be invaluable but themselves can take time particularly if plans and specifications have to be altered and then put through the meeting timetable.

Designing or redesigning property is (as at the time of writing) required to be rejected if it is 'inappropriate to [its] context...clearly out of scale or incompatible with [its] surroundings'. Local authorities have been instructed not interfere with other people's taste 'except where such matters have a significant effect on the character or quality of the area, including neighbouring buildings'.

Regretfully this may be a question of 'do what we say' rather than 'do what we do'. In Epping, Essex there are strict requirements rigorously enforced by the council which (for example) even prevented a resident matching the windows of an extension to the windows of his existing property which left the house looking completely 'unbalanced'. Perhaps this was reason for the council building itself one of the most hideous offices at the end of what was once a reasonably attractive high street.

In Bournemouth, some years ago the local council allowed not only an even more hideous 'pile' (the IMAX cinema) to be built, but also for it to be positioned right on the sea front, where it squats like a massive concrete alien spoiling a spectacular view of Poole Bay and destroying the charm of the approach to the pier and Winter Gardens (although the planners have an answer for that – they are now going to concrete over the Winter Gardens!). In a 2005 survey for the Channel 4 programme, *Demolition*, which drew 10,000 nominations for over 1,000 buildings, the IMAX monstrosity was voted the 'second most ugly building in Britain' – squatting in a prominent position like a "...neighbourhood bully terrorising the town" as the commentator put it. This is even more apposite in the case of the IMAX since it occupies a prime site but for several years has been empty. A former President of the Royal Institute of British Architects expressed the wish that the survey would lead to a fast track for demolition of the entrants to the survey. Whilst this would assist the outlook in the areas currently blighted, what would be far more beneficial would be a revision of the means by which so many such 'uglies' or 'neighbourhood bullies' managed to pass the planning process in the first place.

Of course, planning considerations (and objections to proposed buildings and alterations) work both ways. If a Facility Manager feels a nearby development affects the 'character or quality of the area' or poses problems to his organization's use of its premises (related to noise, traffic, fumes, access and so forth) he should object. The planning office of the local authority is the first port of call and if they reject the application which is then appealed against, they will be able to provide details of the appeal process and to whom further objections should be lodged.

Listed buildings

The process of planning, renovating and repairing is further complicated if the building is listed. Experienced staff should handle such matters and advice should be taken at a very early stage, particularly since any works already carried out may be required to be removed and the original appearance reinstated. Buying a listed building as a prestige head office may be logical, but there may be constraints regarding alterations to make it fit for its purpose. In addition, its status may also militate against its full value being obtained on disposal: not all prospective purchasers will be interested in a property subject to such restrictions.

Other parts planning applications

Local authorities have powers to grant planning applications and also (and subsequently) to revoke or alter the terms of such permission. Anyone who develops land or erects, alters or extends a building without required permission, can be served an enforcement notice by the planning authority requiring compliance (which could include demolition) with the terms of that order. Planning Contravention notices can also be served requiring the addressee to provide information within 21 days. Failing to comply with a demolition requirement or to provide the information is a criminal offence (see USEFUL CONTACTS).

Privity of contract

Introduction

Until January 1996, leases of commercial properties were subject to the ancient Privity of Contract rule i.e. whoever is the first named in the contract retains liability for the obligations in a lease if they sell their interest and the purchaser defaults. The Landlord & Tenant (Covenants) Act 1995 abolished this rule for all leases entered into on or after that day although landlords can require prospective purchasers to give GUARANTEES (which to some extent may have the same effect as the old privity rule) by insisting the lessee enters into an Authorized Guarantee Agreement (AGA).

Definition

Under Privity of Contract, despite subsequent assignment (sale) of the (leasehold) interest in a lease, the original lessee retains the ultimate liability to the landlord for payment of the lease outgoings. The effect is that if the original lessee (X) assigns his interest to a new lessee Z the landlord gains privity of estate against Z. If Z defaults, however, then the landlord can recharge X with the amount of the default. Although initially X may be able to protect his position by checking the financial probity of Z, taking up references etc, this provides no long-term guarantee. He could ask for a deposit of one year's rent in case of default although this may prove impossible to attain. Such protections (limited as they are) are, however, of little use to X, if Z assigns his interest to Y and Y then assigns the interest to W, as it is unlikely, even if X knows of the further assignments, that he can have any control over them. The situation is even worse for individuals that may have given guarantees regarding the original lease to X. If X defaults (e.g. ceases trading) the landlord may well have a right of action against the guarantors. Even though the original lessee retains a financial obligation if later assignees default, it has no right of re-entry to the premises to minimize costs by (for example) using it himself. Obviously once the lease terminates by effluxion of time or by the valid exercise of an OPTION to break, the privity rule ceases to have effect. However, whilst it does, original lessees would be prudent (if allowed by the lease) to consider underletting rather than assignment. Then if the person, to whom they have underlet defaults they can regain possession.

The new law

The 1995 Act's main provisions are as follows:

a) If the lease allows unrestricted assignment, then an assigning lessee is released from the obligations under the lease on assignment.

b) If (as is more usually the case) the lease allows for assignment subject to landlord's consent, then the landlord can impose conditions e.g. that the assigning lessee agrees to guarantee the performance of the incoming tenant to the lease obligations. This is known as an Authorized Guarantee Agreement (AGA).

In such circumstances, of course, the assigning lessee would still be liable in the event of default – but only for the default of the assignee to whom he sold the lease. In the above example, X would be liable if Z defaulted, but not for the defaults of Y or W. If the new lessee wishes to assign then the landlord can ask for another AGA to be entered into – in the example Z could be asked to enter into an AGA in respect of Y and would be liable if Y (only) defaulted and Y could be asked to enter into an AGA in respect of W and so on. The conditions under which an assignment can be granted can be agreed by the parties at the time the lease is negotiated.

c) As far as rent and service charges, the guarantee of the original lessee is restricted to those amounts demanded by the landlord within six months of them falling due. This proviso applies to ALL leases whether they came into operation after 1st January 1996 or were already in existence then.

d) If a lessee is required to pay arrears they can require the landlord to grant them a lease of the premises, thus giving them a new right of occupation of the premises.

Effect

It was anticipated that the effect of the new law would be that landlords would refuse to allow rights of assignment in new leases, although this does not seem to have happened. The counter to that was that lessees would ask for much shorter leases, or require the inclusion of break options, in order to retain flexibility – which is what has happened. Since 1996 the average term of a lease has fallen from 16.8 to 10.7 years and currently 50% of all leases are for five years or less – although this may also be partly a result of the refusal of landlords to abolish the requirement for upwards only rent reviews which are manifestly unfair to lessees.

Q

Quiz   249

Quiz

Introduction

The following case study demonstrates the dangers of signing a lease without fully appreciating the commitment and potential downside. It is based on a real-life situation. It is not a difficult quiz as suggested answers are included as part of the case study but at least its inclusion allows us to complete the alphabet with the only Q we could think of!

Case study

1. The proposal

a) X's son wished to start his own business. A shop was found with a lease with two years unexpired. X agreed to pay £10,000 to the existing lessee for his lease, to gain the advantage of the £18,000 rent then being paid (against a market rent of about £23,000).

b) The premises were in a poor state of repair, and X obtained an estimate that to put them in a state where they could be used for the business would cost around £50,000.

2. The agreement

a) X then agreed to pay the landlord a £10,000 premium for a NEW 15 year lease (with five year reviews and an option to break at year four), commencing immediately at a rent of £23,500 p.a. (The logic of this decision is difficult to understand.)

b) The new lease contained a repair clause which required X to 'put and keep' the premises in a decent state of repair.

3. The problems

a) The idea of buying the tag end of a lease for a speculative project is sound. The tenancy would be protected under the Landlord and Tenant

Act and, on termination, unless the landlord wanted the premises for his own use or for redevelopment, X would be entitled to another lease. Alternatively, after two years X can simply walk away from the commitment – thus flexibility is obtained which is particularly valuable should the business not be profitable.

b) Paying a premium to an existing lessee is logical since the existing lease has a value, its rent (fixed for another two years) being less than rents currently being paid for other shops. However, the existing lease had repairing obligations and the original lessee was responsible for these. Asking for permission to assign the lease would normally prompt the landlord to ensure these repairs were carried out by the existing lessee which would at least be fair since it was during his tenure that the 'damage' occurred.

c) If the repairs were not to be carried out by the existing lessee, X should have had them costed and then insisted either the landlord require the existing lessee to carry them out, or used the estimated cost to reduce or eliminate the £10,000 premium X had agreed to pay, and/or to gain a rent free period whilst the repairs were completed.

d) If the works were not carried out, X could have commissioned a 'schedule of CONDITION' stating (with photographic evidence) the state of the premises stipulating that the repairing obligation on him should be limited to bringing the premises to that and, no better, standard.

e) It might be appropriate to pay a premium for a new lease in certain circumstances, for example, if demand is high for a limited number of properties. The logic here, however, seems odd particularly since the rent for the new lease was at the market rent. Why accept a new lease at £5,500 p.a. more than the existing lease when you can purchase the old lease at a lesser rent?

f) In addition, why go for a new lease with a speculative project? It will probably be known within two years whether the business is viable or not. If it works, a new lease could be negotiated two years down the track; if it doesn't, X can get out of the commitment. With the new lease he doubled his time (and cost) commitment – to four years at least.

g) The one saving grace was the option to break. However, options can be resisted if a lessee fails to comply with lease covenants. Normally it is better to have the date for the exercise of the option following the agreement of a rent review (so that the lessee already knows his future rental commitment) rather than preceding it.

h) Lessees should always avoid 'put and keep' repair clauses: they are an open-ended commitment to the landlord. Here the previous lessee seems to have escaped his liabilities completely leaving X with full commitment and a rather expensive route to gaining a lease to which he is committed for at least four years.

R

Rating   255

Reinstatement   261

Relocation   263

Rent review   271

Repairs and redecoration   285

Risk management   287

Rating

Introduction

Local authorities funding is derived from central government, from occupiers of domestic property via their Council Tax payments, and from occupiers/owners of commercial property situated within its boundaries (via commercial rates). The Council Tax is set by each authority and is a personal tax, whilst the rates on commercial premises are calculated by reference to rateable values of individual properties multiplied by a uniform business rate (UBR).

Uniform Business Rate (UBR)

The UBR was introduced in 1990 at a rate of 34.8p with the intent of being increased annually in accordance with the movement of the Retail Price Index except at the time of a revaluation. This did not happen and at the time of writing the UBR is 44.4p – an increase of 28% after 15 years – well under the rate of inflation for the same period.

Rateable Value (RV)

The Valuation Offices of the Inland Revenue are responsible for assessing the RV of every commercial property. The RV is supposed to equate roughly to the open market rental value of the property. The resultant collection of all RVs becomes the Rating List. To avoid the necessity to revalue every commercial building each year, the RV for new or altered buildings is determined by reference to the valuations of similar properties forming part of the existing rating list. This reference to the 'datum' level of rental values is referred to as the 'Tone' of the Rating list.

Rateable revaluations were intended to be carried out every five years usually resulting in an upwards movement, although due to the slump in demand for property in the early 1990s, the 1995 revaluation showed some substantial reductions from the previous (1990) figures which were arrived at in the aftermath of a property boom.

Amount due calculation

From the Inland Revenue list, each authority extracts the RV for the properties in its area. Under the old system of rate calculation the authority would divide the amount of revenue it needed to raise from the occupiers of business premises in its area, by the total of the RVs of those properties to arrive at a 'rate in the £'. Under the system introduced in 1990 (for England and Wales, the system for Scotland having been introduced earlier) a UBR was established by central Government and commercial rates paid became the product of the new RV multiplied by the UBR.

Central government's intentions

The government at the time of its introduction stated that it intended to increase the UBR and thus the costs of rates by no more than the annual rate of inflation. However, the effect on an individual commercial occupier has varied widely as a result of the five yearly rating revaluation. Following the 1990 revaluation, rates for commercial properties in south-east England rose far more than rates for properties in the north, whilst office and retail premises rates rose more than those for warehouse and factory premises.

Conversely, in the 1995 revaluation which followed the then general slump in property values, many rateable values in the south showed a reduction which was not duplicated in the north.

There was no revaluation in 2000 but the 2005 revaluation has given rise to considerable increases in south east England with much lower increases across the rest of the country – a complete contradiction of the original Government prediction of the revaluation having a 'neutral effect'.

Transitional relief

To offset the impact of the increased costs, transitional relief is available to occupiers in residence, which effectively spreads an increase over a five year period. Similarly, any occupier with a potentially large saving has the annual effect limited by the same phasing concept. There are special arrangements giving relief to small businesses and individual application should be made to the local rating office.

Appeals

Under the previous rating system, the appeal process could be (and often was) used as a device for delaying payment since as soon as an appeal was lodged, rates did not need to be paid. Under the current system, appeals can only be lodged in special circumstances with a Valuation and Community Charge Tribunal (VCGT) whilst in the meantime the rates stated as being due must still be paid. If there is any reduction and thus an overpayment has been made, repayment will be made subsequently. The circumstances under which an appeal can be lodged are:

i) if there is a change of occupation, and the assessment has not previously been tested by a Valuation Tribunal

ii) if there is a change in the property or its surroundings (e.g. if there is considerable rebuilding or redevelopment in an adjoining building)

iii) following the issue of a Notice of Alteration by the Inland Revenue Valuation Office altering the RV. In this case an appeal must be lodged within 28 days

iv) following a decision of a Valuation Office on an appeal concerning a property which affects the RV of the subject property

v) if the assessment refers to a single occupation and is occupied in parts (or vice versa).

Rating appeals can be complicated as there are strict procedures to be observed and expert assistance should be sought. A number of organizations offer such a service, often on a 'no benefit, no fee' basis which can be attractive. However, the skill and experience of some such organizations is suspect and it may be better to use qualified surveyors who specialize in the matter (see USEFUL CONTACTS).

A ratepayer's appeal must follow a number of stages which are codified within the Non-Domestic Rating (Alteration of Lists and Appeals) Regulations 1993 (SI 1993 291). Generally appeals must be made within a year of the creation of a new rating list i.e. following a revaluation. However, in addition to this general right, if a ratepayer feels that the current assessment is incorrect on the basis of the circumstances set out above, then within six months of the change of circumstances a note of the basis of the appeal must be sent to the local Valuation Officer. Within four weeks the Valuation Officer must either acknowledge or reject it as invalid. ODPM has announced a relaxation of the rules so that appeals can be lodged at any time.

An appeal does not have to be in a set format but Valuation Offices have model forms and can advise on their completion. It may be advisable either to deliver the proposal by hand, obtaining a receipt for it at the time, or to send it by recorded delivery. If no reply has been received, a check regarding receipt should be made.

If the proposal is acknowledged, the Valuation Officer will either agree it (and must then alter the Rating List within six weeks) or, assuming he wishes to object, will pass the proposal to the Valuation Tribunal where it will be listed for hearing before the Tribunal. A Tribunal must give 28 days notice of the hearing to both parties. Evidence is normally verbal although written submissions may be allowed. The evidence (i.e. details of rents of other properties in the area) is normally required to be exchanged at least two weeks before the hearing.

The hearing

At the Tribunal the ratepayer can present reasons for requiring the value to be altered, and the Valuation Officer cross-examines this evidence. The Valuation Officer presents his own case which the ratepayer can cross-examine. The Tribunal make their decision, usually orally following the hearing, followed by a written decision. Both parties have a right of appeal to the Lands Tribunal within 28 days of the written decision.

If the Valuation Officer rejects the proposal as invalid, within four weeks the ratepayer must lodge a further proposal. If the ratepayer feels the original proposal had validity, within four weeks of the rejection a notice of 'disagreement' must be served on the Valuation Officer. Within a further four weeks the Valuation Officer must either have accepted the proposal (and passed it for altering the rating list) or lodged an appeal with the Valuation Tribunal where it proceeds as above.

If the ratepayer feels that the original rejected proposal can be amended to meet with the approval of the Valuation Officer then a fresh proposal should be lodged and the process set out above is followed. This amending of an original appeal can only be done once.

Although Tribunals are informal, they can only decide on the basis of the evidence produced. Collecting, collating and presenting evidence is time-consuming and requires considerable attention to detail as well as knowledge of the rating basis, procedure and jargon. As suggested above, appeals may be best handled by experts.

First occupation

When occupying premises, rates become payable from the date when beneficial occupation commences for trading purposes. Authorities view 'occupation of part' as 'occupation of whole' and thus, if even only a small part of new premises is occupied, rates may be payable from that moment on the entire property. The occupier should consider this rule when planning phased occupation, and will also need to confirm the effective date of occupation, to the appropriate authority – although some leeway may be obtained. Authorities can investigate instances of abuse.

Assessment of new premises

Following a notification of occupation, the authority requests the Inland Revenue Valuation Office to make an assessment, which may take several months. On receipt of the Assessment the occupier may appeal against it if he considers the proposed RV is not in accordance with the Tone of the list.

Alternatively, within six months of occupation, and providing there has been no prior proposal, the occupier, being an interested party, has the right to make his own proposal. This should be served on the Valuation Officer who has six weeks to serve a counter-notice stating if he considers it invalid. The occupier has four weeks to appeal against the counter notice. If the Valuation Officer disagrees with a proposal then he must refer it to a VCGT within six months.

Empty property

During the property boom of the 1970s some landlords developed the strategy of keeping property empty whilst rents increased in the hope of achieving a better return when the property was let. To counter this, local authorities were able to charge double rates. This move was countered (particularly as the boom ended) by landlords removing roofs of buildings so that they were unusable and therefore rates could not be levied. Generally, where a property is vacant in most instances local authorities will not charge rates. However, rates are chargeable from the moment the property is 'occupied' (which may be taken from the moment any furniture or machinery is installed).

Case study

In *Hampson t/a Abbey Self Storage v Newcastle upon Tyne Council* it was held that the occupier of premises which, for rating purposes had been divided into seven different premises, did not have to pay rates on those premises (four out of the seven) for the periods for which they were 'non-occupied'.

For rates to be payable four criteria must be satisfied. There must be:

- actual occupation or possession
- exclusive occupation for the particular purposes of the occupier,

whilst possession

- is of some value to the possessor, and
- is for some period which is not transient.

Reinstatement

Introduction

Although landlords will normally allow lessees to carry out alterations to their premises, usually this will be controlled by the landlord stipulating that he be given full details of plans, specifications etc and granting authority to the lessee to carry out the work under a licence or deed of variation or similar legally binding agreement. Regardless of the manner under which authority is granted for the works (it may be possible to gain permission simply by the land-lord signing and returning a copy of the plans covering the works) almost certainly the lessee will be obliged to undertake reinstatement (that is putting the premises back to their original state) before the termination of the lease.

Commitment

With a reinstatement clause or undertaking, the lessee can face a triple cost, since the costs of:

a) the original works

b) the removal of those works (under reinstatement provisions), and

c) making good all damage occasioned by the works being removed (under the same provisions)

must each be met.

On some occasions of course the landlord may prefer to leave the lessee's works in place as they may enhance the appeal of the premises to a new lessee.

Reinstatement may not be just a question of cost but also of time – since the landlord will normally require all works to be completed prior to the expiry of the lease. This could impact the use of the premises in the last few months of the term. If completion of the works is after the lease termination date, rent may continue to be chargeable. It may be possible to negotiate an arrangement whereby the lessee pays a sum to 'escape' the reinstatement liability. How much that will be depends on the negotiations but anything which is less than the combined costs of reinstating and making good is likely to be advantageous particularly as not only will the commitment be known, but also the lessee will avoid the inconvenience of the building works taking place probably whilst they are in occupation.

WARNING: When taking an assignment of a lease, the situation regarding lessees works, and reinstatement in respect thereof, should be checked to ensure the assignee does not acquire an onerous liability, or that due allowance is made for the potential cost in the deed of assignment.

Evidence of the state of the premises

Reinstatement entails putting the premises back to the state they were in before the lessee's works. If the term is of any appreciable length, however, it may be difficult for either party to recall the original state of the premises. It may be preferable to prepare two CONDITION schedules: one showing the premises before the works and one afterwards. The extent of the works can then be evidenced as well as the 'original state' to which it must be returned – which might even encourage the landlord to waive the reinstatement requirement.

Relocation

Introduction

Research indicates that, on average, UK businesses move once every eight years. Virtually every move – even a 'churn' (that is a move within an existing building) – entails a major upheaval and can impair productivity and profitability. Most relocations are dictated by external factors (end of lease, redevelopment of property, requirement to vacate, etc) but there can be other reasons, and a prime consideration should be to define exactly why it is the business wishes to move and then delineate where ideally it wants to go and to what kind of facility. In late 2005, Donaldsons, a leading firm of property consultants, published the results of research regarding lease TERMINATION. This stated that the cost of relocating at the end of a lease on an average building of 20,000 sq ft in the Home Counties could be £1.5 million more than one that had been arranged in advance since 'few companies left enough time to move'.

Financial opportunities

Some organizations have been able to reduce costs and thus increase profitability by relocating the whole or part of their operation away from expensive areas. For example, several companies in the financial services industry relocated from London to Bristol in the mid 1980s. Most managed to dispose of their more expensive offices in London and reduce both location and personnel costs by acquiring property and recruiting employees in the West Country. Had too many operations decided to adopt the same policy, the decision as it affected the last to move could have been flawed e.g. the market in London would have fallen due to a glut of empty offices, whilst the market in Bristol would have risen due to the increased demand. Unless the financial benefits are very large it may be better not to take such a relocation decision purely on financial grounds. (There is a fabled 'rule' which proposes that savings are always 50% less than forecast whilst costs will be 50% more than anticipated!)

First considerations

A move is a major project requiring a considerable amount of planning, organization, arranging, talking (and listening) – all of which are time-consuming, require considerable attention to detail, and have attendant costs. It should not be embarked on lightly – the task is often underestimated. The following are the main reasons prompting a move:

i) Inadequate accommodation and facilities – for example size and/or quality.

ii) Revision or change of business strategy and plans.

iii) Accommodation costs e.g. unsustainable increase in occupation costs.

iv) Change of product mix meaning previously suitable premises are no longer appropriate.

v) Combination of these and other, less important, considerations.

In fact many organizations move because of the combined effects of deficiencies at current locations – rather than a single defect – and because of the defects of existing premises rather than the attraction of new. In other words, they are forced to move, which entails a move under pressure and with insufficient time – not usually a recipe for a successful move.

Appointing the team

Best practice would suggest the project being undertaken by a small team headed by a project manager (PM). That team's remit is to:

- assess the gains and losses

- prepare a budget

- determine the new location

- source a building

- plan a layout

- communicate with all involved

- liaise with all the external agencies

- plan the move (which may be complex depending on the amount of production or computer linked facilities which are to be relocated or the distance between the old and new locations)

- check that all facilities required will be installed at the new location, and

- deal with post-move challenges, and so on.

The project team may best be split into two:

- an external body dealing with the sourcing, acquiring and setting up of the new location (which could include the PM, administrative support, architect, engineer, quantity surveyor, builder, secretary) and

- an internal body dealing with the requirements of personnel and processes required to move (which could include the PM, administrative support, production and office representatives, communications, finance and personnel managers, secretary).

Being on both teams, the PM should provide continuity and inter-communication. Minutes of the meetings of both teams should be distributed widely and could use the 'named person action required' format (i.e. placing the initials of those responsible against the items they are expected to action – possibly with target dates to be met) to engender swift action. Depending upon the complexity of the move and the timescale, meetings of both teams may need to be held monthly, fortnightly or weekly, (the intervals between meetings shortening as the project nears completion – with virtual daily updates as the move becomes imminent).

General considerations

a) Dilution of management attention on the move can create business control problems and there may be an advantage in having as the PM a person (possibly an outsider with relocation experience) able to concentrate on the project exclusively without the distractions of in-company responsibilities. Obviously such expertise needs to be funded.

b) A relocation can have a major impact on staff morale and also potentially on output and productivity – hence good communication is essential although sometimes the need to keep the decision process confidential creates problems among managers who want to take key staff into their confidence and to gain their input.

c) Although the UK is a small country, even a minor move may create problems for both organization and employees relocating. Employees asked to move from south to north may be worried whether, if they ultimately wish to move back, they would be able to afford to re-enter the expensive southern housing market; whereas those moving from north to south may see problems in their current disposable income being decreased – and their 'quality of life' being impaired.

d) Delays are among the greatest problems encountered in moving. Whilst individual delays can be countered, often the problem is the domino effect: earlier delays causing increasing delays in later stages. In generating a timetable the team should consider including 'buffers' of additional time to absorb delays.

e) Employee communication. It is vital to keep everyone involved informed at all times. In advance of discussion or communication of the decision, the organization should decide its relocation assistance package. Once it is known that the organization is moving, those affected will be concerned about their own position and the sooner reassurance (or, at least, certainty) is given, the better for productivity etc. Specific advice may need to be taken on this if experienced personnel staff are not available in-house.

f) Suppliers and customers also need to be made aware of developments – if only to re-assure them regarding future business and supplies. It may also be necessary to advise them regarding any suspension of supplies or re-direction of deliveries.

g) If the raw material being used is heavy and/or bulky and the finished product is small/light it may be cost effective to move nearer the raw material supply. If the reverse is true – it may be better to move near the market. The value of the services on which the organization draws in its current location should not be overlooked – they may only supply minor items but sometimes production lines can be halted for want of one customized bolt.

Identifying the ideal new site

The type, size and character of the new location itself must be identified. To some extent this might be determined by analysing what it is about the current site that no longer makes it viable. The following parameters could be examined:

- Availability of required type of space. Unless there is a reasonable supply of the type of space required, acquisition costs may be disproportionate.

- Existing workforce retention and changes. The skills required for the business in its current location may not be available in the new location unless the workforce – or at least key workers – move with the business. Labour costs and skill availability can have a major impact on a preferred site.

- Design and construction. Specific requirements can narrow the availability of the type of facility being sought.

- Specific needs of occupier.

- Competition for employee and/or products. Neighbours in potential areas may have demand for the skills of recruits the organization requires to replace those not moving with it.

- Systems, spares and equipment support. Some organizations, particularly in manufacturing, may find that in some new locations support for spares, particularly of a bespoke nature, may not be available as quickly as in the previous location.

- Transport (of employees, raw materials, products etc).

- Customer and supplier expectations.

- MAINTENANCE.

- Potential demand in event of disposal. The acquisition of an unusual property (that is one with specific characteristics) may be entirely suitable but could pose a problem of disposal because of those same characteristics.

Location criteria

Criteria for the ideal site/location should be identified, although ultimately some of these may need to be compromised. The following are examples of the initial criteria used by two organizations contemplating relocation searches.

EXAMPLE A

- 30,000 sq ft
- good eaves height
- parking area
- room for expansion
- public transport access
- trunk road access
- residential area
- good delivery access
- light and spacious conditions
- part-time staff available
- within two/three mile radius of Head Office (which was not itself moving)

EXAMPLE B

Initial requirements

- flat green field site
- freehold
- power supplies
- minimum 35 acres (preferably 40)
- no manufacturing neighbours
- high water purity

Detailed requirements

- good communication links (export outlets)
- reasonable access of existing company distribution centre
- good access to international airport
- assistance/grants available (see below)
- component vendors locally

The more specific are the requirements for a new site the longer should be the time allowed for finding and fitting out. Indeed, the benefit of a longer time span is that those responsible for property negotiations are not then pressurized to find a site and/or forced to take 'second best'. Someone who knows the property market in the area of search, needs to be involved. Local agents may well have access to local information which is not generally known and even though there may be a 'finding fee' this might be worth paying.

Note: In Relocation B above, the search was carried out for an organization from the Far East seeking to open a European unit. The search covered the UK, the Netherlands and Germany. Despite the fairly detailed checklist a site in the UK was chosen mainly because there was a preference for an English-speaking workforce. This was a major factor, which despite a considerable amount of thought, was overlooked in the original list, demonstrating how essential it is to delineate exact requirements.

Labour requirements

The specific requirements of the organization in terms of human resources may also need to be delineated, for example:

- availability for general or specific skills
- skilled mechanical and electrical technicians available
- availability of training establishments
- good industrial relations in area
- good supply of local housing
- possible local authority assistance.

Relocation is not just about moving people and processes – that is machinery and machine minders. There are, in addition, all the support services, offices, canteen, reception, as well as stocks and stores, records and record containers. Raw materials, supplies etc may be best run down prior to the move – with later deliveries made to the new site. If so, goods inwards and security staff will be needed at an early stage at the new location.

All facilities under consideration should be fully surveyed. If the building is new, then a list of any defects will need to be prepared and the situation regarding defects liability clarified. If the building is older, then the responsibility for repairs and redecorations needs to be established (usually with a lease this will fall to the lessee, so the wording of the lease needs careful checking).

Services

The services needed to operate the premises must be identified although in a relocation most of this information should be available from the records of the premises being vacated:

- **Electricity**. The development of technology tends to create an ever-increasing demand for electricity and an adequate supply capable of coping with demand for at least (say) three years into the future should be provided.

- **Gas**. The deregulation of the industry means that there is greater competition. However, all suppliers will need estimates of annual and daily consumption. Indeed, the business will want to generate this information to ensure it is placed on the most economic tariff.

- **Compressed air**. Safety considerations mean that often compressed air is used rather than an alternative energy source. The provision needs to be made as comprehensive as possible during fitting out. A site must be provided for the compressor which can create noise and vibration problems – not only for the organization but also for NEIGHBOURS.

- **Water**. Increasingly water companies require supplies to be metered and this may be price advantageous – at least in the short-term.

- **Heating, air conditioning etc**. Whilst these services must or could respectively be provided, care must be taken to ensure that emissions from the equipment are dealt with properly to avoid breaching environment protection legislation.

Fitting out

Customizing an existing property has three implications – consent must be obtained to the works being carried out, time must be allowed to carry out the work, and the costs must be funded. See BUILDING WORKS and LESSEES WORKS.

Post-relocation checks

Ideally the relocation team should be kept in operation to ensure back-up and problem solving whilst the new location and staff settle down. The aim in the first weeks post-move is to recover the pre-move output figures, and then to move smoothly past those figures, and the fact that those responsible for the move are seen to be available may provide valuable morale support. It is also essential that the old site, if not disposed of at the time, is not forgotten. If left unoccupied, it will need security and repair protection until disposed of.

Financial assistance

a) Under the Local Government, Planning and Land Act 1980 the Secretary of State for the Environment can designate areas of the country as Enterprise Zones. As well as the fact that relaxed planning rules apply in the zones, 100% capital allowances are available for industrial and commercial buildings for the ten years during which each zone can exist.

b) Under the DTI Enterprise Initiative there are three types of regional assistance:

i) a Project Grant based on the fixed cost of a project and on the number of jobs the project is expected to create or protect,

ii) a Training grant, and

iii) Exchange Risk Guarantees (which covers borrowers in the UK against exchange risk on foreign currency loans) and grants may also be obtainable from the European Union.

Rent review

Introduction

Reviewing the rent of a lease at predetermined intervals has been the custom for over 100 years. When inflation was low, review intervals could be as long as 21 years but, particularly since the Second World War, much shorter intervals – seven, then five and, in some cases, even three years – have become almost compulsory. Whilst the need for the landlord to ensure their return keeps pace with market forces and inflation is understandable and logical, there is an inherent bias against lessees since they are committed to the balance of the term regardless of the rent being charged. During the 1970s this bias became even more acute as institutional landlords increasingly insisted that on review the rent could **only** be increased (or remain at the same rate). Such 'upwards only rent reviews' (UORR) became the norm in leases. Since the UK recession of the early 1990s, however, demand in some areas for property has fallen – and so have asking rents. In these circumstances it cannot be assumed that at every review date that a rent will rise.

Initial considerations

It is very important that the detail in the review clause is carefully examined and discussed as part of the initial 'lease terms' negotiations. For example, any improvements in value created by the lessee (alterations to the property, goodwill resulting from the lessee's occupation, etc) should be excluded. Some leases stipulate that a certain unexpired term should be assumed, even if this is not the reality of the situation.

For those not conversant with the requirements surrounding the determination of the review, a surveyor or property consultant may be best retained. The temptation to 'do it oneself' to save a professional's fees could be false economy if the result is that too high a rent is agreed, bearing in mind that the increase is not a one-off payment but is charged every year until the next review – and, of course, that rent becomes the starting point for the following review.

Administration

a) Timing

The requirements of the review clause must be strictly followed – particularly any which impose a time limit. Clauses vary from applying strict time limits for the serving of notices and counter-notices, possibly (if time is stated to be 'of the essence') meaning that a review could be missed if the time limits are not observed, to being so loose that even though the review date has been passed, notice can be served and the review completed, with any uplift in the rent back-dated to the review date. Clauses can:

- allow the notice to be served well past the review date but stipulate that the increased rent will not be payable 'until agreed', and/or

- state that unless the review is agreed within a set time it will automatically be referred to a third party.

b) Basis for assessment

The bases on which the review is to be agreed are set out in the lease. Astute landlords will incorporate wording which enables them to charge as much as possible. Conversely lessees will wish to pay as little as possible. The most common bases often inserted in review clauses include the following:

- **Open market rent**. This can be fair to both sides provided there are no restrictions in the lease which apply to the lessee. However, if there is a strict user clause, since it could only appeal to a limited number of lessees who could comply with such a user, the 'open market rent' basis should be rejected.

- **Vacant possession**. In times of buoyant demand property may command a figure higher on the open market than it would with a lessee – particularly if a user clause is restrictive.

- **Length of lease unexpired**. During the life of the lease the unexpired term decreases – as does the value of the lease to the lessee. If, at review, the lease requires the term to be considered as full, even when there is only (say) five years left, the two parties will probably have a differing view of an appropriate rent.

- **Good state of repair**. With a full repairing lease this should have an even effect on both parties. However, if the lessee does not have responsibility for repair, but the landlord does and does not comply, the lessee could be disadvantaged as rent would be based on the property being in a good state of repair when it may not be.

Case study

In *British Telecom v Sun Life Assurance* the Court of Appeal held that where a term in a lease obliged the landlord to keep parts of the property not occupied by the lessee in good repair, the landlord was obliged to keep those premises in repair at all times. The landlord could not have 'a reasonable time' within which the defect should be rectified, but was required to carry out the repairs immediately.

- **Unrestricted assignment and underletting**. If assignment and underletting are at the discretion of the landlord, or are not allowed, then stating a review must be calculated as, if it is allowed it is manifestly unfair to the lessee.

- **Lessee's occupation, goodwill and works**. Stating that additional rent in respect of the lessee's occupation and goodwill should be ignored is fair to both sides. However, if a lessee's works are to be included in the valuation then that is decidedly disadvantageous to them since they will have paid for the works and could, at review, also be charged rent for the works if these have increased the value of the premises (see LESSEE'S WORKS).

- **Floor areas**. The area of the premises must be calculated accurately. Offices are usually valued on a net internal floor area basis; industrial buildings on a gross internal basis and retailing in accordance with ZONING. The problem with calculating areas is that it is amazing, with two people measuring the premises independently, how different they can make the totals, so agreement on the areas should be agreed at an early stage either by negotiation, by reference to previous review measurements or possibly by carrying out a joint measuring session. Conversely arguing about the floor areas may be a valuable stalling device which can be used to 'wear down' the opposition with the purpose of winning concessions.

- **Assumptions re. rent review pattern**. If it is specified that the rent is determined on the review pattern in the lease, this should be reasonable to both sides. However, some leases specify that rent is to be determined (for example) without regard to the review pattern. Since such a wording would be very valuable to the landlord, this could have the effect of inflating the review figure.

Procedure

The review procedure should be laid down in the lease.

i) Usually this will commence with the landlord serving a NOTICE in accordance with the exact requirements of the lease as regards timing and service.

ii) In response to this 'review notice' lessees are often required to serve a counter-notice and if so the exact requirements must be complied with. Some leases, for example, require lessees not simply to respond but also to do so within a specified time and to state the amount they are prepared to pay.

Case study

If time is 'of the essence' should a lessee fail to respond as required to the landlord's notice then it may be that the right to challenge the landlord's figure will be lost – the House of Lords ruling in *United Scientific Holdings Ltd v Burnley Corporation.*

iii) Assuming notices and counter notices have been served, the parties should agree the floor area and, if applicable, any zoning.

iv) The bases on which the lease states the rent is to be determined may or may not be discussed. Since the review process may become a bargaining session, it may be that these matters will not be mentioned initially but used as negotiating points later.

v) Normally the landlord (or agents acting for them) will produce evidence that supports their contention that the rent should be increased. Such evidence should be a reflection of the current rental trend of comparable premises in the locale. Such evidence may be selective, and evidence which does not support the required increase may not be mentioned. There may also be an element of bluff involved in that salient features of the rents quoted may be suppressed. For example, rent of (say) £60,000 may be quoted for the property 'next door' but the fact that the landlord gave an inducement of 12 months rent free may not be disclosed. Since effectively this means that in the first five years the lessee will only pay £240,000, it makes the effective annual rent £48,000.

Similarly, the fact that the review pattern is seven as opposed to five years, which gives that lessee an advantage, might not be disclosed. Lessees should ask for details of the sources of all such information (including names, addresses, telephone numbers etc) so such 'evidence' can be checked independently.

vi) Evidence which negates the landlord's figures and supports the lessee's contention that the increase should be (normally) as small as possible (or even nil, or reduced if there is no UORR) should be presented. This should be sourced, preferably from surveyors who have acted for other lessees in the neighbourhood since they will usually have available the exact terms agreed. If not, then evidence should be sourced direct from other lessees. However, some lessees are very reticent about giving out such details and/or may not know the actual basis of settlement. Nevertheless, even outline figures may assist and, after all, if one side has difficulty obtaining such figures, so too may the other side.

vii) Size is not always indicative of usefulness. In shop, office and warehouse rents the configuration of the unit may militate against its effectiveness. Although floor areas may be identical, if the unit is (for example, triangular or round as opposed to oblong or square) there may be 'corners' or areas which are impossible to be used. In those cases a discount from the overall rent should be sought.

Obtaining evidence

Many lessees when asked for details of agreements, prefer to see something in writing rather than disclose information over the phone or even during a personal visit. The following letter could be used as a draft to source such information.

Name of organization

ADDRESS OF PROPERTY UNDER REVIEW

I am engaged in a rent review of my organization's premises at the above address. Our current rent is £xxxxx p.a. and we are being asked to pay £yyyyy. We believe that it is important for all occupiers that rents out of line with market values should not be agreed, and it would be very helpful if you could confirm the details regarding the premises (address shown below) if leasehold that you occupy. May I thank you in advance for your assistance. Needless to say we are willing to provide you with evidence of the rent that we agree, if and when your own property is subject to review. Should your review/renewal have been dealt with by advisers I should be much obliged if you could pass this letter to them with your request to provide assistance.

PROPERTY ADDRESS _____

OCCUPIER _____

TENURE: _____ Freehold/Leasehold (or Licence)

Note: If freehold – no further action is required – thank you.

LEASE TERM: _____ years from _____ / _____ / _____ to _____ / _____ / _____

USER CLAUSE: _____

RENT FREE PERIOD: _____

Please specify any period allowed at nil or reduced rent. _____

REVERSE PREMIUM (if any): £ _____

Please specify any amount paid as inducement to take new lease. _____

REVIEW PATTERN: Reviews every _____ years

LAST REVIEW: _____ / _____ / _____ RENT AGREED: £ _____

OBLIGATIONS: Insuring/Internal repair/External repair_____

_____ *(Please delete as applicable)*

ACCOMMODATION: Self-contained shop/office/workshop/warehouse _____

Shop/office/workshop/warehouse with shared entry _____

Upper part / flat / storage / garage _____

SUBLETS: £ _____

Please give details including rent of any sublet.

DIMENSIONS: Width _____Length _____

A rough indication of all relevant dimensions would be helpful.

FLOOR AREAS: Basement_____Ground _____

First _____Second _____

Other _____

_____

ZONING: A B C ETC

AGREED ZONE A: _____

OTHER FACTORS: (Please specify any restrictions on use or other factors which could affect the rental valuation e.g. does Privity of Contract apply, is rent subject to VAT, etc)

_____

RENT FREE: (Please specify any period free of rent granted)

_____

CAPITAL CONTRIBUTION: (Please specify if applicable)

_____

Note:

1. Stating details of one's own property may encourage others to disclose their property details.

2. A reverse premium is a sum of money paid by the landlord to a prospective lessee in order to encourage them to enter into a lease.

3. If a lessee receives such letters from other parties in the locale it may be prudent to respond providing the details required and keeping the correspondence so that when a review is implemented there are contacts from whom information can be sought to obtain evidence.

4. Rent free periods and capital contributions (amounts paid by the landlord to assist the lessee fitting out the premises, etc) have the effect of altering the value of the passing rent.

5. The process by which a rental level was arrived at can also be challenged.

Case study

Maynews has a property in a suburb of Leeds. The landlord was being particularly bullish about a forthcoming review and quoted details of a high rent achieved for a neighbouring property that had been newly leased to a high street chain. However, on investigation it was discovered that this letting had been achieved as a form of 'Dutch auction' where two parties had been asked to submit sealed bids of the rent they would pay. Since both were seeking representation in the area they had been forced to pay over the odds to acquire the empty unit. This is hardly open market letting – the basis set out in the Maynews lease – and could thus be discounted.

Determination

With their evidence, the parties try to negotiate a mutually acceptable compromise. The tone of negotiation will depend on the aggressive or otherwise stance of the parties. Some landlords attempt to gain every advantage from the review process – some take a more long-term and pragmatic approach to it. Disagreement is inevitable since the parties have diametrically opposed interests. If agreement is not possible, or not possible within any time limit laid down in the lease then normally the landlord (and sometimes either party) have the right to appoint a third party to determine the review.

A 'third party' is usually appointed by the President of the Royal Institution of Chartered Surveyors (RICS) which lessees could be forgiven for thinking does not seem to be a particularly impartial body (since surveyors fees are related to rents – the higher the rents the higher their fees). More frustrating to lessees is that the RICS will not become involved in disputes regarding the appropriateness of the appointee. Leases generally require the parties to have reached a point where their negotiations have stalled, but landlord's applications to the RICS have been successfully made when no negotiations have actually taken place. Since, in any event, the lessee has to bear part of the cost of the third party appointment, such recourse without the courtesy of any negotiations can be frustrating to a lessee.

After application to the RICS, the office (one of three that the RICS has set up to deal with such applications) notifies both parties of their involvement and selects a Chartered Surveyor knowledgeable of the area in which the subject property is located. If such an appointee is unacceptable to either party (for example, a lessee might not have a normal working relationship with a nominee following an earlier dispute) it may be possible to object and for an alternative to be proposed.

Type of appointment

The basis under which the third party (either as arbitrator or expert) will act should be set out in the lease. An arbitrator acts in accordance with the Arbitration Act and to some extent attempts to find a 'median' position 'fair' to both parties based upon what the parties themselves say. An expert, however, can rely on his/her own knowledge and expertise in addition to that put forward by the parties. An Arbitrator has powers to obtain documents by legal discovery, compel the attendance of witnesses and can hear evidence on oath but an expert does not normally have such powers unless granted by the lease.

The format for the arguing of the case before the third party is determined by the third party setting out a timetable and procedure to which the parties must adhere. They may be asked to attend a meeting to argue their cases or alternatively (and more likely) to make written submissions to the third party. Each party's submissions are set to the other party and each has an opportunity – in a counter submission – to argue against the other party's evidence. Although arguments against statements can be made, the parties may not be allowed to introduce new evidence or facts at this stage. This will be laid down by the third party and may have the effect of forcing both parties to put forward their best case in their first submission.

The third party, who will normally have visited the property and the area, considers the counter-submissions, and makes a decision. The decision is made available when the parties have paid the third party's fees. If the third party acts as an Arbitrator the decision is an Award; if acting as an Expert, it is a Determination.

Fees

A third party's charges tend to be around 5% of the average between the parties original rental estimates. Thus, if the landlord stated they estimate the rent at £40,000 but the lessee felt it was £30,000, the total costs to be charged by the third party would be 5% of 50% of (£40,000 + £30,000) or £1,750. Additionally, the third party's expenses and VAT on the total must be paid. Normally the parties will pay around 50% of the costs each, however, the third party can determine that one party should pay a greater proportion than the other. This might be the case if it is felt that one party has been obstructive in dealing with the review, or acted unreasonably, or been guilty of slowing the process unnecessarily. Since the parties will not know of any split of the costs until they read the determination it is usual for both parties to send the third party 50% of the total cost in order to obtain the decision, and then if there is any split on another basis, for an appropriate adjustment to be made. Alternatively the landlords, who will usually have instigated the appointment, may pay the entire fee to obtain the decision swiftly and then recharge the lessee.

Confirmation

Once the review is determined, either by a third party or by the parties by negotiation, it should be evidenced in writing by means of a Rent Review Memorandum the wording of which should be set out in the lease. Some leases, however, require the landlord's solicitors to prepare such a Memorandum and state that the lessee must pay for it. Given that the purpose of the review is (usually) to allow the landlord to collect an increased rent this may seem iniquitous. All that is required is a simple form of words such as that shown in the draft below. Generally each side should bear their own legal costs (a principle set out in the Cost of Leases Act 1959) however very often this also becomes a matter of negotiation.

REVIEW MEMORANDUM dated _____ to be attached to a LEASE dated _____ and made between _____ (the landlord) and _____ (the lessee) relating to the premises known as _____

By this Memorandum dated _____ 2XXX, the landlord and the lessee hereby record that the rent payable under the lease has been reviewed pursuant to the terms thereof and fixed at [AMOUNT IN WORDS] [AMOUNT IN FIGURES] PER ANNUM exclusive payable from and including the [DATE OF REVIEW] until [DATE OF NEXT REVIEW, subject to further review as provided in the lease] or [DATE OF TERMINATION].

Signed by _____(the lessee) in the presence of

Witness (name) _____

Address and occupation _____

Signed by _____(the landlord) in the presence of

Witness (name) _____

Address and occupation _____

Of course it is possible that at review there may be a nil increase. Even though the rent continues unchanged it may be advisable for this to be stated in a memorandum in which case the following wording might be used in substitution for part of the above draft.

REVIEW MEMORANDUM

Pursuant to and in accordance with the provisions of the lease dated [date] and made between [parties] [name of landlord] the landlord (being the present landlord of the property) and [name of lessee] the lessee being the present lessee of the property, have agreed and determined that the rent payable in respect of the property with effect from [date] being the date on which a review of the rent was due is to be [amount – which will be the same amount as that being paid in respect of the previous review period].

Signed etc. (by both parties)

Once the rent is agreed either by negotiation or by the third party, the amount determined becomes the rent required under the lease and must be paid (with any arrears and interest, if any) by the lessee. If there is no increase it may be advisable nevertheless for a memorandum to be prepared evidencing that the existing rent is to continue to be paid. If there is no UORR of course the new rent might actually be less than that currently being paid.

Cost-effective approach

Rent can be a major factor of business expense and it is normally entirely appropriate for a hard line to be taken by a lessee in trying to reduce a rental figure asked for by a landlord. Thus pushing the determination to a third party may be logical. However, such determination is risky and the effect of the costs to be borne need to be considered.

Case study

A lessee had a shop unit slightly off the main area of retailing demand. The landlord asked at review for a rent of £40,000 – a 100% increase – using the rents in the prime area (which commanded proportionately higher rent) as its evidence. By negotiation the asking price was reduced to £30,000 – still a 50% increase. However, the lessee did not feel the rent should be more than £27,500 and believed they had evidence to support it and that the landlord had not given enough recognition to the fact that the shop was not in a prime position. It was decided to resist to the point of third party determination, particularly as there was no interest payable in respect of a late agreement on review, and the determination by a third party would take at least two months. It was pointed out that to incur a third party determination, a surveyor would need to be appointed to prepare the submission and any counter-submission (fee plus expenses say £1300) and the lessee would also bear at least 50% of the costs of the third party. Since the lessee's opening submission would be £22,500 and it was estimated that the submission from the landlords would start at £35,000 this would cost (including expenses) around £1500.

It was felt that for a one-off cost of around £2,800 it was worth forcing the point. In the event, the third party was required to act as an expert. As a result of his own investigations, he discovered additional evidence that neither party had put forward and determined the rent at £30,000. In addition, he determined that the lessee should pay 75% of his costs.

This demonstrates the risky nature of the process. Indeed even had the expert accepted the lessee's assessment, the first year's gain (£30,000 less £27,500) would have been virtually wiped out by the costs involved. Had an offer of, say, £29,250 been made, the landlord might have accepted.

Analysis

Very often the landlord will require the lessee to evidence the analysis of the rent agreed. Lessees may best try to avoid this since it provides evidence that can be used in other negotiations and indeed there are several ways of splitting the total to reflect the various aspects of an agreed figure, particularly in retail leases. A form such as the following may be required.

PROPERTY _____AREA _____UNIT _____

Landlord _____

Lessee _____

Agent _____

Lessee Agent_____

Lease terms – that is the basis on which the review was required to be agreed.

_____

Current rent_____Effective date of review _____

Agreed new rent _____

ANALYSIS	USE		SQ.FT	£PER SQ FT
SUBTOTAL				
Floor areas	Basement	Store		
	Ground	Retail		
	Ground	Office/Store		
	1st floor	Store		
	2nd floor	Store		
ALLOWANCES/ADDITIONS				
		Use	%	
		Prominence	%	
		Return frontage	%	
		Awkward shape	%	
		Agreed rent	£	

Approved by landlord/agent _____

Approved by lessee _____

Note: Percentage allowances are set out for a number of bases. If use of the premises is restricted by the lease then a discount must be allowed for this. Similarly, an allowance may be granted because the shape of the unit does not lend itself to ease of use, and so on.

* *

Renewal

On renewal, if the lessee wishes to remain in occupation, the main item to be agreed is the rent. A similar process of each side putting forward rental evidence is used. However, should the parties not agree terms, reference has to be made to the Court for determination. Of course, at renewal the landlord's protection of 'upwards only' rent reviews is lost. If surrounding rents are static (or even falling) landlords can protect their position by 'inactivity' i.e. not terminating the lease but simply letting it run on at the existing rent. In such a case the lessee can terminate the lease (by giving three months notice) with the aim of being able to renegotiate the rent referring to open market evidence without being hampered by the 'upwards only' clause. This, however, has a danger since if the lessee gives notice they lose the protection of the Landlord and Tenant Act and have no 'right' to a new lease. If the landlord could find an alternative lessee the original lessee could be out of the location.

Repairs and redecoration

Introduction

Some of the most important – and potentially expensive – lease COVENANTS undertaken by the lessee are those requiring that the premises be kept in a good state of repair and be redecorated regularly. Non-compliance can be sanctioned by the issue of a DILAPIDATIONS schedule and non-compliance with that schedule is not only a further breach of the lease potentially leading to its forfeiture, it also gives the landlord the right to enter the premises, carry out the work and to charge the costs to the lessee. Such costs will almost certainly be greater than those the lessee would have incurred had they commissioned the works themselves (not least since the landlord must manage the works) – and probably far more than would have been incurred by complying with the repair and redecoration covenants in the first place.

Reasonable state

The fact that the premises must be brought to 'a reasonable state' – the wording used in most leases – does not mean the premises must be in excellent condition. Defining what is 'reasonable' may be difficult, particularly if the building is old – or has been well-used. It is usually easier to keep a new building (erected with the benefit of modern materials etc) in a good state of repair and redecoration than an older building.

Accordingly standards of reasonableness may vary and if a dilapidations schedule has been served then, following the completion of the works, the landlord or his surveyor should be invited to inspect the works and, with the lessee, jointly agree a list of any items which are not at the standard required. This may result in argument and/or negotiation, particularly if the lease is nearing the end of its term, since the landlord will want the property in good condition particularly if it is to be marketed to prospective lessees.

The materials used in carrying out the repairs and redecorations should be of good standard but wording that appears in old leases such as 'paint with three coats of oil paint' should be challenged since using modern materials should remove the need for multiple coats – indeed repeated application could be detrimental.

Frequency

Redecoration is normally required every three or five years externally and five or seven years internally. In addition a final redecoration may be required in the last year of the term. Failure to comply with regular redecorations is widespread but may be short-sighted as landlords rely more and more on the use of Schedules of Dilapidations to force compliance. Paint can sometimes conceal serious problems and compliance with redecoration clauses may avoid needing to comply with far more onerous requirements. The best solution may be to prepare a redecoration programme, to develop which the preparation of a property register with the layout illustrated in KEEPING THE RECORDS may be invaluable. An 'at a glance' projection of the salient aspects of properties occupied provides a yearly guide to those obligations. There may be leeway in the timing of the works. For example, in some cases, the redecoration schedule may mean that there is an obligation to carry out such works in consecutive years. In a 13 year lease, with an obligation to externally redecorate every four years and in the last year, the lessee would have to redecorate in both the twelfth and thirteenth years of the term. It may be possible to gain a concession from the landlord to combine the two – or simply to ignore the requirement in the twelfth year providing it is carried out in the thirteenth.

Risk management

Introduction

Employers are legally required to control the risks to which all users of premises – employees, contractors, and visitors – might be exposed, and to bring these to their attention. Risks thus need to be assessed but although it is sensible to remove any risks that can be removed, or to try to mitigate their effect, there is no requirement to eliminate risks – not least since it will be impossible to eliminate them. An employer's duty is to identify the risks and communicate them to those who could be affected.

Obligations

By virtue of their commitment to the requirements to which they must subscribe for their shares to be quoted on the London Stock Exchange, listed PLCs are required to adopt the Turnbull Committee recommendations regarding risk assessment. However, these recommendations can usefully be applied to all commercial organizations. 'Turnbull' requires Boards of Directors to assess all the risks to which their organizations could be exposed and to take action to prepare contingency plans and minimize risk. The recommendations suggest that:

- internal risk control should be embedded in the company processes. This means that at every stage, risk should be considered. It should not be seen as a separate exercise,

- the Board should prepare and regularly review contingency and disaster recovery plans,

- risk control should be responsive to changing circumstances, in particular to new risk areas,

- organizations should customize their plans, allocating the responsibility to a senior member of management to ensure the matter is given a priority,

- management at all levels should be involved and given clear objectives which should be checked for completion,
- the responsible manager should identify all risk areas, prioritize such risks, establish risk management reduction programmes, and regularly update the procedures.

Assessment of risks is increasingly required (see new FIRE legislation) of all bodies, for example governors of State Schools, despite them being unpaid volunteers, have a legal obligation to prepare and update disaster recovery plans; they also have potential liability in the event of failure.

Preparation

The foundation for any risk management process is the preparation of risk assessments. Normally there is little that is difficult about their preparation other than where there are complex working environments or specific dangers, and thus there should be no need in most instances to commission experts. Assessments may be best compiled by those in charge of the operation – after all who should know the operation better? A standard format should be used, particularly if the assessments are to be compiled by several managers. Each assessment should be reviewed every time there are changes in:

- working practices or procedures
- the environment and/or facility

and perhaps, if neither of the above have occurred in the previous year, at least once a year.

Content and purpose

An assessment of risk:

- seeks to identify all the hazards posed in a particular situation
- considers ways in which, if possible, hazards can be minimized or eradicated
- identifies who it is that is at risk
- evaluates the risk, the likelihood of occurrence, the number exposed to the risk, the severity of injury and the existing control measures

- decides on any necessary new control measures to reduce or eliminate the risk

- implements the controls and monitors their effectiveness

- records the assessment and brings it to the attention of those affected

- sets a timetable within which the situation will be re-assessed or reviewed.

Some risks cannot be removed or even minimized and where this is the case, the risk must be brought to the attention of all likely to use the area and suitable advice provided. Property administrators should consider the competency of those likely to be at risk and take note where skills, experience etc are not felt capable of dealing with the risk – and make suitable arrangements to protect those at risk. Risk assessments should be prepared throughout the operation and made available in written form – although this would not prevent an employer being held liable if a risk could have been minimized or removed and was not, or suitable preventative measures, which could easily have been implemented, were not in place.

Case study

In *R v Rhone Poulenc Rorer*, an engineer went on to the roof of an industrial building. Like many such roofs it was not designed to bear the weight of a human being and a notice stated the roof was fragile and that 'crawling boards should be used' was displayed. Ignoring this advice he stepped onto the roof plunged through and was killed. His widow sued the company whose defence was that because he was an engineer and thus competent, he must have known the risks and they could rely on the notice. The Court stated that they could not rely on a sign: there needed to be practical preventative measures.

Many may think that the Court was asking an impossibility and that the engineer was master of his own destiny. However, there are steps an employer could – and currently would – be expected to take. Preparing a risk assessment along the lines of the following might provide a defence.

Example

The employer could stipulate the following:

1. Roof work is restricted to competent personnel.

2. The work to be done must be assessed and the dangers identified and minimized or removed. Those that remain must be brought to the attention of those involved and a plan of work prepared.

3. Roof access is only possible via possession of a key, retained by a manager

4. The manager, when asked for the key, must:

   a) ensure the person is competent to undertake the work

   b) accompany the person to the roof (i.e. not simply hand him the key).

5. Before opening the door, the manager must state that access would only be granted on condition that the crawling boards provided would be used.

   (The employer would need to be able to show that these were in good condition and fit for their purpose to avoid liability.)

6. The manager must instruct the person to put on a full protection harness which, if he did fall through, could prevent him hitting the ground.

7. Before stepping on to the roof, the person might even be required to sign a statement that all the foregoing had been explained to him.

8. Whilst the roof door was open, the manager must remain there to ensure no-one else (unless under the requirements set out above) went onto the roof. Obviously the manager would not be able to force the employee once on the roof to wear the harness (or to stop him removing it if donned prior to access) or to use the crawling boards, but should an accident occur in those circumstances it seems likely that the Court would feel that the occupier had done as much as they could to protect the person and thus liability might be avoided – or at least minimized.

Note: This is an example only – a detailed risk assessment would be needed.

Examples of areas of attention

There are many areas where attention needs to be directed to ensure safe use – and to avoid abuse not only in terms of personal danger, but also security generally. Most risks can be reduced by the introduction of procedures and checklists which are regularly policed, breaches are investigated and those responsible made subject to sanction. Requirements regarding pregnancy risk assessment is an example of an area related to property occupation. Just under 50% of the UK's working population are female and a considerable proportion of them are in the age range usually regarded as being of 'child bearing age'. Research indicates that although most UK employers know they are required to prepare risk assessments generally, far fewer know that under the Management of Health and Safety at Work (Amendment) Regulations 1994, employers are required in anticipation of a woman of child bearing age entering their employ to carry out an assessment detailing risks to a woman and her unborn child that are inherent in the workplace (i.e. the property) as well as those related to the procedures on which she is engaged.

A. Maternity

Case study

In *Day v T. Pickles Farms Ltd*, the EAT stated that if an employer fails to assess the risks to a pregnant woman in the workplace (or even fails to carry out such an assessment in the anticipation of a woman of child bearing age entering their employ) this amounts to a detriment within the meaning of the Sex Discrimination Act 1975 and thus the employer could be liable for discrimination penalties.

The risk assessment process (which covers those who have recently given birth and are breastfeeding as well as pregnant women) requires employers:

a) to assess all risks to which such employees might be exposed

b) to ensure they are not exposed to those risks, and

c) if a risk remains, despite preventative and other actions, terms of work (hours, place, etc.), to offer such employees alternative work or grant them paid leave if this is not available.

The HSE identify five general risks that there are to pregnant women in the workplace but these should be taken as guidance only since each workplace will inevitably be different. Each employer should identify the particular risks related to their own operation

1. Working with unhealthy substances

Perhaps the most widely encountered substance with which a pregnant woman and new mother might come into contact is lead. Any use of lead should be identified and women of child bearing age prohibited from working anywhere near its use or handling products which have been in contact with lead.

Similar restrictions apply to a range of other substances -e.g. radioactive material, whilst under the Control of Asbestos at Work Regulations, those who occupy buildings as well as those who own them have an obligation to identify, record, monitor and assess the risks from asbestos in their building.

2. Violent or stressful environments

What some people find acceptable, others may find stressful e.g. some people can stand loud music, others cannot. The environments within which people work should be assessed and, those working in areas felt to be potentially stressful should be specially advised and if and when a woman states she is pregnant she should be asked if she wishes to transfer elsewhere. The situation of a pregnant or new mother working within an environment which is 'rough' or 'tough' or in any way violent, needs to be assessed very carefully with specific guidance depending on individual problems and risks.

3. Lifting

Employees are generally prohibited from lifting loads heavier than around 20 kilos or 55lbs without manual or mechanical assistance. However, applying this weight restriction could be unwise for many pregnant women and a more realistic maximum load is perhaps 4 kilos or 10lb. The volume of a package is also important since a light weight but bulky object might pose considerably greater danger than a small but heavier item. This may be particularly a problem in office environments e.g. simply dealing with stationery supplies.

4. Confined working space

The simple increase in body size due to pregnancy, can create problems of its own if the working environment is at all confined or small, or there is a restricted access etc. Such items should be identified. If it is impossible to change them, the possibility of the woman working elsewhere should be considered.

5. Using an unsuitable workstation

Where the woman is using a visual display unit, the ergonomic arrangement of such equipment may often leave much to be desired. Whilst this may be acceptable in the ordinary course, there may be specific dangers to a pregnant woman whose condition requires attention to posture etc. Those using VDUs should:

- have a comfortable, adjustable chair – with good back support
- have a surface which allows them to position the VDU at least 25cms from their head and provides sufficient space for other working papers
- have a monitor which is not situated so that it creates a reflection or glare, and generates minimal radiation
- keep the screen clean and adjust brightness and contrast to create a good working light
- take regular rests (not necessarily from work but from the VDU work) and allow the eyes to refocus on a more distant subject than the VDU screen
- sit so that the wrists are parallel with the keyboard, 'float above it', and can rest on a support regularly
- place the feet either on the floor or on a raked footstool to remove strain from the back; thighs should be parallel with the floor.
- either the user should face any window, or natural light should be capable of being filtered with blinds or curtains.

Possible procedure

1. Accompanied by a pregnant woman (or a woman who has given birth) tour the whole area where the pregnant woman/new mother might work – identify all risks.

2. Consider whether any risks can be removed or minimized – and, if so, implement changes to effect this.

3. List risks which cannot be removed and/or minimized on a written risk assessment.

4. Immediately a woman indicates she is pregnant, give her a copy of the risk assessment (possibly touring all the areas to which she will have access and identifying the risks with her).

5. Invite the woman to advise the employer if she notes any additional risks so that the risk assessment can be updated.

6. Regularly review and update the risk assessment.

Action

If there are serious risks, during the time she continues working, a pregnant woman has a right:

a) to have the risks removed from her normal place of work. If this is impossible then she can

b) carry out her work elsewhere where there are no risks. If this is impossible then she can be asked

c) to work on other tasks (without any detriment regarding salient features of her contract – hours, pay, benefits etc). If there is no work she can undertake she has the right

d) to be suspended on full pay until such time as her maternity leave commences.

B. Terrorism and criminality

Some practical suggestions regarding precautions related to the effects of terrorism are made in that section. However, employers are responsible for the safety of their employers and thus failing to prepare assessments of risks associated with the effects of terrorism could mean that an employer could be held liable. Similarly, where the activities are such that there is a possibility of employees being injured as a result of other criminal activity, the employer could be held liable. For example, banks and building societies try to protect their employees by installing glass or metal grills which can be activated at the touch of a button to protect both them and the money. Since hold ups are an occupational hazard for such properties, failing to provide such protection could itself mean the employer could be liable in the event of any injury.

Case studies

In *Dutton & Clark v Daly*, a building society clerk who had experienced two armed raids, resigned and attempted to claim unfair constructive dismissal. However, it was held that since the employer had taken steps to protect employees (installing screens etc) that these could not reasonably have been improved upon and her claim failed.

In *Keys v Shoefayre*, however, when an employee after a robbery was told there was nothing that could be done and resigned, she successfully claimed unfair constructive dismissal, since her concerns were dismissed without investigation.

C. Young people

Young people are perceived to be particularly at risk – not least since due to their inexperience, they may be unwilling to speak out about their concerns. Thus employers are specifically required in respect of those under 18 to assess the risks to which they could be subjected and take action to:

- minimize these
- take into account their inexperience within the working environment
- consider whether any of the work (and risks attached thereto) prohibit execution by young people
- inform parents and guardians of the risk assessment.

S

Safety communication	299
Security	307
Service charge	319

Safety communication

Introduction

Under the Health and Safety and Welfare at Work Act (HASAWA) 1974 employers have an explicit legal requirement to provide a safe place of work for their employees and their visitors. They must also provide a Safety Policy for each property in which work is being carried out, and must bring the contents to the attention of those employed and/or working in those premises. The facility administrator needs to ensure that not only are the premises subject to HEALTH & SAFETY considerations but also that occupants are advised of this. Ideally, a copy of the Safety Policy should be given to every person using the facility. This provides a prompt for action as well as a criteria for guidance. Increasingly property occupiers can expect to become answerable if injury or death occurs in premises under their control (see RISK MANAGEMENT).

Consultation

Under Health and Safety (Employee Consultation) Regulations, employers must consult with their employees on matters of health and safety which affect them, and are required to provide:

- employees with all information so that they can participate fully in such a consultative process

- representatives elected by their employees with suitable facilities and paid time off for training and to carry out their duties.

Promulgation

As well as giving every individual employee a copy of a Safety Policy, it may be advisable to post in every place of work (and on every floor where there is multi-floor occupation) a readily identifiable and visible folder within which could be kept a number of documents for individual and ad hoc reference. The (visible) front sheet of such a folder could include a checklist of items demonstrating the time each was checked (for example, fire evacuation, equipment inspection dates etc) so that employees own viewing of the folder can operate as a reminder if it is too long, for example, since the last time there was a fire evacuation practice.

Such a folder (see following example) could contain details of those responsible for safety, the safety policy, a reminder diary, FIRE and FIRST AID procedures. It could also contain a supply of hazard reporting forms, the principle behind which is that the sooner the organization knows of a hazard, the better the chance of avoiding injury by being able to effect some remedial work.

WORKPLACE SAFETY

CONTENTS

1. Safety and First Aid Policies (& date of last issue)

2. Fire escape precautions procedure (also posted on fire exit routes and by fire alarms)

3. Hazards in workplace – assessments, list, plan, procedures and risk prevention data

4. Accident/Hazard report forms

PERSONS RESPONSIBLE

At workplace _____

In organization _____

POLICY

Accident and hazard reporting procedure:

The [organization] wishes to hear immediately of any hazards or potential hazards occurring in the course of its operations. To do this it has devised Hazard Reports (HR) (supply in this wallet) which can be completed by any employee becoming aware of a hazard. HRs are to be passed to the person responsible at the workplace and by them, to the person responsible in the organization (see above). HRs should also be used to confirm details of all accidents which may need to be reported under the Reporting of Injuries, Diseases, and Dangerous Occurrences Regulations and/or recorded in Accident Book B1510.

DIARY

Staff reminded of fire procedure precautions   Date_____

Most recent fire drill (check Fire Certificate for obligations
for frequency – usually twice p.a.)_____

Staff reminded of danger areas_____

Staff reminded of hazard coping/reducing/procedure _____

Staff reminded not to tamper with machinery etc. _____

Equipment inspection dates Item _____

                            Item_____

                            Item_____

[Note: Dates are included so that all can see the last time an item was 'examined'. If the last date entered was some time previously this should act as a prompt for further attention. Thus the pressure of employees' attention can be harnessed. A similar tactic applies to the provision of Hazard reporting forms in each folder.]

Health and safety policy

1. AIMS

a) To ensure, as far as is reasonably practicable, the health and safety of all employees whilst at work.

b) To comply with all relevant health and safety legislation, regulations and codes of practice.

c) To provide safe and healthy conditions of work, plant and systems.

2. RESPONSIBILITIES

Of company

i. To work towards the achievement of these policy aims.

ii. To provide appropriate training, advice, protective clothing, equipment and documentation as is necessary or advisable.

iii. To carry out assessment of risks and endeavour to reduce or eliminate these.

iv. To provide written systems of work for all and any procedures which are exposed to hazard.

v. To record notification of hazards and accidents and incorporate improvements suggested as a result of investigations conducted following such notifications as soon as possible.

Of [named director]

To ensure that all the requirements of this policy and ancillary procedures are implemented with the overall aim of ensuring as safe a place of work as is possible.

Of managers and supervisors

i. To be responsible for the execution of the safety policy as far as the department/employees for which he/she is responsible.

ii. To be responsible, as far as reasonably practicable, for the safety of all persons working in or visiting his/her department, and for all plant/ equipment under his/her control.

iii. To ensure, in the event of accident, that prompt and appropriate First Aid is administered, that further medical assistance is obtained if necessary, that the circumstances of the incident are investigated and reported on, and that recommendations made as a result of an investigation are implemented.

iv. To ensure the Workplace Safety folders are kept and displayed, that their contents are brought to the attention of every employee, and that all employees are conversant with such data.

v. To ensure protective clothing/equipment is used at all times where and when necessary.

vi. To ensure that employees are conversant with the accident/hazard reporting procedure and that notification of hazards is passed to the appropriate person for action.

Of employees

i. To make themselves familiar with, and adhere to, safety procedures, including the fire alarm procedure and evacuation route(s).

ii. To wear protective clothing/equipment as and when necessary, and to report any defects in such clothing/equipment to their supervisor.

iii. To report all accidents/incidents to a supervisor, and to carry out instructions given by a supervisor.

iv. To report all safety and health hazards and machinery defects using the Hazard report procedure.

v. To co-operate with the organization at all times on matters of safety

Of safety representatives (if applicable)

i.   To assist the employer (and employees) in the assessment and reduction of risk and hazards, by being aware of the implementation and effect of procedures and work in the workplace.

ii. To advise the employer on matters of concern evinced by employees and liaise/help in rectification thereof.

iii. As a member of the Safety Committee to take full part in its deliberations and operations.

Of Safety Committee (if applicable)

i.   To further the interest of all involved in the reduction and/or elimination of risk, or, failing this, of its control.

ii. To advise management on safety matters.

iii. To assist in the education of employees in operating safe working practices.

iv. To raise awareness of the need for high-profile safety policy/procedure.

3. ADMINISTRATION

The Safety Director is [name] and is responsible for overall attainment of safety principles and the creation of places of work that are as safe as reasonably practical.

The Safety Officer is [name] (Deputy) and is responsible for:

i.   Preparing, reviewing and updating this Policy, accident/hazard reporting procedures, fire and safety procedures and evacuation guidance.

ii. Accepting and actioning Accident/Hazard Report Forms.

iii. Ensuring compliance with the responsibilities laid down in this policy. statement – and reporting failure to comply to senior management for sanctions to be applied.

iv. Liaison with health and safety offices, insurers, factory and environmental health officers, fire brigade etc and ensuring appropriate recommendations are effected.

v.   Implementing the requirements of the Reporting of Injuries, Diseases and Dangerous Occurrences Regulations 1986 (RIDDOR) and all such other legislation or requirements as may be enacted from time to time.

Signed _____Managing Director _____Safety Officer

Date of issue_____To be reviewed on [date]_____

(FIRE PRECAUTIONS procedure – see separate section)

HAZARD REPORT FORM

Organization name _____

To: Safety officer/facilities manager   From: Name _____

Date: _____Safety Rep. for _____Area*

Time: _____Form number _____

Place: _____

Please note that at the above time/place I became aware of what I consider to be an
unsafe/unacceptable / dangerous *

building or part thereof*

practice,*

machine,*

procedure,*

other (specify)*

Comments/additional information _____

_____

Signed _____ Date _____

Copies: Safety committee, works manager * Delete as necessary

- -

ACKNOWLEDGEMENT/REPLY SLIP   NO_____

From: Safety officer/facilities manager   To: _____

Date: _____Time: _____

Thank you for bringing the details set out on this HR to my attention. I am arranging to take
the following action _____

_____

Signed _____Safety officer/facilities manager   Date _____

Since legally employers are required to try to make the workplace as safe as possible for both employees and visitors and advance knowledge of a danger provides an opportunity to avoid accidents, an effective hazard reporting process could be invaluable. RISK ASSESSMENTS (RA) are legally required for all workplaces, and notification of hazards can provide information to help update RAs.

Personal liability

Since 1980 there have been over 30,000 deaths and serious injuries at work in the UK for which employers may have been responsible. During that period there have only been a handful of successful prosecutions of those believed to have been responsible – all of small organizations. This trend is stated to be due to the fact that success is easier when prosecuting smaller companies as the 'controlling mind of the organization' can be identified. Cynics might comment that it is more likely to be due to the fact that larger organizations are able to afford the best legal defence. To try to bring those culpable to justice, it is currently proposed to implement new 'corporate killing' legislation which could result in the fining of an organization held responsible for death or serious injury of an employee, worker or member of the public.

Earlier suggestions that prosecutions could be brought against individual directors and managers which, if successful could have resulted in a sanction of imprisonment of anything between five years and life, have been dropped, but the employing organization could still be held liable – for an unlimited fine.

To be held culpable an organization must:

- owe a duty of care to the victim connected to work undertaken by it,
- be in breach of that duty of care in the organization of its activities, and
- be responsible for the victim's death by its managerial failure.

The breach of the duty must be gross (i.e. 'conduct falling far below what can reasonably expected of the organization in the circumstances')

Security

Introduction

Security challenges arise in a wide range of circumstances. These could include admitting and controlling visitors (and resisting and/or rejecting the unwanted), dealing with deliveries to the premises, preventing confidential material finding its way into the possession of those antagonistic to the organization, trying to prevent theft from the organization's property and minimizing the potential risk as a result of unwanted visitations (e.g. from TRESPASSERS).

Visitors

Visitors should only be able to enter via a 'guarded' main entrance. Although control is understandably important, in the current climate, it is preferable always to require visitors to sign in AND out – an aspect overlooked by many. Some organizations require visitors to wear a badge – although, again, those who either refuse to wear it and keep it in their pocket or who lose it are rarely challenged mainly since employees seeing a new face can, understandably, assume that the person is a new employee. Perhaps the only way round this is for everyone authorized to be in the building (i.e. whether employed or visiting) to be required to wear identification at all times – at least then visitors feel less like a 'package'. A system such as the following might be used

❋ ❋

Administration procedure

A. Employees
   1. Employees can only gain access to the premises of the organization using the electronic key cards (issued on commencement of employment) in the employee entrances. The card must be inserted each time an employee enters or leaves the premises. The use of an individual's card is restricted to the person named on it.

2. If an employee loses their card the fact must be reported to the [Facilities Manager (FM) or Personnel Administrator (PA] immediately and a new card obtained. In the event of second or subsequent replacement cards being required, the company reserves the right to charge for these.

B. Visitors

3. All visitors are requested to sign in on a daily registration sheet in Reception. They are required to state their time of arrival, name and organization, the name of the person they are visiting and, if their car is parked on the premises, its registration number.

4. Each visitor will be given a badge bearing a reference number (corresponding to the number in the registration sheet) and a copy of the security guide (see below).

5. A copy of the [organization's] health and safety policy will always be displayed on the coffee table in the Reception area.

6. At the end of their visit, the badge and guide must be returned to Reception and the person should sign out on the registration sheet indicating their time of departure.

7. If a visitor remains after Reception has ceased to be manned, the person they are visiting is responsible for complying with item 6 above.

8. Reception staff are responsible for keeping the registration sheets, replacing pages each day, ensuring badges are returned, checking discrepancies, and reporting them to the FM or PA. The sheets will be kept for one year.

9. Employees wishing to arrange a site visit for members of their family, or for members of a school or other organization, should apply to the PA giving full details of the organization, numbers involved etc. Visits are restricted to one each month, so it may be necessary to book such a visit well in advance. All members of a party visiting the premises are subject to the rules that apply to employees: they must keep to the designated routes, wear appropriate clothing and observe all necessary safety and other rules.

10. Children under the age of 12 are not normally allowed in the plant. Employees who require children to attend the plant (e.g. to await the end of a shift being worked by a parent/guardian/relative) should make arrangements with the PA for the child(ren) to wait in the [specify] Department. Employees are fully responsible for the actions of their child(ren) whilst on the premises, and the organization will not accept any liability arising as a result of this concession

C. Security guide

'Welcome to [organization]

In the interests of your own safety please take a few seconds to read the following:

1. Visitors are required to announce themselves at Reception, to sign the daily registration sheet, to wear the badge given to them at the time and to return it to Reception on departure, noting their time of departure on the registration sheet.

2. Visitors must be escorted at all times.

3. If the fire alarm [description needed] is activated, please evacuate by the nearest Fire Exit to which you are directed and assemble at [location].

4. All visitors are covered by, and expected to comply with, the [organization's] health and safety policy, a copy of which is available for inspection at Reception.

5. In the event of a visitor suffering an accident, a First-Aider should be summoned. Visitors are expected to act in accordance with the suggestions made by the First Aider.

6. Visitors are requested to respect the [organization's] non-smoking policy.

If visitors are to wear badges and to register on arrival, then the requirement that they surrender their badges and sign out (or are signed out should they leave after Reception has ceased to be manned) should be strictly enforced. Failing to collect badges could mean that either accidentally (by being discarded carelessly) or deliberately, undesirables can obtain evidence of apparent access authority.

Reception areas should always be tidy, not only to give a good impression to visitors but also to help prevent theft. Untidy workplaces can generate theft (the fact that something has gone missing can be blamed on the lack of organization of the items) and in certain circumstances can also be the basis for damage both to premises and people.

Deliveries

Most organizations will have deliveries ranging from stationery and office supplies to large amounts of raw materials. Inevitably there need to be procedures for the proper and secure reception (and onward storage) of such goods not only to check that what has been delivered is what was ordered and that the quality and quantity was correct, but also to preserve the security of the system (i.e. that the payment for the goods is correctly processed, and so on).

Theft

Sadly theft is on the increase – much of it carried out by employees. Whilst ensuring that every part of the workplace is kept tidy and well-organized can itself reduce the incidence of theft, more obvious action may also be necessary. Restricting exits from commercial premises can reduce the potential for employees moving their employer's assets away from the facility to finish under their own control. Where there are many and unsupervised exits from the premises this can act as an encouragement to the light-fingered. If the organization has valuable raw material and or products – particularly if these are small and/or portable – it may be advisable to introduce a 'right of search' (see Search policy, below). It is widely recognized that there is what could be termed a 'vicious circle' of employee theft.

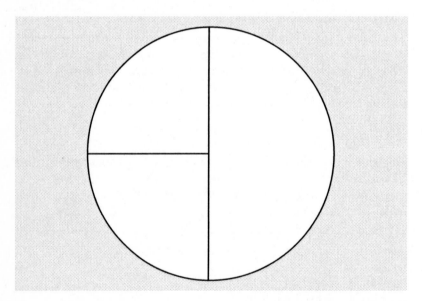

The vicious circle of employee honesty

It is suggested that of the total employees in the average organization, 25% are honest and another 25% are dishonest. The remaining 50% are said to be as honest or dishonest as the procedures of their employer will let them be. Adequate procedures and regular policing of such procedures are essential to minimize theft and they should be adhered to strictly. Once the rule has been breached, and is known to have been breached, its effectiveness may be at an end.

Case study

In Pilkington v Morrey and Williams, the Employment Appeals Tribunal noted that the employer was aware that employees routinely claimed for expenses which had not been incurred and these were paid with the employer's knowledge. Because of this precedent, the dismissal of two employees for similarly claiming expenses was found to be unfair. The two employees successfully claimed that they were 'confused' about the situation.

Wherever there is doubt or uncertainty, that situation can be exploited.

Buying product

Many organizations allow their employees to purchase their own products or discontinued lines, at a discount. Since this legitimate removal of such items from the premises can be abused, a well-advertised policy document should be drawn up and strictly monitored.

Draft policy

1. All employees are expected to respect, to protect and to retain for the exclusive use of the organization, all property in the ownership of the organization. Such property includes samples received by and prepared by the organization, discarded product and raw material, and all waste on the premises or belonging to the organization but held by others on behalf of the organization.

2. Such property may not be removed, damaged or destroyed without the prior express and written permission of the management. Unau-

thorized removal will be regarded as theft, dealt with under the theft policy, and be subject to prosecution as well as dismissal.

3. Surplus items, supported by a Material Destruction Note signed by the management, will be channelled through the staff shop, together with product authorized for such disposal and other items as management may from time to time determine, and will be made available to employees at advantageous prices for their own use, (and for the use of their immediate families) and not in any case for resale. All such purchases will be evidenced with a receipt and the receipt must be retained (and if necessary produced on request) as proof of purchase.

4. Employees may not conduct any other business which is, or may be, in competition with the business of the organization, or any other business without the prior, express and written permission of the management, and may not divulge to any other party, information concerning the organization or its products or plans.

5. Any employee breaking these rules will be considered to be guilty of gross misconduct.

Search policy

Since personal searching is (perhaps understandably) repugnant to many, the manner in which it is introduced must be carefully considered, and there should be consultation with employee representatives. Implementation should not be rushed – every opportunity should be taken to explain the rationale and need. The framing of a policy and procedure should stress that all searches will be carried out tactfully, confidentially and at random.

Draft policy

1. Unless the organization has clear reason to suspect an employee of theft, those to be searched should be chosen entirely at random (e.g. picking from anonymous payroll numbers rather than from a list of names).

2. Confidential rooms for the conduct of searches will be provided and the searches will be conducted by members of the same sex as the subject. If requested by the employee, a witness acceptable to both parties should also be present.

3. The searcher should indicate to the subject that the organization has a right to search and ask if the subject has any objection, pointing out (if applicable) that a refusal to allow the search will be regarded, in the absence of mitigating circumstances, as gross misconduct. If the

employee refuses, the effect should be carefully explained again. If, following such explanation, there is still a refusal, the employee should be suspended on full pay for 24 hours pending consideration of the case under the disciplinary code.

4. Employees should be asked to open bags etc and the boot/rear of any of their vehicles parked on the premises.

5. On no account should any comment be made on any private item seen during the conduct of the search. The process should be carried out with tact and respect.

6. The day (as well as the time should there be a shift system in operation) should be varied, and occasionally two (or more) searches should be carried out within a short space of time (even sequentially). The random nature and unexpectedness of the procedure is one of its main strengths.

7. Every search should be conducted swiftly. This is particularly important, since, if there is any delay, it may result in the search being carried out after working hours – which should be avoided.

8. If any employees (or agents, consultants, etc) have a legitimate need to remove a product and/or raw material, etc they should be given a suitable letter of authority for use should they be chosen as a subject for the search process.

9. Employees who have been authorized to remove a product from the premises should be prepared to produce the receipt if requested.

Destruction of confidential material

In The *Fleet Street Sewer Rat* (Artnik) Mark Watts recounts the experience of Benjamin Pell who, it is claimed, has made a comfortable living by rummaging through the plastic bin bags left for rubbish collection by lawyers and other organizations in London, and selling some of the 'secrets' he discovered there to competitors, newspapers and publicists. He is rumoured to have made around £250,000 a year through such activities. The value of the information Mr Pell 'liberated' may have been exaggerated, but it is possible to discover quite valuable information from such discarded 'rubbish'. During Sir Richard Branson's successful libel action against British Airways, BA's 'dirty tricks' operation commissioned not only a search of Branson's office waste, but also his domestic waste, trying (and failing) to discover unsavoury 'facts' with which they could try to blacken his name. Direct competitors able to read draft minutes of meetings and/or reports can discern the progress on development of products etc. That 'information is power' is certainly true here. Organizations should develop rules requiring all such information either to be shredded and/or incinerated.

Authority chart

It may also aid the control of authority (and thus help preserve security) if the organization adopts, promulgates and regularly updates an authority chart.

Draft authority control chart

Philosophy: For the proper control of the company, approval should be granted to contracts by suitably appointed personnel, and for the allocation and disposal of money and stock assets of the organization that authority is granted at an appropriate level.

Contracts

All contracts between the company and third parties, other than those covered by items specifically set out below, must be channelled through the Company Secretary's office to ensure correct status (i.e. whether it is to be regarded as a Deed or not) and approval.

For a document to be sealed or signed as a deed at least two weeks notice of the effective date of approval should be given and, should it consist of more than [say, five pages] a synopsis should be provided.

The Company Secretary will arrange the passing of suitable Board resolutions granting approval to specified person(s) to sign on behalf of the company. It should be noted that sufficient time to obtain such a resolution should be allowed.

Contracts of employment for those earning in excess of [sum] must be signed on behalf of the company by [name]. Contracts for those earning less than this sum must be signed by [name].

CASH COMMITMENT

Capital projects	Responsibility
Authority for all projects (note: No low cutoff)	Board
(All items must be supported by a Capital Expenditure (Capex) form Repairs and renewals, purchase of furniture and fittings (All items must be supported by a Capex form)	
Up to £1000	Manager – level ...
Over £1000 and up to £5000	Director
Over £5000	Board
Vehicles (Supported by Capex form, for new allocations, or replacement form (for write-offs and replacements)	Board

ALL PURCHASES TO BE IN ACCORDANCE WITH POLICY

Expense items:

Up to £500	Manager – level ...
Over £500 and up to £1000	Senior Manager
Over £1000 and up to £5000	Director
Over £5000	Board

Committed expenditure:

Rent, rates, utility costs – where no change or increase is less than rate of inflation	Manager – level ...
Where change has taken place	Director
All other property expenditure	Facility/Property
(if within projected terms)	Administrator

Bought ledger:

Raw materials, services etc in accordance with budgeted level of production	Purchase Manager
Not in accordance with level of production	Director

PERSONNEL

Wage adjustments:

Annual review	Board

Other than annual review, or for new staff, or replacement at other than at old rate

Salary up to £10,000 p.a.	Manager – level...
Salary over £10,000 p.a	Board

DISCIPLINE

Warnings (written – grades [x] to [y])	Director
(written – other grades)	Manager – level...
Warnings (verbal)	Manager – level...
Dismissal	Director

SUNDRY TRANSACTIONS

Credits (cash or stock), samples, etc.

In accordance with policy and less than £1000	Manager – level...
Over £1000	Director

Gifts, donations (cash or stock)

In accordance with policy and budget	Personnel Manager

Stock write-off and/or authority to dispose in stated area
(e.g. to market trader, staff shop, by gift, etc)

Up to £1000	Sales Manager
Over £1000	Sales Director in liaison with finance director

EXPENSES

Personal expenses (inc. telephone bills etc)

Up to £500	By level above level submitting the expense claim (i.e. using the required company form
Over £500	By level two levels above person submitting expense claim.

Removal expenses

In accordance with range of reimbursement agreed at time and may only be authorized by a Board Member. All invoices should be submitted in the name of the company to allow recovery of VAT.

TIPS AND INDUCEMENTS

Other than normal business entertaining and acknowledging special service, the provision of inducements bribes etc in the name of the organization is expressly forbidden being a criminal offence. Any instance where this is expected or required should be referred to [name] for guidance. Any instance where this is expected or required should be referred to [name] for guidance. Breach of this rule is gross misconduct.

Price fixing

It is illegal for any organization to conspire with another to fix the price of any product or service – indeed even discussing prices might infringe the rules. Sanctions include imprisonment. On no account is any employee permitted to discuss prices with a competitor or to enter into any arrangement regarding prices no matter how informal. Any instance where this is expected or required should be referred to [name] for guidance. Breach of this rule is gross misconduct.

Issued by (Finance Director) on (Date) _____

To be updated (Date) _____

Note:

Whilst this authority chart may help minimize unauthorized commitment of the organization's resources, cash spend may not necessarily be the best criteria in terms of **risk** to the organization. For example, two contracts might have the same cash value but one (if, for example, the specification is incorrect) could involve the organization in substantial loss.

⁎ ⁎

Example

Two identical value contracts are placed:

    A.   One for the supply of office furniture. The risk here is virtually nil since if the items are wrong, very often they can be replaced – probably without charge and certainly without any knock on effect.

    B.   The other for the supply of computer software to a specification generated by the organization. If incorrect there could be serious financial and other consequences to the organization.

It may therefore be advisable to incorporate an added dimension – 'risk to the organization' – to the simple levels of authority, requiring the originator of the order to obtain higher level of authority where the perceived risk (for example) exceeds the value of the contract.

Service charge

Introduction

Where a property is in sole occupation, responsibility for upkeep of the premises, repairs, redecoration, security, parking etc will usually be that of the lessee or occupier in accordance with the terms of the authority (lease or licence) to occupy. If, however, the premises are in multi-occupation, it is usual for the cost of upkeep etc of common areas and of services which benefit all occupiers, to be sourced centrally and for each occupier receiving benefit to contribute to such costs by means of a service charge.

Authority

In occupying premises which already have a service charge in operation there may be little a lessee can do other than ensuring that:

a) the proportion of the whole that they are required to pay is fair,

b) the items included in the charge are for items from which the lessee derives a benefit, and

c) lessees in occupation are not charged for a proportion of a service charge which covers empty properties.

Case study

A company occupied a unit in a shopping centre which had restricted parking facilities. One day when checking the service charge, an advisor asked where the shop's two parking bays were in case he could use one on his next visit. The owner stated she had no parking bays for each of which she was being charged £16 per week! When queried, it was admitted that her unit did not have two parking bays and the charges already made – and paid – on two previous occasions were refunded.

When taking a new lease it may be possible to negotiate which items are to be charged and on what basis the apportionment is to be made. However, ultimately the landlord will have a list of items and costs and will be determined to recover these costs from lessees.

Apportionment

If the demised premises are separately rated then the rateable value can be used as a basis for the determination of the proportion of the total charge to be borne by each lessee. Such an externally sourced value has the advantage of being independently assessed and recognized by all. It also reflects the fact that common parts allied to, say, a ground floor suite, may tend to have a higher value than those allied to, say, a fifth floor suite. However, the ground floor lessees could argue that they should not pay a proportion of the cost of maintaining a lift which they do not use and, if agreed, there may be some items for which a modified basis of charge may need to be used. If using the rateable value as a base, care should be taken to ensure that the valuations are current and that none are subject to appeal or redetermination (or, if they are, that they are adjusted accordingly). Floor areas can also be used as an apportionment base.

Accuracy

Lessees might request either that they inspect the contracts and/or invoices for the supply of the items included in the service charge, or that there is provision for some independent authority to check the calculations and proportions and confirm to the lessees the accuracy of the charges. Often a firm of accountants is appointed to do this.

Default

Charges are levied on the landlord who recoups the cost from all lessees. In the event that one or more lessee defaults on payment, the attitude of the remaining lessees should be that this is a loss to the landlord and should not be re-charged to the remaining lessees. Lessees will rarely have any control over who occupies the other areas in the property whereas the landlord does – thus it is the landlord's responsibility to ensure adequate collection etc.

Payment

Payment should be required after the services have been provided, although in practice in many modern leases, a sum of money (usually a major part of the total expected) is demanded as a deposit, either a year in advance or sometimes in quarterly instalments with any balancing charge being collected once the final charges are known. Interest is sometimes stipulated to be added in the event of delayed payment of sums demanded.

Complaints

The provision of services by an absent landlord to lessees is prone to problems of poor execution or even non-completion. Lessees should note all service provision failures. This can then stand as evidence in the event of later dispute and as a means to obtain an improvement in the future.

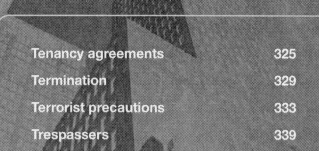

Tenancy agreements   325

Termination   329

Terrorist precautions   333

Trespassers   339

Tenancy agreements

Introduction

Many units, particularly shops, have residential areas which, whilst they may not be of direct use to the organization, can be a valuable source of income. Ideally flexibility of possession should be preserved i.e. vacant possession should be able to be obtained swiftly. Letting premises on a shorthold tenancy basis either to a tenant directly or via a Housing Association could be considered.

Shorthold tenancy agreement

Tenants can be given a limited right of occupation via the grant of a short-hold tenancy (see below). This limits the right of occupation to six months, although there is nothing to stop a further tenancy being granted at the end of each six months. To terminate such an agreement, however, two full calendar months notice must be given in writing. It may be prudent to require tenants to deposit the equivalent of four or six weeks rent with the organization against damage to premises or fittings. A deposit may also help provide against loss should the tenant depart secretly leaving unpaid rent and/or having damaged the property.

Wording for such an Agreement follows, although legal advice should be taken.

AGREEMENT

for letting unfurnished dwelling house on an assured shorthold tenancy under Part 1 of the Housing Act 1988 (as amended by the Housing Act 1996).

Date: _____

Parties: 1. The Landlord – [name] _____

2. The Tenants – [name] _____

Property: The flat situated at [address] _____

_____

together with the fixtures and effects therein.

Term: Six months from [date]_____

Rent: [£Amount] per calendar month payable on the 1st day of each month. _____

1. The Landlord lets and the Tenants take the Property for the Term at the Rent payable as above.

2. This Agreement creates an assured shorthold tenancy within Part 1 Chapter II of the Housing Act 1988 (as amended by the Housing Act 1996) and the provisions for the recovery of possession by the Landlord in Section 21 thereof apply accordingly save where the Landlord serves a notice under paragraph 2 of Schedule 2A to that Act.

3. Where the context admits:

   a) The Landlord includes the persons for the time being entitled in reversion expectant on the tenancy.

   b) The Tenant includes the persons deriving title under the Tenant.

   c) References to the property include references to part or parts of the property and to the Fixtures, Fittings and Effects or any of them.

4. The Tenant will:

   a) Pay the rent at the times and in the manner specified.

   b) Pay for all gas, electricity, water and sewerage services supplied to the property during the tenancy and the amount of all charges made for the use of the telephone (if any) at the property during the tenancy or a proper proportion of the sums demanded for the aforesaid utilities and facilities to be assessed according to the duration of the tenancy (for the avoidance of doubt such payment will be due in relation to amounts attributable to standing charges annual rates or levies or the like and to VAT as well as to actual consumption).

   c) Not damage or injure the property or make any alteration in or addition to it.

   d) Preserve the fixtures, furniture and effects from being destroyed or damaged and not remove any of them from the property.

   e) Yield up the property at the end of the tenancy in the same clean state and condition as it was in the beginning of the tenancy and make good pay for the repair of or replace all such items of the fixtures, furniture and effects as shall be broken, lost, damaged or destroyed during the tenancy (reasonable wear and damage by fire excepted).

f) Leave the furniture and effects at the end of the tenancy in the rooms or places in which they were at the beginning of the tenancy.

g) Pay for the washing (including ironing or pressing) of all linen and for the washing and cleaning (including ironing or pressing) of all counterpanes blankets and curtains which shall have been soiled during the tenancy (the reasonable use thereof nevertheless to be allowed for).

h) Permit the Landlord or the Landlord's agents at reasonable hours in the daytime to enter the property to view the state and condition thereof

i) Not assign sublet or otherwise part with possession of the property without the prior written consent of the Landlord.

j) Not carry on at or in the property any profession, trade, business or let apartments or receive paying guests on the property or place or exhibit any notice board or notice on the property or use the property for any purpose other than that of a strictly private residence.

k) Not do or suffer to be done on the property anything which may be or become a nuisance or annoyance to the Landlord or the tenants or occupiers of any adjoining premises or which may vitiate any insurance of the property against fire or otherwise or increase the ordinary premium for such insurance.

l) Permit the Landlord or the Landlord's agents at reasonable hours in the daytime within the last 28 days of the tenancy to enter and view the property with prospective tenants.

m) Perform and observe any obligation on the part of the tenant arising under the Local Government Finance Act 1992 or regulations made thereunder to pay council tax and indemnify the Landlord against any such obligation which the Landlord may incur during the tenancy by reason of the tenant's ceasing to be resident in the property.

n) Within seven days of the receipt by the tenant of any notice given under the Party Wall etc Act 1996 to give a copy thereof to the Landlord and not to take any steps in consequence thereof unless required to do so by the Landlord.

o) Provide the Landlord with a bond equivalent to one months rent (i.e. £........) and not set this off against rent payable.

5. Provided that if the rent or any instalment or part thereof shall be in arrear for at least 14 days after the same shall have become due (whether legally demanded or not) or if there shall be a breach of any of the agreements by the tenant the Landlord may re-enter on the property (subject always to any statutory restrictions on his power to do so) and immediately thereupon the tenancy shall absolutely determine without prejudice to the other rights and remedies of the Landlord.

6. The Landlord agrees with the tenant as follows:

   a) To pay and indemnify the tenant against all assessments and outgoings in respect of the property (except any council tax and any charges for the supply of gas, electricity, water and sewerage services or the use of any telephone payable by the tenant under clause 4 above).

   b) That the tenant paying the rent and performing the agreements on the part of the tenant may quietly possess and enjoy the property during the tenancy without lawful interruption from the Landlord or any person claiming under or in trust for the Landlord.

   c) To return to the tenant any rent payable for a period while the property is rendered uninhabitable by fire, the amount in case of dispute to be submitted to arbitration pursuant to Part 1 of the Arbitration Act 1996.

7. This Agreement shall take effect subject to the provisions of section II of the Landlord and Tenant Act 1985 if applicable to the tenancy.

8. Notice under section 48 of the Landlord and Tenant Act 1987 – the tenancy is hereby notified that notices (including notices in proceedings) must be served on the Landlord by the tenant at [address]

AS WITNESS the hands of the parties hereto the day and year first above written

Signed by and on behalf of [name] (the Landlord) by

_____[Name]

Date _____

Signed by the above-named tenant(s)

_____ [Name]

in the presence of (as witness) _____(signature)

Witness name (block capitals)_____

Date _____

If using such an agreement, a diary note should be made to check intentions prior to the ending of each tenancy period.

Termination

Introduction

Despite a lease expiry date being stipulated within it and that date having been reached, a lease does not automatically terminate. Notice must be given by one or other of the parties to terminate. If the landlord does not give notice to terminate then the lessee continues in occupation until either landlord or lessee gives notice.

Landlord's termination

Leases are either within the protection of the Landlord and Tenant Act 1954 (LTA) or not. If within the LTA, lessees are protected in a number of areas not least that they have the right, subject to exceptions, to a new lease at termination. However, a lessee who is, party to a lease outside the LTA, has no such right to a new lease. To take a lease outside the LTA, both parties must agree to this at a hearing at Court (which acts to protect lessees) and that fact must be stated in the lease.

To bring a lease (which has LTA protection) to an end, the landlord must serve a minimum of six months notice stating whether they are prepared to grant a new lease and, if so, how much rent will be expected. Normally notice will be served sufficiently in advance that it brings the lease to an end on the termination date set out in the lease – but it must not be served more than 12 months before the termination date. If, however, the notice is served 'late' (i.e. less than six months before the lease termination date) the lease terms continue and the lessee continues to pay rent at the existing rate until there is a termination date. This is termed 'holding over' under the lease and a lessee can continue to 'hold over' until either the expiry of the term of a notice served by the landlord (six months) or by the lessee (three months).

A landlord giving notice can indicate they are not prepared to grant a new lease if:

- they want the premises for their own occupation, or
- they wish to redevelop the premises.

If a new lease is not granted then the lessee is entitled to compensation – normally twice the rateable value of the subject premises.

Until June 2004, within two months of the serving of the landlord's notice, a lessee had to serve a counter-notice stating whether they wanted a new lease and if so how much they were prepared to pay. The requirement to serve a counter-notice has been scrapped, but if the lessee (tenant) does not make an application to the Court to protect their position, they could lose their security of tenure rights (which was the point of serving the counter-notice).

Negotiations ensue during which the parties try to agree terms for a new lease. If the process drags on either party can apply to the Court (before the notice termination date, or, by agreement, thereafter) and the Court may set a timetable for agreement – or determine the matter itself.

New lease application

Under Section 26 of the LTA 1954 (as amended) a lessee can give notice to their landlord of a request for a new lease. Such a notice must be given not less than six months (and not more than 12 months) before the lease expiry date and the lessee must stipulate the lease terms. To ensure their right of security, a lessee must also apply to the Court – legal advice should be taken.

Termination (post expiry)

Should the lessee wish to terminate occupation after the end of the lease (when the landlord has not served notice) then they must serve notice. Legal advice should be taken, but the principle is that three months notice must be served on the landlord. Action by the lessee terminating the lease could be considered where the lessee feels the existing rent is higher than might be the case with a new lease. Whilst the rent cannot be reduced at review this may be able to be applied at renewal. Knowing this, the landlord might not wish to bring the lease to an end but merely allow it to continue – at the existing rent.

Despite the potential advantage of a achieving a lower rent, there is a danger in the lessee giving notice, since the lessee cannot force the landlord to offer a new lease. The lessee having given notice to terminate, the landlord is released from the LTA obligations and no longer has to offer a new lease to the existing lessee.

Preparation needed

Six months notice to terminate occupation is not a great deal of time, and lessees who do not plan for the possible termination of their occupation could find them-selves facing a large increase in rent if it is too late to source an alternative. In late 2005, Donaldsons, property consultants, calculated that UK businesses 'waste up to £10 billion a year on rent' simply because they fail to make arrangements before their leases expire. The survey stated that between 70% and 80% of commercial leases were terminated by landlords with the minimum six months notice forcing businesses to renew on 'expensive or inappropriate terms' simply because they did not have enough time to make alternative plans. The state-ment 'not enough time' is obviously a nonsense since every lessee knows the date of termination of the lease from the date they agree to take it – what many fail to do is plan ahead for the effect of such termination. Donaldsons went on to state that the cost of relocating at the end of a lease, on an average building of 20,000 sq ft in the Home Counties, would be £1.5 million more than one that had been arranged in advance as 'few companies left enough time to move'.

Terrorist precautions

Introduction

Either as a deliberate target or incidental to a neighbourhood-based action, property occupiers can become subject to damage and loss, and their employees and visitors to injury as a result of terrorist activity. Organizations should have policies for dealing with everything from telephone threats and suspect packages, to full evacuation as a result of a bomb threat – real or hoax – or actual explosion or should access be denied to their own premises.

Publicity

Organizations must decide whether to disclose their precautions to their employees. Some may prefer, to avoid undue concern, to make the procedures known only to a few. Conversely, others may feel it may re-assure their staff to know there are precautions. Often the responsibility for this will devolve to the Property or Facility Administrator. Sadly, no warnings have been given for the most recent and cowardly terrorist activities and most of such precautions may need to be reactive.

Telephone threats

The police estimate that over 95% of telephoned threats are hoaxes made by disaffected employees or ex-employees. Indeed, the percentage of hoaxes may be even higher as many such calls are not reported. Receptionists and telephonists should be coached to deal with such calls.

Threat reaction procedure

1. Taking a threat call

   i.   Accept the call in a calm, unhurried manner. Ask caller to repeat the sentence or message to give yourself time to recover and possibly, without alerting the caller, to advise someone who can listen in.

   ii. Keep caller talking, "I'm sorry this is a bad line – I can't hear you clearly", or "I don't understand what you mean – could you repeat that please so that I get it right" or "Did you say...(repeat the statement the caller made)?" etc.

   iii. Discover as much information as possible. Take particular note of any unusual words or phrases used in case these contain a code word.

   iv. Find the answers to the following questions:

        a) Where is the bomb?

        b) What type is it: incendiary, explosive, gas, etc?

        c) Who put it there, and when?

        d) Who is the caller, and who does (s)he represent?

        e) Does (s)he have any police identification code?

        f) When will bomb go off?

        g) Why is the person taking this action against organization?

        h) Does (s)he have a grudge against this organization?

        i) Nature of this complaint?

        j) Will bomb affect fire evacuation routes? [If it will, do not activate fire alarm, as this could put employees at greater risk.]

   v.   During, or immediately after, conversation, make note of caller's characteristics:

        • Young, old, male, female, English, foreign?

        • Special accent or speech defect?

        • Drunk or drugged, lucid, rambling or incoherent?

        • Did it sound as if message was being read?

        • Any background noises, or anything else of note?

        (Note: Organizations with a record of such alarms could arrange to link a tape recorder to the switchboard ready for immediate operation.)

vi. As quickly as possible, notify [state title – with deputy] who will need to make decision whether to evacuate or not, and will contact police/fire brigade. Before arranging evacuation, fire evacuation routes should be checked for suspicious packages. If suspicious packages are found, an alternative means of escape should be used.

(Note: The police may advise not to use the fire alarm as its noise and/or vibration can detonate some devices.)

Staff should be requested to take personal belongings with them, so that as many potentially suspect packages as possible are removed prior to a police search.

vii. When the police arrive, staff should act in accordance with their instructions. The police will normally request that an employee accompany them during the search to identify, and thus eliminate, harmless packages.

Suspect packages

Receipt of a suspect package brings the potential danger into the premises without warning. Staff whose responsibility it is to handle the post should be coached accordingly.

Suspect package reaction

1. The organization will publish (and update), a list of countries from which they would expect to receive post and packages. Odd looking or smelling packages from these countries and all packages from other countries should be treated with extreme caution.

2. All packages which are:
   - oddly addressed or presented
   - show signs of staining from a liquid
   - display metal protrusions
   - seem to contain machinery not likely to be of interest to the recipient
   - have broken coverings
   - have contents which are ticking (or making a similar noise)
   - smell of almonds or marzipan, etc.

(This list is not meant to be exhaustive – it should be treated with considerable suspicion and placed within the secure section in the Post Room.)

3. The department, and surrounding departments, should be cleared, the matter should be reported to [stipulate title and deputy] who should summon the police.

* *

Liability insurers need to be kept informed regarding:

1. employees accompanying police when checking for suspect packages, and/or

2. whether the organization has decided to ignore bomb warning calls (and thus employees do not evacuate the building on receipt of a telephone threat), and/or

3. whether the organization leaves the decision of whether to evacuate or not to individual employees.

General emergencies

Terrorist activity, such as the Canary Wharf or London Transport bombs, can be foreseen generally even if not specifically. It is likely those based in cities, on or near major transport facilities, or near widely recognized landmarks are most likely to be at risk. If privately owned, organizations, so based, owe it to both their shareholders and their employees to at least plan for such eventualities. Acceptance of the existence of the threat is the first major challenge. In the aftermath of the Bishopsgate bomb at the height of the IRA mainland bombing campaign, many organizations realized their vulnerability, not so much for the initial damage about which little could probably be done, but in terms of the subsequent dislocation to their business. Obviously the sooner they could get back in business, the lower their overall losses as a result of the post-incident hiatus.

Case study

Gee Publishing was located in a building next to Canary Wharf in part of London's old rejuvenated docklands. One Thursday in February in the mid 1990s, I delivered the manuscript of my latest updating manual to Gee's offices for publishing and was horrified at 7.00pm the following day, to see on television, the same office where I had walked the day before devastated by the Canary Wharf bomb. Yet early the following Monday morning I received a phone call from my editor checking that I had my own copy of everything passed to her the previous Thursday.

Because of the lessons learned from the Bishopsgate bomb, Gee had detailed contingency plans having realized that being located immediately next to a very recognizable landmark, their premises and business were vulnerable. During the weekend after the bombing they had 'moved' (in the widest sense of the word as they were not allowed back into the premises for several months) to other premises. Whilst inevitably there was disruption and a severe loss of records etc. a substantial part of the business was up and running, understandably imperfectly, but virtually without the loss of a working day.

'The morning after the disaster before' is far too late to consider action. Those located in high risk areas should do what an increasing number of organizations (particularly those service-based) have done and commissioned 'back up' premises in which they keep copies (regularly updated) of their most important files, with duplicated computer equipment etc. Indeed, the current trend to senior people working at home, may provide the means by which back-up records etc can be easily kept off-site.

Action points to be considered

1. Adopt CONTINGENCY PLANNING. Consider what is needed to effect recovery from all the worst case scenarios.

2. Identify and train Crisis Management Teams. There could be several of these, differently composed, depending on the nature of each emergency.

3. If utilizing alternative premises:

   a) these should be relatively, but perhaps not too, near the original location

   b) use these additionally for back-up documentation (see ARCHIVING).

4. Advise everyone of the contingency plan, with key personnel retaining copies of the latest version. At least one copy should be kept off-site – perhaps in the alternative premises but also in the private residences of senior personnel (see HOMEWORKING).

5. Identifying threats, setting them down in the plan and considering and recording suggested reactions should help build resilience amongst all involved which may help when they have to switch into a 'recovery frame of mind' after the initial shock.

6. A free contact number should be provided, known by all (including relatives) and manned immediately an emergency has occurred. Very often in the aftermath of a catastrophe 'lack of information' may be one of the greatest problems. If there is no news – rumours will abound.

7. A senior person should be nominated to interface with the media. This person may need training in dealing with what can be searching or even deliberately intrusive questioning.

8. Contact numbers of local hospitals, police, fire, hotels and other authorities as well as insurers, builders, surveyors should be compiled and included within the contingency plan (in the back-up premises).

9. If the emergency occurs in working hours, detailed evacuation procedures (perhaps based on the FIRE evacuation procedure) must be known to everyone, with arrangements to check for all employees and visitors, including any contractors on the premises. Provision might need to be made for shelter, FIRST AID and transport home and/or local accommodation if more appropriate. (Subject to emergency services' requests, retaining key personnel near the facility may help communication and recovery.)

10. If the emergency occurs outside working hours key personnel will need to be contacted. They in turn should have lists of numbers to advise other employees of what to do in the aftermath (e.g. using the 'ripple effect' in that no one person needs to call more than, say, ten people)

11. Update all the above at least once a year AND, after each occasion that any part of it is implemented, having conducted a post mortem on the effectiveness of the reaction, revise the plan accordingly.

Trespassers

Introduction

Anyone not working in, invited to, or lacking a right to be in the facility can be regarded as a trespasser or, if they seem to have taken up residence, as a squatter. Although neither trespassers nor squatters have any right to be on the premises, however, the owner or occupier may still have obligations to them – particularly *vis-à-vis* their safety. Many trespassers do so in order to commit crime – particularly arson. 25% of those asked stated their businesses had suffered a crime in the previous 12 months (the figure for small organizations is 58%); whilst a survey by the Institute of Directors found the average cost to business victims of crime is £5,000.

Prevention

The facility should be made as secure as possible to render such unwanted access difficult. Too often too little is done to clarify that access is only permitted to authorized personnel through designated entrances and at certain times. Boundary walls and fences should be kept in a good state of repair with defensive measures (high walls surmounted by barrier wire, etc) installed; gates should be sturdy and kept locked, whilst notices should be displayed stating that not only is access denied to the unauthorized but also there is danger to unauthorized persons from illegal entry. If security is a major issue, additional safeguards such as regular inspections and/or closed circuit television could be installed although the expense that both of these items entail, may militate against this – basically the potential loss needs to be compared with the costs of the added protection.

Unrestricted control over access lends itself to the:

- unauthorized access of those intent on stealing from and/or damaging contents and/or the building
- ability of those persons to disrupt the operation of the organization

- inability of the organization to ensure that its facilities, personnel, operations, systems, records, product development and trade secrets are adequately protected

- creation of a perception that 'nothing there is worth much so they won't miss it' potentially leading (almost encouraging) to increased employee theft as well as other pilferage and damage

- fostering in the minds of observers (particularly employees) that they do not need to be careful regarding the foregoing – which could have a knock on effect on the performance of their duties.

Hazards

Despite danger warning notices, however, the occupier is not absolved from liability if a trespasser, particularly a child, is injured on the premises. Hazards such as wells, ladders and flat roofs may also need to be guarded. Using guard dogs to improve security, unless on a leash or under supervision, may itself pose a hazard. Any facility which contains what could be described as 'an enticement' to children, should negate its appeal and try to prevent access. Under various Occupiers Liability Acts, those who visit commercial premises, even when they have no right to be there, may have a right of action against the owners or occupiers if they are injured whilst on the premises. This extends to trespassers – particularly children whose inquisitiveness may outweigh their sense of danger.

Instructions regarding the organization's and any contractors' equipment should recognize this potential for injury and liability, for example:

- No ladders should be left erect unless unavoidable in which case a scaffold plank should be attached vertically to the rungs to reduce ease of access.

- Ladders left demounted should be padlocked to a stanchion or similar so that they cannot be used either extended or not.

- All mobile plant should be parked facing and touching either a wall (or another item of mobile plant).

- All ignition keys should be removed from mobile plant and any other vehicle parked on the premises.

- Visible barriers should be left secured on flat roofs. (After work is completed flat roofs could be protected with hazard wire.)

- Lids should be securely attached to the openings of vats, barrels, silos etc

- All raw materials (paint, plaster, cement, fixatives, etc) should be stored internally.

- All mobile and hand tools should be stored in a locked store (preferably inside the premises).

- Any electricity or other power supply to the works should be isolated if the latter have to be left unattended.

- No rubble and/or rubbish should be left so that it can be accessed by uninvited persons.

- No means of access should be left adjacent to scaffolds or access platforms.

Case studies

1. By climbing onto the roof of Container Care park in Bootle, nine year old Carl Murphy trespassed with a group of similarly aged children. He fell through the roof and, as a result of his injuries, claimed to have developed severe behavioural problems which led to him being expelled from school. He was then taught by a private tutor – an arrangement that ended when he threatened the tutor with physical violence. He went to a school for children with such problems but was expelled from that school. He lives with his grandmother as his parents are in jail for running a crack cocaine business from their council house. In 2005, to an understandable adverse reaction from many groups representing victims of crime, he was awarded £567,000 compensation for his injuries.

2. In *Margereson & Hancock v J W Roberts Ltd*, the company was held to be liable to the widow of a man who had contracted a disease as a result of him playing, when a child, in the asbestos-ridden dust of their company's loading bay – where he had no right to be.

3. A Federation of Small Businesses survey disclosed that 58% of small businesses had been the victims of crime. The FSB crime spokesman stated that, "The UK is facing a crime epidemic and no-one cares. Sentences are lower for commercial burglaries than domestic burglaries, and criminal damage and theft from commercial premises have been effectively de-criminalized." Such an attitude can only lead to increasing numbers of crimes against businesses.

Squatters

Whereas most trespassers remain on the property for a relatively short period – to steal from or cause damage to the property, or, as far as children may be concerned, simply to explore and play there – squatters tend to occupy the premises or part of them on a long-term basis for 'housing'. It may be difficult to eject them and specific advice needs to be taken in such circumstances. It should not be assumed that simply because they have to right to be there that they can be ejected forcibly. It can take up to two months to gain legal access and eject them. Legal advice should be taken.

Under the Land Registration Act 2002, if a squatter wishes to claim title to a property, an owner must be notified – thus giving an owner the chance to object and to fight to retain ownership. This Act has been reinforced by a 2005 decision of the European Court of Human Rights in the *J A Pye (Oxford) Ltd* case. The ECHR held that where a squatter obtained rights of ownership by virtue of time expired in possession (usually 12 years), the owner was still entitled to compensation since otherwise this was a violation of Article One of Protocol One of the European Convention of Human Rights.

U

Underletting   345

Upwards only rent review (UORR)   347

Use and user clause   349

Underletting

Introduction

Lessees can cut short their lease commitment, by assigning it. However, the danger is that, for leases entered into before 1st January 1996, should the person acquiring the lease (the assignee or a subsequent assignee) default, the original lessee could be required to refund any shortfall in amounts due under the lease to the landlord (see PRIVITY OF CONTRACT). The lessee has no right of re-entry and/or re-occupation of the premises whereby these costs could be minimized or offset. As an alternative to assignment, lessees could consider underletting.

Basis

An underlease passes on all the responsibilities of the original lessee to an under-lessee who will also benefit, at the lessee's discretion, from the rights under the lease. It is prudent for the term allowed to an underlessee to be slightly shorter than that to which the lessee is entitled – to provide a buffer of time to ensure that vacant possession can be given when the original lease expires. If the under-lease terminates a month before the lease, the original lessee has the opportunity not only to ensure the underlessee has left the premises but also left them in a reasonable condition, before the due date that they in turn must vacate.

Permission

A lessee has no automatic right to underlet the premises – indeed many are actually prohibited from doing so, since their lease will either contain a covenant requiring them, other than for short periods, to 'remain in occupation' or prohibit them from underletting at all. A right to underlet the whole should be insisted on during acquisition negotiations. Normally the landlord will only allow this, subject to their control evidenced by words such as 'with the permission of the landlord' to which the lessee in turn should add the words 'such permission not to be unreasonably withheld'. If wishing to sublet, the lessee will need to submit full details of the proposed underlessee for approval to the landlord. Normally the landlord will wish to see evidence of financial reliability and to be assured that the organization or person is likely to be a responsible tenant and one that will keep the premises in a reasonable state etc. Indeed these requirements may be as much in the interests of the original lessee as those of the landlord (since the provisions of the original lease are still effective) and so should have already been investigated. A deed granting the landlord's permission to the underletting will be prepared to which the landlord, the lessee and the proposed underlessee should all be parties.

Underletting the whole only

Normally a lessee will only be able to underlet the whole premises and unless the premises are large and easily dividable, it may not be in anyone's interest to consider underletting parts of the property to different underlessees. Unless there is strict and effective property management, unrestricted partial underletting can lead to a situation where unauthorized underlettings proliferate, and sub-sub-tenancies are created so that the effect is of a number of 'occupations' resembling a rabbit warren. The difficulty in this situation may not only be understanding the relationships between underlessees but also regaining vacant possession of the whole since so many parties may be involved. The responsibility for repairs and redecorations may also be unclear.

Lessee removal

Where a permitted underletting has been arranged, and particularly where a profit rent has been obtained, the landlord can require the original lessee to drop out of the relationship on lease termination. In such a case the landlord can negotiate new lease terms direct with the underlessee thus acquiring the benefit of any enhanced rent for itself.

Case study

In *Graysim Holdings Ltd v P&O Property Holdings Ltd.*, because the lessee had sublet the areas, the House of Lords found that they then had no protected holding when the landlord served notice ending their business letting.

Upwards only rent review (UORR)

Introduction

When annual inflation was low, the initial rent of a lease tended to remain unchanged throughout its term. As rates of inflation increased, in order to protect their income, landlords inserted the right to increase the rent. Initially the gaps between such reviews were lengthy e.g. every 21 years – but gradually they reduced – to 14, seven, five and even three years. It is customary nowadays for leases to be subject to a five year review. During the 1970s, however, it became increasingly common, particularly when retail units were being taken in the new shopping centres being built at that time, for landlords to insist that at review, rent could only remain the same or be increased. This was copied for office leases and generally elsewhere. 'Upwards only' rent review (UORR) clauses were born.

Principle – and flaw

The UORR principle is very simple: before the effective date of a review, the two parties agree what the new rent should be – except that it can either remain the same or move upwards. If there is no rent inflation in the area (or even a downward trend) the rent must remain at its existing level. The perceived logic is that rents will always increase which is, of course, a complete fallacy. For all sorts of reasons, rental levels around the subject property might not sustain the level attained when the original rent or a previously reviewed rent was set. Hence at review, the lessee should be able to argue that the rent should be reduced to reflect the downturn in values demonstrated by such evidence. If the lessee has agreed to the inclusion of an UORR this cannot happen and thus rent will continue to be paid in excess of the local level for new lettings.

Legal intervention

For many years there has been a campaign to outlaw UORR clauses, and several years ago the Government suggested to the commercial property 'industry' that it should initiate a voluntary code to try and limit the effect of such reviews. A 2003 survey found that out of 1334 leases examined, 92% contained UORR. The Government concluded that since no voluntary code was working it should legislate to ban them. However, landlords responded by pointing out that lessees were able to circumvent the effect of UORR – and had done so simply by insisting on shorter lease terms. The average lease life had by then shortened from over 16 to just over ten years with over half leases being for five years or less. The Office of the Deputy Prime Minister was active in pressing for legislation to ban UORR although to date no such legislation, even in draft, has been proposed and it seems that the move may have been defeated by the vested interests of landlords. This view will have been strengthened as a result of a 2005 report by Reading University which found that more than half the leases it studied contained no rent review clauses (mainly since lease terms had shortened so that there was no need for a review at all). Conversely most of the other leases did contain UORR. The British Retail Consortium is still urging the Government to legislate to ban UORRs maintaining that they impede British competitiveness and slow the UK's economic growth.

The results of Reading's survey may not be surprising. Although landlords, and particularly institutional landlords, knew of the adverse pressure and the survey, it is unlikely that many lessees knew of it and thus their opinions may not have been made known (the number surveyed was relatively small). My experience of lessess, particularly retail lessees, is that they are virtually unanimous in objecting to UORR.

Note: Reading University monitors the property industry's Code of Practice (available from British Property Federation, www.bpf.propertymall.com) and flexibility of lease terms.

Practical action

Even in the most popular locations, lessees should try to resist the inclusion of such a clause. If unavoidable, then a shorter term or a lessee's option to break the lease should be insisted on. Such an option should ideally be timed to operate after a rent at review has been determined so that the lessee knows what rent they will have to pay before the time limit applies to imposition of the clause that allows them to escape their liabilities.

Use and user clause

Introduction

If freehold, the use of a property may be constrained by planning considerations, which could restrict such matters as hours of work e.g. if a factory is located within a residential area. If leasehold, the use of the premises may be constrained by the above as well and more pertinently by lease clauses specifying the uses and non-uses e.g. some leases prohibit the use of the premises to sell alcohol, conduct auctions, etc of the property.

Operation

When negotiating lease terms the prospective lessee should check the impact of any and all restrictions on the operation of the business that are included (see COVENANTS).

Case study

The *Something Special* bridal hire business was negotiating a new lease. Included in the lease was a requirement that the business should be open (and only open) between the hours of 8.00am and 6.00pm on Monday to Saturday. To most service-orientated businesses these hours might have caused no problem. However the business had no need and no intent of opening before 11.00am each morning – its main business being conducted between 4.00pm and 8.00pm on weekdays and Saturdays and also for a few hours on Sunday. Hence the apparently innocuous use restrictions via the authorized hours of business would have had a crippling effect on the business had these not been challenged during negotiation – when of course there was some room to manoeuvre.

That case study illustrates another problem for lessees. The lease with those 'restrictive hours' trading had already been vetted and approved for signature by the lessee's solicitors, not realizing the effect of that clause. It is important that all lease covenants and details are examined by someone with knowledge of the **practical** requirements of the business.

Planning use

Generally the classification of uses under the Town and Country Planning (Use Classes) Order 1987 (as amended by the Use Classes (Amendment) Order 2005) is as follows.

Note: Only a brief outline of items under each class has been given in the following list.

- Class A1 – Retailing of items for sale generally
- Class A2 – Financial and professional services
- Class A3 – Restaurants and cafés
- Class A4 – Pubs and bars
- Class B1 – Offices/research and development/light industry
- Class B2 – General industrial
- Class B3 – Industrial use as defined by the Alkali Works Regulations 1906
- Class B4 – Industrial use (smelting, galvanising etc.)
- Class B5 – Industrial use (bricks, crushing, fuel ash etc)
- Class B6 – Industrial use (oil, stoving, rubber, chemicals etc.)
- Class B7 – Industrial use (boiling, fish, skins, fats etc.)
- Class B8 – Storage and distribution
- Class C1 – Hotels and boarding houses
- Class C2 – Residential homes, hospitals, nursing homes etc.
- Class C3 – Dwelling house/small businesses at home
- Class D1 – Non residential premises (day nurseries, places of worship, libraries etc.)
- Class D2 – Assembly and leisure premises (cinemas, theatres, dance halls, swimming baths etc)

Premises are not permitted, without a lease variation, to be used for a purpose other than that for which they are designated.

Use clauses

Although clauses that stipulate for what purpose the premises must be used are particularly relevant to retailing, leases for offices, warehouses and even industrial buildings can contain restrictive use clauses. When agreeing terms, all the purposes for which the premises will be used should be included. If not, and the premises are then used for a purpose other than that specified, the lessee could be in breach of covenant. Normally alterations to a user clause are allowed, subject to the permission of the landlord. To alleviate the potentially restrictive nature of such a clause, the words 'such permission not to be unreasonably withheld' should be added. Without such wording it may allow some landlords to negotiate additional rent when a request for additional use was made on the basis that if the rent agreed was fair for the original use, any additional use should attract greater rent. For example, when the National Lottery was introduced and retail units were granted the right to sell lottery tickets, some landlords attempted to increase the rent those units were paying, arguing that selling lottery tickets was an extension of the permitted use. The wording should be studied carefully although sometimes the wording can work to the benefit of the lessee.

Case study

Boots the Chemist operate several hundred shops (some leased, some freehold) throughout the UK. One leased shop in the Midlands had as its user clause, 'the shop can be used for the retailing of goods normally sold in a Boots store'. This virtually negated any controls in the user clause since Boots only need introduce products to one of their freehold stores to be able to stock such products in that unit.

Effect on rent review

There may be some logic in a landlord attempting to gain additional rent in exchange for allowing the premises to be used for additional purposes, providing that the original rent was fixed at an appropriate level because of the restricted user. Further the logic of 'restricted user = restricted rent' should also hold good when it comes to review and any wording such as 'any restricted user is to be ignored in assessing the rent to be paid on review' should be deleted. Lessees who use premises for purposes other than those allowed under the lease commit a breach, and may find their rights etc under the lease are impaired or, ultimately, that they lose the right of occupation by forfeiture.

V

Valuation   355

Variation of orders/lease   357

VAT on rent   361

Valuation

Introduction

Property can, for many organizations, be among their most valuable assets. If so, the current value of such assets should be known at all times. This should be a continuous process since property values are constantly changing, simply due to supply and demand – as well as to a variety of other factors. If the true value is not known, appropriate decisions concerning the assets cannot (or should not) be made.

Staged valuation

Many property owners adopt as a policy the concept of revaluing (say) a third of their portfolio every year meaning that over a period of three years the value of their whole portfolio will have been updated. Not only does this mean that at any time the value of no property should be more than three years out of date but also it spreads the valuation cost over the same period (indeed it can become a regular annual charge). If a system of recharging an INTERNAL RENT against those parts of the business that occupy the premises, the valuations themselves can serve as a base for the calculation.

As an alternative, staged revaluations over a five year period can be used, although property values tend to be somewhat dynamic and to leave a valuation of part of the portfolio for five years may mean that the value of some properties are seriously out of date. In addition, the valuation itself could be a major addition to costs in that year.

Instruction

For valuations to be reliable and of use, particularly as part of the financial accounts of the organization it will be necessary for qualified surveyors or valuers to conduct the work – and to provide written confirmation of their assessments. If such advisers regularly carry out work for the organization, and/or a commitment to repeat the process regularly is given, it may be possible to negotiate a reduced fee. If the same valuer is used repeatedly, a reduced fee may be negotiated at the time of the second or subsequent valuation, as a certain amount of information and knowledge of the property should have already been assimilated by the valuer with records compiled and a history of the organization's occupation being available.

Other matters

As part of a valuation, particularly one required for a proposed purchase, checks can also be made on floor loading, security and the exact position of boundaries etc. Some firms can also provide valuations of plant and machinery. For the purposes of insurance cover it may also be necessary to obtain valuations although here it is normally the cost of rebuilding that may be required. The valuation figures could be incorporated in the (KEEPING) PROPERTY RECORDS and also in the YEARLY PROJECTIONS to assist in the taking of informed decisions.

Variation of orders/lease

Introduction

Few building contracts run to completion without at least one variation of the original specification. Whilst some of these may be the result of unforeseen snags and/or be requested by the builder, most tend to emanate from the client as a result of second thoughts. Second thoughts may be sound and logical – but they can also be expensive, particularly if work has already begun or been completed on the area now to be changed. Lease terms may also, with consent, be varied which will usually entail both parties signing a Deed of Variation.

Building works control

Only one representative of the client should be empowered/authorized to agree variations and that name/title should be inserted within the contract with the instruction that unless that person agrees the variation in writing the contractor should not proceed. This should mean that unless the contractor has authority from the person the variation is unauthorized and, at least in theory, the contractor cannot charge for it.

Originally the contract should have specified both time and price for the works. Changing the specification may not only mean a variation of the price, it could also affect the time specified. If the contract stipulates that there is an agreed time (and particularly if there are penalties linked to a failure to keep within such time) all variations should address additional (or reduced) 'term' as well as 'cost'. If not, the contractor may, should the contract overrun, be able to claim, with some justification, that the variations themselves were directly responsible for the contract being late and thus the impact of damages for late completion may be negated.

The following example of a contract variation form requires completion of both cost and time alteration boxes. Most organizations will also insist that a variation can only be authorized provided any additional cost (perhaps subject to a minimum threshold) is firstly authorized by the approval of the capital expenditure at the level of authority required.

Variation Form

ORGANIZATION NAME   PROJECT

VARIATION ORDER NO

This order is made this _____ day of _____ 20XX and varies the term/amount*
of order no _____ placed on _____ (builder/supplier) on _____ (date).

Details of alteration _____ Value/Time _____

1.

2.   etc.

Total value addition/reduction   £ _____

(as approved by CAPITAL EXPENDITURE form ref _____)

Total time addition/reduction   Days _____

Authorized by _____ (signature)

_____(position) _____(date)

Received by _____(builder/supplier)

_____(position) _____(date)

Copies to:

Builder/Supplier

Architect/Surveyor/Building Project Manager

Finance Dept.

(Others) _____

Alterations to the original contract may only be made following the issue of an authorized
Variation Order, and to the extent of the amount of cost/saving/time as shown thereon.

WARNINGS:

1. If the works covered by such a variation order are substantial, the safety plan prepared previously may have to be reviewed.

2. If the premises are leased, the prior permission of the landlord may need to be obtained and confirmed in writing. In addition, the landlord may require reinstatement of the premises on lease termination.

Lease variations

The covenants and provisions of a lease are binding on both parties. However, with the agreement of the parties such terms can be varied e.g. removing the effect of a schedule of condition, relaxing the ban on subletting part of the premises, and so on. Whilst such a variation can be based and rely on correspondence, it may be better for a Deed of Variation to be signed by both parties and kept with the lease. Inevitably there will be costs involved in this and the parties will need to agree who should bear these – normally the party requesting the variation.

VAT on rent

Introduction

As a result of a regulation which many people feel is somewhat odd, Value Added Tax at the full rate (currently 17.5%) can, at a landlord's discretion, be added to the passing rent.

Rent demand

Rent must be paid on the due date (or by the end of any days of grace allowed) whether demanded or not. Thus, if a landlord has decided to charge VAT, the rent element should be paid on the due date regardless of whether a demand has been received. However, it is at least arguable that the VAT element should not be paid unless and until a VAT invoice is received. If paying the rent minus the VAT, this should be advised.

Effect

Imposing VAT on the rent for any VAT registered business will have little effect other than on cash flow. Not all businesses are VAT registered, however, and thus, to such organizations, the effect is an increase of 17.5% in their occupation cost. This could mean, should the organization wish to assign their lease, that the numbers of potential assignees might be reduced. When seeking rental evidence e.g. for a review, the effect of VAT has also to be taken into account.

Other charges

Landlords will normally have the right not only to require the preparation of a schedule of DILAPIDATIONS but also to charge the lessee for the surveyor's work preparing it and the solicitor's work for serving it. Invoices for both services will normally be made out to the landlord and bear VAT. Those issuing the invoices should be required to produce a VAT invoice made out in the name of the lessee.

W

Waste   365

Work/leisure occupation   373

Waste

Introduction

In the immediate aftermath of World War ll the UK created relatively little waste since most surplus materials were re-used or recycled (either automatically or as a result of government initiatives). Nowadays a great deal of waste is created and only a small (although increasing) percentage is recycled. Since the capacity of the world in general, and the UK in particular, to absorb the waste being created is totally inadequate, increasingly all producers of waste are under pressure to reduce the creation of material that will be waste and/or to recycle wherever possible – the possibilities (as the recycling advertisement states) are endless. The responsibility of Facility Managers which may in the past have been limited to ensuring that waste was collected internally and transported to external repositories from whence collectors would dispose of it, should be extended to ensure that proper recycling facilities are provided.

Legal obligations

The Government has published strategies to reduce the production of waste and the risk of pollution or harm to human health from waste disposal or recovery, with the twin aims of encouraging everyone to generate less waste and recycle more. The Secretary of State is also empowered to make regulations concerning 'producer responsibility' in order to increase the re-use, recovery and/or recycling of products or material for which initiatives there is increasing pressure from the European Community. A considerable amount of waste is created by packaging and in this respect the EU's Packaging (Essential Requirements) Regulations 2003 will increasingly bite.

The DTI's note on these regulations stipulates that packaging shall be manufactured so that:

- the packaging volume and weight are limited to the minimum adequate amount to maintain the necessary level of safety, hygiene and acceptance for the packed product and for the consumer

- the presence of noxious and other hazardous substances and materials... is minimized with regard to their presence in emissions, ash or leachate when packaging or residues from management operations or packaging waste are incinerated or landfilled

and

- it shall be designed, produced and commercialized in such a way as to permit its recovery, including recycling, and to minimize its impact on the environment when packaging waste or residues from packaging waste management operations are disposed of.

Companies with over 200 employees are to be required to publish environmental policies covering waste, and to devise and implement systems to give effect to them. The Business Resource Efficiency & Waste (BREW) programme was launched in April 2005 and has available £284 million to assist businesses:

- minimizing waste
- diverting waste from landfill, and
- improving resource efficiency.

Future fund allocation will be effected via the Department for Environment, Food and Rural Affairs – see DEFRA website www.defra.gov.uk.

In addition, the 2001 Waste Resources Action Programme (WRAP) has as its aim 'the creation of stable and efficient markets for recycled materials and products for the 100 million tonnes of waste [created by] commerce, industry and municipalities'. This is a major task and one that in time will no doubt impact individual Facility Managers. WRAP's budget has risen from £40 million initially to £85 million (in 2005/6).

DEFRA has announced that the business targets for recovered or recycled paper packaging are to increase by 1% per year from 65% in 2004 to 70% by 2008.

Not all waste may need to be disposed of, however, some may have a potential for re-use.

Case studies

1. A pine furniture producing company had high wastage. Whilst steps were taken to reduce the wastage itself (by designing products which could utilize offcuts), it was realized that the surplus could be utilized as fuel. A wood-burning boiler was commissioned and the costs of heating the factory and ancillary offices were reduced by around 20%. This also enabled the relatively costly procedure for bagging and transporting away substantial quantities of pine to be avoided.

2. A similar approach was adopted by Swinton Park – an ancestral home – which switched its heating source to a woodchip burning boiler using the fallen wood and surplus timber from its 20,000 acre of woodlands. The annual saving was £18,000.

3. The Bank of England printing works in Essex constantly withdraws old and damaged notes from circulation. These are burnt in its own incinerators (for understandable reasons) which are linked to the printing works internal heating system.

Note: Although a commendable use of waste products, in both these (and all other similar systems) waste (ash) is created and itself must be disposed of, whilst the process of burning creates emissions which are subject to controls.

Obviously employees have a role to play in trying to help minimize commercial waste. In the UK, recycling of household waste doubled in the four years to 2005. English households now recycle over 23% of the 25 million tonnes of waste they create annually. It should not be difficult to harness the same commitment from those individuals when at work.

Waste carriers

Registration is required of anyone who transports waste with the local authority in which area the principal place of business is situated. Registers giving details of all carriers are maintained by the authority and are open to free inspection by the public. Where a facility is creating waste it has an obligation to ensure that the waste carrier they are proposing to use is properly licensed for the waste they are generating. Licences are only issued to 'fit and proper' persons, who should be technically qualified, have appropriate financial resources and should not previously have been convicted of a relevant criminal offence. Facility managers should keep a copy of the licence – and any renewal.

Those undertaking waste disposal have a 'duty of care' to:

- prevent unlawful deposits or act other than in accordance with and as authorized by a licence
- prevent the escape of waste
- transfer waste to an authorized person with an accurate and adequate written description to enable the transferee to deal with the waste appropriately.

There is a code of practice to help Courts determine whether these duties have been discharged. Breach of the duty is a criminal offence with a maximum fine of £20,000.

Obviously one must expect the costs of waste removal/disposal to rise – in April 2005 the standard rate of landfill tax applying to active waste increased 20% to £18 per tonne. Further similar sized increases are to be expected in the near future to reach a long-term rate of £35 per tonne. Obviously any reduction in waste generated helps occupiers reduce the costs of its removal.

Case study

In the case of *Pharmacos*, because the company did not have the raw materials to enable it to repackage chemicals, the Managing Director instructed two chemists to use a more hazardous process. As a result, poisonous gas escaped into the atmosphere, and mercury into the River Thames. He ordered the process to be repeated with greater controls but again poisonous gas escaped. The two chemists were dismissed and they reported the matter to the HSE.

As a result of the ensuing prosecution the Managing Director was disqualified from acting as a director for four years and fined £2,500.

Where an organization creates waste or emissions which create a risk to the environment they must apply to the local Inspectorate of Pollution or Local Authority Environment Health Officer. Disposing of waste in other ways will generate fines.

Case study

Trojan Developments, a building company, disposed of 300 tonnes of controlled waste including toxic chemicals by building a 20ft bonfire which they set alight just after Guy Fawkes Day 2003. They were fined £5,000 plus £1,995 costs.

'Take back'

The Waste Electrical and Electronic Equipment (WEEE) directive amongst other obligations, requires producers and retailers to take back certain products from customers. Commercial requirements are overseen by the Environment Agency whilst the DEFRA leads on certain parts of domestic implementation: guidance, assessing producers' compliance with the collection of waste, recycling and recovery targets.

As a result of the Hazardous Waste (England and Wales) Regulations 2005 (SI 2005/94) and List of Waste (England) Regulations 2005 (SI 2005/95) which came into effect a month before WEEE, the disposal of a number of routine office equipment items became controlled. Items such as fluorescent light tubes, computer monitors and televisions are now classified as 'hazardous' and their disposal should be undertaken only via waste collectors registered with the Environment Agency. This is a considerable problem in the UK since we throw away over one million tons of electrical equipment each year – most of which contain a variety of toxins, 90% of which previously finished in landfill sites which formerly created 25% of the UK's methane emissions. Those needing advice should contact the Environment Agency.

Due to a lack of preparedness for the effect of these regulations, the operative date was deferred to June 2006 but at the time of writing has been further deferred for the same reason.

Public statement

Increasingly larger/higher profile companies provide a public statement (usually within their Annual Report) of their attitude to, and means of, attaining Social Responsibility including use of resources and means of dealing with the waste created by their activities. This is a trend which is likely to continue and be more widely adopted since it will come to be expected not least by the 'good employees' – those who progressive employers should wish to recruit. Such persons will want to know:

- what the organization stands for
- how it wishes to trade (attitude on safety, value, quality, recycling, waste control etc)
- how it interacts (i.e. with society as a whole, as well as with suppliers, customers, employees, shareholders etc), and so on.

Organizations that fail to address this need may find they lose their cutting edge.

Obviously the paper commitment must be evidenced in practice. The first essential of such a programme is a willingness to commit to the principle of having a duty to trade in a way that enhances society, uses materials in as 'non-wasteful' a way as possible, treats all-comers with respect and so on.

NOP conducted a survey for the Institute of Directors in June 2002 and discovered that:

- in roughly 50% of the 500 organizations contacted, the Board discussed social responsibility (66% of large companies did so)
- 60% discussed environmental issues (66% of large companies and 85% of those engaged in manufacturing did so)
- 36% had a Board member whose responsibilities included social issues
- 48% had a Board member whose responsibilities included environmental issues.

Board activity

Recommendations of Association and British Insurers (Disclosure Guidelines on Social Responsibility) encourage institutional investors to require their companies to answer questions such as the following in their companies' Annual Reports.

- Does the Board regularly review Social, Ethical and Environmental (SEE) matters?

- Has the Board reviewed both short and longer term risks arising from SEE matters?

- Has the Board adequate information for this purpose and does it train directors and managers in SEE matters?'

The future

Waste prevention, recycling and control is one which can only command more and more attention. Facility Managers need to become conversant with the requirements and be proactive in dealing with what is generally a growing problem – particularly as a priority trying to encourage occupants to minimize the creation of waste in the first place. When the BREW initiative was launched it was stated that 'a wide range of industries can save literally billions of pounds a year by cutting waste and improving resource efficiency often with little or no investment. [If industries get involved in BREW] businesses of all size are set to boost profits whilst reducing environmental impacts'.

Work/leisure occupation

Introduction

Modern day working requires many executives and others to spend longer and longer at their desks and computers – very often in addition to spending long hours commuting to the working location. Conversely, some employees would like to have the option of working hours to suit themselves rather than their employer – these numbers (which seem to be fast growing) include many in addition to those who have legal rights to have such a request considered objectively because they have parental responsibility. The widely-used phrase 'work:life balance' (which should more accurately be 'work:leisure balance') has caught the imagination of many. Given this scenario it is perhaps unsurprizing that HOMEWORKING is expected to grow rapidly since this enables working hours to be constructed to suit the individual. Alternatively, instead of bringing the work to the home, some organizations are investigating the possibility of taking the home to the work.

The 'life/work' concept

Many local authorities, particularly those with responsibilities in older cities with central and other areas from whence trade and occupation have moved, are currently investigating converting erstwhile commercial, retailing and industrial buildings into small units of low cost housing. These units would then be made available to lower paid workers unable to obtain funding from housing facilitators to enable them to purchase their own homes. For many years local authorities have urged owners and occupiers to fit out disused upper parts of older retail properties so that these could be used (either on a commercial basis) or funded by housing associations or even public funds, to provide accommodation for the homeless and/or lower paid employees. It has been suggested that a similar concept could be used for a range of properties to satisfy a perceived demand from better paid employees.

The 'work/life' concept

An alternative proposal has now been mooted by Sir Terence Conran, designer and founder of retail chain 'Habitat'. Sir Terence has proposed to the Office of the Deputy Prime Minister that all empty office space in UK cities should be converted into residential apartments for younger workers. His firm, Conran & Partners, has published a brochure, *Work/live, a proposition*, outlining this concept which is aimed at around 10% of the workforce – predominantly young single professionals working in the financial, legal, insurance or media sectors of commerce. The brochure states that providing customized flats for younger workers adjacent to their workplace could:

- increase the number of homes in inner cities

- reduce traffic congestion (and pressure on public transport)

- reduce wasted energy in buildings

- enliven business districts at weekends

- reduce the stress and cost of commuting, and

- save money for businesses by utilizing otherwise redundant or unused space.

Whilst some might welcome the idea, many would feel the last thing they want, despite the wasted hours travelling, would be to 'sleep at the job'. For many the commute in and out to the place of work is a chance to gear up for and wind down from the working environment. However, some employees might welcome the idea either as a permanent home or at least as a 'Monday night to Friday morning' 'pied a terre'.

Granting rights of occupation of any such converted premises would need careful consideration. For both freehold and leasehold occupation, planning consent will be needed to convert commercial premises to domestic use, whilst lessees will also need the permission of their landlords. Insurers will also need to be advised. Whilst the tenant remains an employee, there may be no problem but should they leave, there may be difficulties in regaining vacant possession – legal advice should be taken. In many ways this concept has memories of 'reinventing the wheel' since back in the 19th century manufacturing organizations often created living accommodation virtually at the factory door for their workers – thus confectioners Cadbury built 'Bournville', a village, for their employees.

X

Xmas precautions 377

Xmas precautions

Introduction

Employers can be held liable for compensation in respect of claims resulting from inappropriate activities – fueled or not by alcohol – of employees (and their guests) at employee parties, dances etc. If the only reason for the participants (or most of them) gathering is their link as 'employees of the organization', then the occasion regardless of location and who funds it, may be held to be an 'extension of the workplace'. Whilst trying to protect the organization from transgressions may be more a challenge for the personnel or human resources department, it may have ramifications for the Facility Manager, particularly if it is proposed to use an employer's facility for the celebration. Nowhere is this more likely to be a problem than during the festive season.

Commentary

In *Watching the English*. Kate Fox, a social anthropologist, reviewing the 'goings on' at workplace Christmas parties writes '[people] misbehave because misbehaviour is what Christmas parties are all about: misbehaviour is written into the unwritten rules governing these events.' She points out that there is nothing particularly depraved or wicked 'just a higher degree of disinhibition than is normally permitted among the English'. Unfortunately it is exactly this 'degree of disinhibition' that is a matter of concern for employers particularly as she goes on to record that '90% of respondents [to her surveys] admitted to some form of misbehaviour at their employers' Christmas parties'!

Without wishing to restrict enjoyment it may be advisable to issue a warning in advance of the proposed celebrations.

Example of warning clause

1. The [organization] in sponsoring [event] hopes every employee [and guest] will enjoy it and that they will appreciate that the following guidance is meant to achieve that. At all such events (whether we sponsor and/or fund them or not, at which the attendance is related to the fact that those present or some of them are employees), the [organization's] employees and their guests are expected to act in accordance with this guidance.

2. At these events the normal rules and guidelines regarding attitude and behaviour in the workplace apply – particularly rules regarding substance (including alcohol) abuse, harassment, 'horseplay', and any acts that could be construed as discriminatory etc.

3. Moderation and a consideration and respect for others is expected at all times.

    Breach of these guidelines cannot be tolerated and will render employees responsible subject to disciplinary action, and others to claims made by the [organization].

4. All persons in a position of authority must remember their responsibilities. Whilst being relaxed and informal, they should not act in any way such that their position and/or respect will then or subsequently be undermined.

5. Drivers are reminded of the legal requirements regarding consumption of alcohol – particularly if also taking medication which could cause drowsiness.

Alcohol

The reminder about alcohol and driving is perhaps obvious. However, employers could be held liable if, for example, they provide a 'free bar' with no control placed over the number of drinks consumed.

Case study

A brewing company operated a residential training facility. After the day's training the delegates had use of a free bar. On one occasion several delegates drank too much and a manager was attacked. The employees who had attacked the manager were dismissed but were successful in their claims of unfair dismissal. It was stressed that if a company provides a free bar without control over consumption it creates a situation where excess consumption – and its results – is almost inevitable.

FOOTNOTE: The Inland Revenue tax free limit that employers can spend on entertainment for their employees and guest is £150 per person (that is per employee plus one guest). However, if the spend is £151 or more per person then tax is payable on the whole amount (not just the excess over £150).

In-house celebrations

Perhaps the safest rule is to prohibit any celebration within the working environment and always ensure that purpose-designed facilities – public halls, hotels, restaurants, public houses etc are used. If commercial premises are to be used, care should be taken to ensure that working facilities, machines processes etc are cordoned off and those present made aware that only the area in the immediate vicinity plus toilet facilities are to be used. An in-house restaurant or social area may be the most suitable location provided it can be isolated from the rest of the facility. Employees should be able to exit the site without having to re-enter working areas. Any alcohol must only be consumed within the area reserved for the function.

Case study

In an insurance company, it was common at Christmas for there to be many departmental parties within its Head Office. These became quite well-organized with employees contributing food as well as drink. On one Christmas Eve, a couple were discovered 'in flagrante delicto'. Immediately a complete ban on internal parties was imposed as well as a rule that once people left the building during the last working day before the Christmas holiday (usually to go to one of several public houses) they would on no account be left back in the building – even if they only wished to collect coats etc.

Y

Yearly projections   383

Yearly projections

Introduction

At least annually Facility/Property Managers should project location costs for the year ahead as well as reviewing their long-term responsibilities and duties. Indeed, this is probably a necessity for budgetary requirements. If a property register has been kept updated this should provide an ideal base for both long-term and yearly planning.

Budgetary projections

Provided the information suggested for retention in KEEPING PROPERTY RECORDS is constantly updated, identifying expenditure expected in the budget period becomes a relatively simple operation. From the 'at a glance' layout, the coming year's obligations regarding repair, redecoration and so on, should be easily identified.

Anticipated expenditure may not, however, be restricted to these items, since where there are leased premises, should there have been a previous history of a failure to comply with repairing covenants, it might be advisable to allow for expenditure related to the serving of a schedule of DILAPIDATIONS.

Movement in portfolio costs

The projection also identifies when leased property occupation could be terminated and/or incur higher costs. Such movements could result from:

- the ending of a lease either by effluxion of time or by the exercise of an option
- the creation of a new lease
- timing of rent reviews, and so on.

The Property Manager needs to feed such information through to those responsible for trading and also for those who may need to make a decision about retention or disposal.

a) Rent reviews, renewals etc

To assist with the assimilation of information needed for financial planning as well as basic unit administration, an analysis, regularly updated as each situation alters, should be presented to the Board.

Projection for financial year ending 30th June 2006

Unit		R due	Rent now	Estimate	Action	Expires	Investment
(02)	Hunt	8/01	£8300	£10000	Still O/S	2010	£14k
(02)	Hunt	8/04	'£8300'	See above		2010	
(25)	LawW	12/01T	£8000	£10000	Still O/S	(2001)*	£54k
(11)	LPlaz	9/02T	£7000	£9000	Still O/S	(2002)	£4k
(20)	Tong	5/03	£6600	£7000	Still O/S	(2006)	£74k
20)	Tong	5/06T	'£7000'	See above		(2006)	
(15)	ParlSt	3/04T	£27250	£35000	Still O/S	(2004)	£33k
(24)	Shire	5/05	£11200	£14000	Notice rec'd	2010	£55k
(07)	Morl	8/05	£15000	£18000	L'lords@ £17k	2010	£30k
(19)	Pock	7/05	£13000	£14000	L'lords @ £15k	2008	£9k
(47)	Donc	3/06	£19000	£23500	Option (6m)	06/11	£25k

Date of issue: Jan. 2006

Explanatory notes

This is a cost projection for rents expected to review/renew for this portfolio for the financial year July05/June06 with additional information (e.g. the investment in the premises) to aid decision-making:

- 1st column – unit reference number.
- 2nd col – abbreviated unit name.
- 3rd col – date of renewal (T = termination of lease) or review.

- 4th col – rent currently paid.

- 5th col – estimate of possible rent to be paid on review/renewal assessed as a result of information of rents in locale or of similar properties.

- 6th col – provides a guide to the status of the event.

- 7th col – gives the termination dates of the lease.

- 8th col – gives the written down value of the investment in the unit which, should a lease not be renewed or be sold, would have to be written off or set off against sale proceeds.

At the date of this report:

1. Landlords have not activated the process that would lead to an agreed review or the negotiations for new leases for five units (or, more correctly, seven, given that there are two reviews outstanding on each of two properties).

2. Notices have been received in two cases stating the review progress is starting but no figures have been received to commence negotiations.

3. Notices have been received in another two cases stating the figures suggested by landlords for the revised rents.

4. There is an option to break on Unit 47 so the lease could end either in 06 or, if the option is not exercised, in 2011.

b) Costs of repairs/redecorations

In year 2010 in the schedule in KEEPING THE RECORD, there are three lease-hold properties in respect of which there are either internal or external redecoration obligations and another with both. This provides a base to assess the cost of such redecoration both individually and collectively. Since some land-lords will fail to remind the organization of the redecorating covenant there may be flexibility regarding the expenditure. If the budget is tight then the redecoration of the freeholds can be postponed although this may create a need for greater expenditure in the future.

c) Revaluation costs

If the system outlined in VALUATIONS has been adopted, the manager should know which properties are to be revalued in the coming financial period and can thus estimate these costs. A further column giving the latest valuation (with a note of the date) of each property could be added to the above schedule.

General duties

Items in the following checklist should be reviewed at least one a year – and any inherent costs associated with the answers need to also be built into the budget.

* *

The A-Z of a facilities manager's duties

Have we:

a) Kept the property records (including building(s) plans) updated to the most recent alterations?

b) Ensured the records are kept securely – with copies stored in a remote location?

c) Generated a long-term plan of the organization's property utilization?

d) Negotiated all the rights inherent in our occupation – and are these rights still current?

e) Kept all statutory bodies – planning, building regulations, health and safety, environment, etc – advised of information regarding our operations and any changes thereto?

f) Reviewed our obligations under the new Fire Precautions regulations to ensure adequate preparation?

g) If in shared occupations, have we ensured that the landlord has reviewed obligations under the new Fire Precautions Regulations for common areas?

h) Interfaced with bodies having a right of access, ensuring their requirements are carried out and that employees know what to do when such inspections are required?

i) Updated contracts for all building services – cleaning, security, reception, safety etc, and are the services provided adequate?

j) Updated specifications and job descriptions for cleaning, security, reception, etc., employees or specifications for bought-in services?

k) Regularly checked that fire escape routes are clear, tested fire bells or alarms, and carried out evacuation drills and reviewed risk assessments?

l) Complied with all repair and redecoration covenants in leasehold premises and/or formulated and complied with such a schedule, if freehold?

m) Ensured our housekeeping provisions in general and/or as part of risk assessment/prevention procedure, are adequate?

n) Carried out all requirements made of us by all insurers – particularly regarding recommendations regarding lifts, boilers etc (which have statutory implications)?

o) Pursued all insurance claims?

p) Overseen builders and/or subcontractors effectively?

q) Ensured all variations to such contracts were properly controlled, budgeted for and authorized?

r) Conducted spots checks to test the effectiveness of our security arrangements?

s) Updated, tested and evaluated our contingency or disaster plans?

t) Checked that we have complied with all safety requirements?

u) Interfaced with our neighbours and dealt adequately with trespassers?

v) Acted promptly and efficiently regarding notices and schedules received from landlords etc?

w) Ensured new facilities performed in the way required – and, if not, is there anything we should note in case other such facilities are to be commissioned?

x) Disposed of all redundant facilities?

y) Commissioned and relocated to new facilities satisfactorily?

z) Prepared the expenditure budget for the coming financial period?

Z

Zoning   391

Zoning

Introduction

Comparing what can be widely differing shapes and sizes of retail units can be difficult. To facilitate such comparison, units are normally 'zoned' with the varying areas in each zone adjusted arithmetically to give what is termed a 'zone A equivalent' (ZAE). If a market rate is then applied to the ZAEs the rent for the property can be calculated.

Setting the zones

Zoning is perhaps most appropriate for larger units – that is, large supermarkets or departmental stores. For smaller and very often more narrow units the principle is less appropriate, although it can still be utilized. Looking from the pavement towards the rear of a shop, the first 20ft (regardless of width) is Zone A. The next 20ft of depth is Zone B, the third area of depth is Zone C and the fourth Zone D. The rental charge for any other space is then a matter for negotiation. In the following illustration, a plan of the shop was incorporated into the lease itself. Not only does this clearly show the zoning 'by 20ft increments' but also the areas of the three zones can be seen and the overall ZAE.

Using the ZAE

In the illustration the lease states that the area of Zone A is 299.56 sq ft, the area of Zone B is 328.04 sq ft and that of Zone C is 361.88 sq ft. To arrive at the Zone A Equivalent (ZAE), the area of Zone B is usually divided by two, Zone C area by four, Zone D divided by eight and any other areas by 16 (although this is often varied). In this example the three areas have been totalled and this is the ZAE. If this figure is multiplied by the rent demanded for Zone A the result is the rent for the whole. Here the result is 554.05. The rent of this shop at the time was £23,500 so ignoring any charge for any other areas the Zone A rent is £42.41 per square ft. However, the ZAE can be adjusted if there is agreement that other areas not within the Zoning (storage areas for example) should be charged at nominal levels.

For example

Garden area (to rear of this café – used as summer seating)

500 sq ft @ £2 = 1000.00

Storage – Ground floor and basement

360 sq ft@ £3 = 1080.00
_____
£2080.00

This would leave £21,420 to be split between the other zones (554.05 sq ft) which now gives £38.66 per sq ft for Zone A.

Whilst zoning helps comparability it is still open to query and dispute particularly regarding the treatment of ancillary areas.

The divisors

Although Zone B being half and Zone C being a quarter of the Zone A rate is very common, it is arguable that with narrow shops like that illustrated these may not be entirely applicable. Generally customers are averse to long narrow units, feeling that they may trapped – and possibly 'forced' into buying something that they do not want. Larger divisors than two and four could be argued. This is particularly true in this unit. Zone B includes within it an area of food preparation and it is at least arguable that a greater divisor than two should be applied to that portion. Further over 75% of the area in Zone C is food preparation and again it is arguable that a greater divisor than four should be used here. Obviously a certain proportion of every shop must be storage, services etc and these cannot command as great a value as retail space.

Unfortunately when trying to agree a rent review it is possible for the two sides not to be able to agree with the treatment of all the areas. If, for example, a unit is an odd shape (triangular), this could mean that although the total rent is agreed that because of the awkward shape a discount is applied having calculated the rent in accordance with the zoning principle.

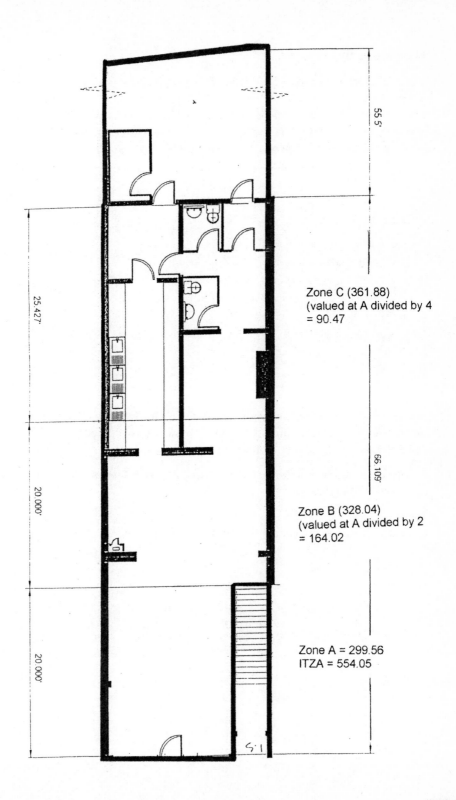

Zone C (361.88)
(valued at A divided by 4
= 90.47

Zone B (328.04)
(valued at A divided by 2
= 164.02

Zone A = 299.56
ITZA = 554.05

55.5'

25.427'

20.000'

66.109'

20.000'

Adjusting the figures

With very small shops zoning may not be entirely appropriate. The current rent of a small shop in the city of York is £27,250. The unit is not only very narrow with part of the rear ground floor only accessible via two steps (which is very offputting for customers) it has both a basement and two upper floors neither of which can be used by the retailer. The following split of areas and charge per sq ft was agreed at the time of review as:

Zone A 214 sq ft £109	=	23,326
Ancillary A 132 sq ft £12 (rear of the shop but up two steps)	=	1,584
Basement 314 sq ft £5	=	1,570
1st floor 42 sq ft £4	=	168
2nd floor 302 sq ft £2	=	604
		£27,252

However, the Zone A value could easily be adjusted. If we halve the 'rent' charged for the Ancillary and other areas, their rent value would be reduced to £1,963 and the Zone A to £25,289 or £118 per sq ft.

Conversely, if the other areas were given twice their value, the Zone A would be reduced to £90 per sq ft.

Sometimes arguing a review is as much about agreeing the values to be given to the ancillary areas as about the evidence from other units.

Useful contacts 397

Cases 401

Useful contacts

The contacts listed below may be of use to facility and property administrators in dealing with some of the challenges highlighted here, but no endorsement or recommendation is intended by such inclusion.

Accident prevention – HSE documents *Major accident prevention policies for lower tier COMAH establishments and A new duty to investigate accidents* are available from HSE Books, PO Box 1999, Sudbury, Suffolk, CO10 6FS.

Archiving – Sources of advice. Institute of Chartered Secretaries Document retention handbook. Tel: 0207 580 4741

LexisNexis Butterworth Tolley's *Company Secretary's Link*. Tel: 0208 686 9141 Auditors, solicitors etc can also provide advice

Dilapidations schedules disputes – The Royal Institution of Chartered Surveyors (RICS) offers a service to try to find an amicable solution to or arbitration of disputes concerning serving and content of dilapidations schedules. Contact: Dispute Resolution Service, RICS, Surveyor Court, Westwood Way, Coventry, CV4 8JE. Tel: 0207 3343806.

Energy control – The Carbon Trust promotes the Enhanced Capital Allowance (ECA) scheme for energy saving investments. The trust can conduct a free survey of the facilities of larger energy users, making suggestions for saving energy etc. Via the ECA scheme businesses can write off 100% of the cost of energy saving equipment against their profits in the first year of use. Also available is the trust's free booklet *FOCUS – a practical guide to reducing energy bills*. Tel: 0800 085 2005 or www.thecarbontrust.co.uk

Environmental matters advice – Envirowise, a government funded organization, provides guidance to businesses on how to make environmental regulations work for them.

- (www.envirowise.gov.uk)

- Environment Agency (www.environment-agency.gov.ulk)

- Chris Blandford Associates (Environment, Landscape, Planning), The Old Crown, High St, Blackboys, Uckfield, East Sussex, TN22 5JR. Tel: 01825 891071. 1 Swan Court, 9 Tanner St., London, SE1 3LE. Tel: 0207 089 6480 or www.cba.uk.net

Graffiti – Anti-defacing paint: Dacrylate Margard Water Washable Graffiti system. Dacrylate Paints. Tel: O1623 753845 (www.dacrylate.co.uk)

Land registry – The Land Registry operates via 26 regional business units and can, on a fee basis, provide those interested in land matters (including owner-ship) with details. The Registry handles around 30 million enquires per year generating a revenue stream of £390 million (2004/5). Tel: 0207 917 8888 (head office for details of local offices).

Neighbour difficulties

- Community mediators – www.mediationuk.org.uk

- Hedgeline – http://freespace.virgin.net/clare.h

- Office of Deputy Prime Minister:

  - Trees and high hedge advice – www.odpm.gov.uk/treesandhedges

  - Publications: *High hedges – complaining to the council*
    Over the garden hedge

Noise

Noise reduction at work – www.soundoff.co.uk or 0207 921 8066

Planning, environmental matters, architecture, rating etc – Terence O'Rourke is a 100 strong, employee-owned company which for over 20 years has provided nationwide assistance in the above and other related areas. Contact: Everdene House, Deansleigh Rd, Bournemouth, BH7 7DU (www.torltd.co.uk)

Planning permission

Department of the Environment's booklets *Planning permission – a guide for small businesses and Planning appeals.*

Purchasing office supplies – CNG Business Services Ltd offers the supply of discounted photocopiers, electricity, emergency glazing, office supplies, ATMs etc. 17 Marylebone High Street, London W1U 4NZ. Tel: 0207 224 2822/01904 692232 or www.cngbs.com.)

Recycling

Computers – tinyurl.com/d2asb for a list of recycling firms who may be prepared to take old computers. (Local authorities may under legislation, which should have been introduced in 2005, provide recycling sites.)

Office furniture – Furniture Re-Use Network (FRN) – 01942 375252 (www.frn.org.uk) cannot take electrical goods; and soft furnishing goods must have an up-to-date fire label.

Gas cookers – (Must be disconnected by a CORGI registered fitter) FRN may be able to provide details of local projects that could use such items.

Mobile phones and chargers, printer and copier cartridges – Several charities (Oxfam – www.oxfam.org.uk, Action Aid (www.actionaid.org.uk) RNLI (www.rnli.org.uk) etc) can accept these although many suppliers state as part of the use agreement that their cartridges will not be donated for such recycling.

Paint – Community RePaint (www.communityrepaint.org.uk) is a national organization that can accept usable leftover paint for distribution to those unable to afford to buy it.

Stamps – The Royal National Institute for the Blind (RNIB) (www.rnib.org,uk) will accept stamps which it sells to collectors and dealers. The Institute asks donors to leave around 1cm around the stamps and ideally likes them sorted into class type (1st, 2nd, foreign).

Retention time limits – See *Company Secretary's Link* published by LexisNexis/ButterworthTolley – 0208 662 2000; company auditors or solicitors may also provide guidance.

Risk planning – Willis Ltd (contact Martin Bennett, Project Director, One Camomile St., London EC3A 7LA, Tel: 020 7975 2393, www.wills.com).

Toys – National Children's Home (NHC) may take items into its local shops but not on a central basis (Great Ormond Street Hospital may also be unable to accept them). Soft toys may be best disposed of in local textile banks although local schools may welcome donations to be sold at fetes etc.

Waste – For Electrical and Electronic Equipment: www.dti.gov.uk/sustainability/weee

For the Waste & Resources Action Programme etc: www.wrap.org.uk

Waste collection – Try local council

Windpower – DTI's Community Renewables Initiative. Clear Skies renewable energy grants – www.clear-skies.org

General contacts

Alternative Dispute Resolution Service – Guidance booklet and details available from local courts

British Institute of Facilities Management – 67 High St, Saffron Walden, Essex, CB10 1AA. Tel: 01799 508606 (www.bifm.org.uk)

British Security Industry Association – www.bsia.org.uk

Facilities Management Direct – www.find.co.uk

International Facilities Management Association – 1, E-Greenway Plaza, Suite 1100, Houston TX77046-0194, USA www.ifma.org

Royal Institution of Chartered Surveyors – *Getting serious about your business premises* (covers service charges, rent reviews, tax allowances, disputes with landlords, homeworking, subletting and renting and buying business premises) Tel: 0870 333 1600 (www.propertyinbusiness.co.uk)

Service Works Global, Facilities and Property Management Software, 2 Burston Road, Putney, London SW15 6AR (Tel: 08707 36 0000, www.swg.com) can provide software to assist property management

Cases

- British Telecom v Sun Life Assurance (*The Times* 3.8.95)
- Co-op v Argyll Stores (trading as Safeway) (1996 9 EG 128)
- Day v T Pickles Farms Ltd (1999 IRLR 217)
- Denco v Joinson (1991 ICR 172 EAT)
- Dutton & Clark v Daly (1985 IRLR 363)
- Graysim Holdings v P&O Property Holdings Ltd (*The Times* 24.11.95)
- Hampson t/a Abbey Self Storage v Newcastle upon Tyne Council
- Havenbridge Ltd v Boston Dyers Ltd (*The Times* 1.4.94)
- J A Pye (Oxford) Ltd (*The Times* 25.11.05)
- Jervis v Harris (1996 10EG159)
- Margereson & Hancock v J W Roberts Ltd (*The Times* 17.4.96)
- Pilkington v Morrey & Williams (1990 EAT 307/89)
- R v F Howe & Sons (Engineers) Ltd (*The Times* 27.11.98)
- R v Rhone Polenc Rorer (1996 ICR 1054 CA)
- Rainham Waste Recycling & Sullivan
- Retail Parks Investments Ltd v Royal Bank of Scotland plc (*The Times* 22.4.96)
- Ryland v Fletcher (1866)
- Trojan Developments (*The Times* 16.1.04)
- United Scientific Holdings Ltd v Burnley Corporation